Prose for Comparison

* * * * * * * * * * * * * * * * * *

Edited by

ELEANOR TERRY LINCOLN

Smith College

W · W · NORTON & COMPANY · INC · *New York*

PRINTED IN THE UNITED STATES OF AMERICA
FOR THE PUBLISHERS BY THE VAIL-BALLOU PRESS

Prose for Comparison

Contents

❀ ❀ ❀ ❀ ❀ ❀ ❀ ❀ ❀ ❀ ❀ ❀ ❀ ❀ ❀ ❀ ❀ ❀

———————————— III ————————————

Victorian Setting

———————————— IV ————————————

Small Town, U.S.A.

———————————— V ————————————

Waterloo

——————— VI ———————
Dunkirk

——————— VII ———————
London Fire

——————— VIII ———————
Flight

——————— IX ———————
The Pullman Strike, 1894

—————————————— X ——————————————

Woman Suffrage

—————————————— XI ——————————————

Merry England

—————————————— XII ——————————————

The Gilded Age

──────────────── XIII ────────────────

The Sea

──────────────── XIV ────────────────

The Great Plains

──────────────── XV ────────────────

The American

──────────────── XVI ────────────────

The Gentleman

XVII
Tragedy

XVIII
The Idea of Comedy

Preface

❀ ❀ ❀ ❀ ❀ ❀ ❀ ❀ ❀ ❀ ❀ ❀ ❀ ❀ ❀ ❀ ❀ ❀

It is hoped that the initial shock to the reader who makes an exploratory survey of this volume will be the discovery of some inferior writing. This discovery may be precipitated, it will undoubtedly be emphasized, by parallel examples of very good prose. The reader who has such an experience understands at once the purpose of this anthology. It is a collection of prose readings grouped around the same or closely related subjects. The arrangement is designed to concentrate between two covers a variety of works which illuminate one another, to produce, in fact, what Corbyn Morris called "the Lustre resulting from the quick Elucidation of one Subject by a just and unexpected Arrangement of it with another Subject."

In the course of years a thoughtful reader develops literary judgment largely through repetition. His observation of related books and articles sharpens his knowledge of techniques and matures his recognition of quality in literature. These grouped examples are chosen to insure that the repetitions are frequent within a short time and a short space. Presentation in brief, easily remembered units makes it possible to keep one example in mind while reading the next, thereby developing literary understanding more rapidly and with more interest than would be the case in extended and random reading. The authors represented, writing upon the same topics for different purposes and from different points of view, achieve, of course, different results, often with varying degrees of success. Conflicts in the various treatments of a theme offer the reader the stimulation of both contrast and comparison and give support to controversial judgments.

The relationship between like and unlike elements is one of the most useful adjuncts to thinking. It is a key, therefore, to both reading and writing. Recognition, realization, understanding, even imagination, all are founded upon comparisons: of a familiar object or experience or idea with a new one, of a concrete conception with an abstract one, of a known situation with an imaginary or a concealed one. Oft-repeated anecdotes like that of the tourist who recognized the beauty of the Parthenon because it looked like the post office in Jefferson are true to a degree of every traveler, whether in space or in print. Most of us apprehend the true extent of a one-mile walk by remembering an old familiar mile trudged in our childhood from home to school or from a farm to a swimming hole. Every metaphor or simile, every diagram, every Christmas nativity play is founded upon the often intuitive recognition of the importance of comparison in all kinds of apprehension.

Readers and writers, at whatever level of development, are enlarging their powers of perception by a series of experiences, each of which illuminates or helps to expand the others. It may be concluded that taste itself and critical judgment are based upon an endless chain of comparisons ascending from simple works to more complex, from the obvious to the subtle, from the work itself to the imaginary conception of ideals which we call standards of taste.

It is unreasonable to expect the developing reader to skip too many links in the chain of experiences which makes it possible for him to come to a considered judgment about a literary work. Under pressure of time he is too often asked to express an opinion about writing in which his random reading has given him little experience. His responses are vague; because the passage seems to him unique, it is isolated, and his judgments are undefined and unmeasured. He may be able to feel the quality of the work on a more or less satisfactory level, but to understand what he feels and to express it, he requires comparative reading by which to measure results and with which to develop and support his own imaginative construction of what the work might be, for better or for worse, if it were different.

Nothing in the plan or arrangement of these selections should encourage the reader to regard them as a hierarchy of merit or the steps in an ascending scale of perfection by which to establish a critical yardstick. The passages are designed to make the reader *think* about the relative success of different methods but not to decide for him upon the basis of absolute standards of literary achievement. In fact the presentation of alternatives will almost inevitably make the *easy* decision of what is good or what is bad more difficult to accept and harder to defend.

The reader of these selections must not fail to see, lest comparison become dogmatic and literature seem simply mechanical, that no two of the passages are upon exactly the same subject or written with the same object in view. It would be relatively easy to select from several sections in this volume examples which are comparable in more truly fundamental characteristics than the obvious likeness in subject matter which is the basis for these groups. The reader is asked to grant a willing acceptance of an artificial arrangement. The likenesses are by design both obvious and superficial because it is the differences which are most significant and most interesting. It is not the reduction to a formula which the exercises suggest but the multiplication of possibilities in meaning and method. Writing develops from reading, and both from imagination. The object of these artificially concentrated examples is liberation from the conventional and strictly congruent, is recognition, in fact, that nothing in literature is ever a stereotype.

This is not a collection of prose models. It should be expressly noted that the selections are of unequal merit; they were chosen as examples which demonstrate that there are several ways of doing the same thing. In fact, one of the chief purposes of this kind of study is to break down the unquestioning acceptance of the published page; to provide evidence that the printed word is not the last or the only or the best word. It is hoped that this anthology will help to develop readers who see not only what is written, but also what else might have been written.

The order of attention to the selections may be treated with the utmost freedom. The juxtaposition and progression in the present order is not the only one, nor is it based upon a scheme of development. The readings may be useful in another sequence and in whole or in part. Readers seeking examples of definition will find them in the sections on Tragedy, The Gentleman, The American, and others. Short nonfiction narratives, useful for transition to the short story, are found in the account of President Buchanan at Washington Junction (p. 296), the British Soldier's Retreat, the accounts of Waterloo. Setting, character, and action pertinent to the problems of the short story are variously illustrated in sections grouped together for a different emphasis. It is interesting, also, to consider the types of writing which are represented here and there in these groups. Individual readers may study the differences between history and fiction and belles lettres, or analyze the problems of organization, emphasis, and choice of detail which are peculiar, for instance, to the news report.

Material in this collection is presented in brief excerpt to enable the reader to concentrate on vocabulary and detail; it is presented in contradictory or contrasting relationships to challenge attention to the subject matter and the words which are an author's raw materials. But the reader should be cautioned against stopping before the significance of the minutiae has been considered in the framework of the whole paragraph and of the whole intention. Even in short descriptions, the single idea or attitude or impression which is the core of the passage dictates the choice of each word and the order of every sentence.

All of the prose passages included in this collection, with one or two exceptions, are excerpts from longer works. Many of the abridgements have a form or design of their own which can be studied usefully. Yet by the very nature of the project the passages must be fragmentary, are frequently condensed, and are, in a sense, dislocated. The selections should be accepted in this form, simply as an exercise in the study of prose, and in full recognition of the fact that such excerpts are often an unfair, certainly an incomplete, representation of the author's position and of his ability.

In abridging these passages, I have followed a practice, common in anthologies, of not indicating the omissions by dots. (In cases where dots appear in the source, they have been retained.) I do not altogether approve of this method, but it is practically necessary for the appearance and readability of the page. Further it may be observed that the use of dots is a completely inadequate indication of either the length of a deleted passage or its importance.

The headnotes to the groups of readings are intended to explain why the passages were chosen rather than to dictate a critical estimate of them. They provide a brief setting or background for the group as a whole; in some instances they suggest an attitude toward the reading, but they are designed to open the subject, not to close it.

No one writes a book without exploiting his friends and incurring debts in gratitude which pervade far beyond the limits of recognition. To my colleagues at Smith College, who generously accepted and tried this idea, I am indebted for its first lively months and its "shakedown cruise." I am grateful in particular to Professor Katherine G. Hornbeak, who has purged the manuscript of sins against both reading and writing. First and last, however, tribute is due to Professor Mary Ellen Chase, who first dealt severely with my sentences some thirty years ago and whose Introduction, after all those years, is first in this book.

E. T. L.

October 2, 1955

Introduction

❋ ❋ ❋ ❋ ❋ ❋ ❋ ❋ ❋ ❋ ❋ ❋ ❋ ❋ ❋ ❋ ❋ ❋

DURING years spent in teaching English composition to college students I have wished fervently that some other happier term than *exposition* might be used to describe that type of writing which is so variously and richly illustrated by this fine collection of readings. For the word in itself conveys to the imagination little or nothing of what it actually embraces. Lacking in connotation both in sound and in appearance, it is unlikely to suggest initially either grace or excitement to those entering upon its study and practice. And yet in its wider meanings of interpretation, portrayal, persuasion, disclosure, discovery, and even revelation, it affords without doubt the most reasonable and most natural type of writing for college students, once they have become aware of its almost unlimited possibilities.

Other forms of composition sometimes required (in my opinion unwisely) of those beginning to learn to write on the college level, notably fiction in the form of the short story, but occasionally drama and even poetry, are clearly discouraging, not to say impossible for any but the gifted. All imply a maturity of outlook, a grasp of language, and a sense of structure, skills rarely possessed by the average young person; and all, moreover, suggest a moving away from familiar experience, or at least a difficult translation of it into relatively unfamiliar and equally difficult forms. Surely to attempt to utilize that experience in the simplest, yet most flexible and generous form of writing is the more natural and wise procedure whether for the talented students, who dream of authorship in the future, or for those, the vast majority, who are inexorably required to write here and now.

Nor is personal experience, as a basis for truly creative writing, in any sense limited, as these selections prove. It may range from memories of childhood and from people and places one has known to adventures in reading and to ideas concerning literary values; from conceptions of historical figures and scenes to evaluations of their contributions to human society; from actual and concrete happenings in the past or in the present to imaginary events in some far distant and even hypothetical age; from accepted and traditional ideas to the most daring of opinions and surmises. It includes one's background, one's foreground, and one's future; predilections, pleasures, and prejudices; observations both of the simplest and most complex sort. It affords material for persuasion, controversy, evaluation, interpretation, and reflection.

Inevitably the writing based upon such individual experience, whether required of the student or examined by him in such comparative readings as are contained in this book, shares the breadth and variety of experience itself. The possibilities of literary method are many: the narrative method, the descriptive, historical, biographical, journalistic, critical. The ways of approach to material and the means of its development are equally generous. One learns through both reading and experiments in writing the meaning and the importance of point of view, selection, illustration, emphasis, allusion, understatement, economy, comparison and contrast, analysis, the choice of detail, and various telling forms of sentence structure. Through the careful study of isolated units, the paragraph or even the sentence, made possible through prose selections such as these, students can be made aware of those minutiae upon which the intention or the impression of the entire selection so often depend: the word order, the choice of words singly or in combination, their sound, aptness, imagery, connotation, the richness or poverty of figures of speech—in short, all those countless traits and even tricks by which written expression gains, or loses, its appeal and value. Nor is such analysis in its efficacy unrelated to other forms of writing. The study of scenes of action like those in the accounts of Dunkirk; or of character portrayal in the delineations of Queen Elizabeth I and of Lincoln; or of setting in the various Victorian backgrounds are clearly pertinent to the later study and writing of fiction.

At Smith College where I have for many years taught composition both to freshmen and to more advanced students, we have discovered that an early and close study of prose selections, accompanied by frequent short themes suggested by them, is of immeasurable constructive value to the average as well as to the gifted student. Without it, the average flounders hopelessly when required to write longer, more sustained papers; with it, the more able increases her powers not only in writing but in reading discriminatingly and well. The selections which follow were originally prepared for our Smith College classes, and, in mimeographed form, have been used now for two years by the members of our English staff with marked success and pleasure. The decision of their collector and editor to publish them in more permanent form has been largely influenced by the enthusiasm of students and teachers alike who have found them to be both an indispensable preparation for further and more advanced work in the writing of English and an exciting adventure into wide fields of reading.

Much of the value of the selections lies in the fact that they were not chosen as a collection of models for the writing of prose, but, instead, that they purposely represent varying and diverse standards of literary excellence. Thus they do not encourage unquestioning acceptance or admiration so much as they arouse curiosity and stimulate comparison and discrimination in the minds of their readers. They illustrate the several or many methods possible in treating a given subject, methods dictated as much by the personality as by the craft, or art, of their respective authors.

And quite apart from the values they possess as a means of teaching and study and as a foundation for critical judgments, is their engaging character as pieces of prose, their variety and range, their diversity in practice, the introduction which they give to the work of many writers over a wide period of time. Drawing together as they do the most modern and the long-established both in authors and in the subjects which claim their interest, controversial, aesthetic, social, political, critical, they offer not alone to college students, but to any intelligent reader hours of enjoyment, excitement, and fresh discovery.

Mary Ellen Chase

Prose for
Comparison

I

Queen Elizabeth I

❀ ❀ ❀ ❀ ❀ ❀ ❀ ❀ ❀ ❀ ❀ ❀ ❀ ❀ ❀ ❀ ❀

ELIZABETH TUDOR, an enigmatic character in her own time, has continued to be a controversial figure in history. Artists, historians, biographers, novelists have celebrated her variously, as a woman, as a queen, as England: flesh and blood, political force, symbol. In these six distilled descriptions several varieties of treatment are presented in uncomplicated brevity. The order of arrangement is roughly that of Elizabeth's growth from the girl of twenty to the great queen. It is also an order of ascending complexity and technical interest. It is no mere coincidence that maturity contributes majesty. The successive descriptions take on depth of meaning, the words become more poignant, the portraits more skillful, as the character of the queen assumes broader implications for England and for history.

Even the shortest and simplest of these portraits, that of Neale, attests to the complexity of Elizabeth's character; qualifications and contradictions are suggested: "rather comely than handsome," "more red than yellow," "fine, though . . . olive." At the opposite extreme Virginia Woolf apparently describes only a "ringed hand in water," yet it is an abstract design caparisoned with all the conflicting suggestions of kingship.

❀ ❀ ❀ ❀ ❀ ❀ ❀ ❀ ❀ ❀ ❀ ❀ ❀ ❀ ❀ ❀ ❀

ELIZABETH AT TWENTY

J. E. NEALE · 1934

Elizabeth was just on twenty, in the full bloom of life. Some thought her very handsome, others rather comely than handsome. She was moderately tall, with a fine figure to which her dignified carriage lent impressive majesty. Her hair was golden, but more red than yellow; her skin very fine, though of an olive complexion. She had striking eyes, and above all, beautiful hands which she knew how to display.

From *Queen Elizabeth*, by J. E. Neale. London: Jonathan Cape, Ltd., 1934. Reprinted by kind permission of the publishers.

ELIZABETH AT TWENTY-FIVE

J. R. GREEN · 1878

England's one hope lay in the character of her Queen. Elizabeth was now in her twenty-fifth year. Personally she had more than her mother's beauty; her figure was commanding, her face long but queenly and intelligent, her eyes quick and fine. She had grown up amidst the liberal culture of Henry's court a bold horsewoman, a good shot, a graceful dancer, a skilled musician, and an accomplished scholar. From her father she inherited her frank and hearty address, her love of popularity and of free intercourse with the people, her dauntless courage and her amazing self-confidence. Her harsh, manlike voice, her impetuous will, her pride, her furious outbursts of anger came to her with her Tudor blood. She rated great nobles as if they were schoolboys; she met the insolence

Abridged from J. R. Green, *A Short History of the English People*, 1878.

of Essex with a box on the ear; she would break now and then into the gravest deliberations to swear at her ministers like a fishwife. But strangely in contrast with the violent outlines of her Tudor temper stood the sensuous, self-indulgent nature she derived from Anne Boleyn. Splendor and pleasure were with Elizabeth the very air she breathed. Her delight was to move in perpetual progresses from castle to castle through a series of gorgeous pageants, fanciful and extravagant as a caliph's dream. She loved gaiety and laughter and wit. A happy retort or a finished compliment never failed to win her favour. She hoarded jewels. Her dresses were innumerable. Her vanity remained, even to old age, the vanity of a coquette in her teens. No adulation was too fulsome for her, no flattery of her beauty too gross.

Yet, luxurious and pleasure-loving as she seemed, Elizabeth lived simply and frugally, and she worked hard. Her vanity and caprice had no weight whatever with her in state affairs. The coquette of the presence-chamber became the coolest and hardest of politicians at the council-board. Fresh from the flattery of her courtiers, she would tolerate no flattery in the closet; she was herself plain and downright of speech with her counsellors, and she looked for a corresponding plainness of speech in return. No nobler group of ministers ever gathered round a council-board than those who gathered round the council-board of Elizabeth. But she was the instrument of none. She listened, she weighed, she used or put by the counsels of each in turn, but her policy as a whole was her own. It was a policy, not of genius, but of good sense. Her aims were simple and obvious: to preserve her throne, to keep England out of war, to restore civil and religious order.

If Elizabeth could be said to love anything, she loved England. "Nothing," she said to her first Parliament in words of unwonted fire, "nothing, no worldly thing under the sun, is so dear to me as the love and good-will of my subjects." And the love and good-will which were so dear to her she fully won.

QUEEN ELIZABETH, 1598

PAUL HENTZNER

Next came the Queen, in the sixty-fifth year of her age, as we were told, very majestic; her face oblong, fair, but wrinkled; her eyes small, yet black and pleasant; her nose a little hooked; her lips narrow, and her teeth black (a defect the English seem subject to, from their too great use of sugar); she had in her ears two pearls, with very rich drops; she wore false hair, and that red; upon her head she had a small crown, reported to be made of some of the gold of the celebrated Lunebourg table; her bosom was uncovered, as all the English ladies have it till they marry; and she had on a necklace of exceeding fine jewels; her hands were small, her fingers long, and her stature neither tall nor low; her air was stately, her manner of speaking mild and obliging. That day she was dressed in white silk, bordered with pearls of the size of beans, and over it a mantle of black silk, shot with silver threads; her train was very long, the end of it borne by a marchioness; instead of a chain, she had an oblong collar of gold and jewels. As she went along in all this state and magnificence, she spoke very graciously, first to one, then to another, whether foreign Ministers, or those who attended for different reasons, in English, French, and Italian; for, besides being well skilled in Greek, Latin, and the languages I have mentioned, she is mistress of Spanish, Scotch, and Dutch. Whoever speaks to

From *Travels in England*, 1598. Translated from the German by Richard Bentley (1662–1742).

her, it is kneeling; now and then she raises some with her hand. While we were there, W. Slawata, a Bohemian baron, had letters to present to her; and she, after pulling off her glove, gave him her right hand to kiss, sparkling with rings and jewels, a mark of particular favour. Wherever she turned her face, as she was going along, everybody fell down on their knees.

ELIZABETH AND ESSEX

LYTTON STRACHEY · 1928

Elizabeth herself—from her visible aspect to the profundities of her being, every part of her was permeated by the bewildering discordances of the real and the apparent. Under the serried complexities of her raiment—the huge hoop, the stiff ruff, the swollen sleeves, the powdered pearls, the spreading, gilded gauzes—the form of the woman vanished, and men saw instead an image—magnificent, portentous, self-created —an image of regality, which yet, by a miracle, was actually alive. Posterity has suffered by a similar deceit of vision. The great Queen of its imagination, the lion-hearted heroine, who flung back the insolence of Spain and crushed the tyranny of Rome with splendid unhesitating gestures, no more resembles the Queen of fact than the clothed Elizabeth the naked one. The lion heart, the splendid gestures—such heroic things were there no doubt—visible to everybody; but their true significance in the general scheme of her character was remote and complicated. . . . her true history remains a standing lesson for melodramatists in statecraft. In reality she succeeded by virtue of all the qualities which every hero should be without—dissimulation, pliability, indecision, procrastination, parsimony. Such was her nature—to float, when it was calm, in a sea of indecisions, and, when the wind rose, to tack hectically from side to side. Her femininity saved her. Only a woman could have shuffled so shamelessly, only a woman could have abandoned with such unscrupulous completeness the last shreds not only of consistency, but of dignity, honour, and common decency, in order to escape the appalling necessity of having, really and truly, to make up her mind. Yet it is true that a woman's evasiveness was not enough; male courage, male energy were needed, if she were to escape the pressure that came upon her from every side. Those qualities she also possessed; but their value to her—it was the final paradox of her career—was merely that they made her strong enough to turn her back, with an indomitable persistence, upon the ways of strength.

QUEEN ELIZABETH

GEORGE MACAULAY TREVELYAN · 1926

There was in her a certain hardness and coarseness of fibre, necessary perhaps for her terrible task in life. As a private person she would scarcely have been lovable, perhaps not even very admirable. But lonely on the throne she knew all the arts to make herself adored by her Court and her people. Without ceasing to be a woman and while loving life in all its fullness, she made everything subservient to purposes of state. Her learning endeared her to the universities, her cour-

From *A History of England,* by G. M. Trevelyan. London and New York: Longmans, Green & Co., 1926. Reprinted by permission.

age to the soldiers and sailors. Her coquetry became a means of keeping her nobles and courtiers each in his place, and exacting from each one the last ounce of personal devotion in the public service. Leicester's neck might be tickled by the royal hand, but his rival Cecil would be trusted in matters of high policy. Her love of hunting and dancing, masque, pageantry and display, was used to strengthen the wider popularity which was her ultimate strength; her public appearances and progresses through the country, which she thoroughly enjoyed, were no dull and formal functions, but works of art by a great player whose heart was in the piece, interchanges of soul between a Princess and her loving people.

THE GREAT QUEEN

VIRGINIA WOOLF · 1928

Orlando, overcome with shyness, darted off and reached the banqueting-hall only just in time to sink upon his knees and, hanging his head in confusion, to offer a bowl of rose water to the great Queen herself.

Such was his shyness that he saw no more of her than her ringed hand in water; but it was enough. It was a memorable hand; a thin hand with long fingers always curling as if round orb or sceptre; a nervous, crabbed, sickly hand; a commanding hand; a hand that had only to raise itself for a head to fall; a hand, he guessed, attached to an old body that smelt like a cupboard in which furs are kept in camphor; which body was yet caparisoned in all sorts of brocades and gems; and held itself very upright though perhaps in pain from

sciatica; and never flinched though strung together by a thousand fears; and the Queen's eyes were light yellow. All this
he felt as the great rings flashed in the water and then something pressed his hair—which, perhaps, accounts for his seeing
nothing more likely to be of use to a historian. And in truth,
his mind was such a welter of opposites—of the night and the
blazing candles, of the shabby poet and the great Queen, of
silent fields and the clatter of serving men—that he could see
nothing; or only a hand.

II

Abraham Lincoln

❋ ❋ ❋ ❋ ❋ ❋ ❋ ❋ ❋ ❋ ❋ ❋ ❋ ❋ ❋ ❋ ❋ ❋

FEW AMERICANS can project themselves into a dispassionate consideration of the character of Lincoln. Almost no one living in the twentieth century can recapture by whatever power of imagination the feelings of doubt, insecurity, snobbery, fear, uncertainty, hope against all assurance of hope, with which Lincoln was greeted in the first years of his presidency. The first six of these selections were chosen because they are primary sources, descriptions written in the early years of Lincoln's public life, when opinion of him was shifting and uncertain, and when it was uncolored by martyrdom. They were chosen, moreover, to represent the varied opinions of well-known Americans. Howells's *Life* was written as a campaign biography; Whitman's comment is a vivid example of a poet's prose, very different in character from the poems on Lincoln which he wrote later, though the ship image is already suggested. Conant's account reveals the artist's perception of what was actually his experience in doing a portrait of Lincoln at the time of the first presidential campaign. Howells and Hawthorne employ even in such short passages the methods of the novelist. Herndon was, of course, the man who knew Lincoln best; and Charnwood, the Englishman of a later century who admired him most. Unlike the others these two write with knowledge of Lincoln's whole career and in the light of his assassination.

❋ ❋ ❋ ❋ ❋ ❋ ❋ ❋ ❋ ❋ ❋ ❋ ❋ ❋ ❋ ❋ ❋ ❋

THE SEPARATE STREAMS

DR. J. G. HOLLAND · 1866

The writer has conversed with multitudes of men who claimed to know Mr. Lincoln intimately: yet there are not two of the whole number who agree in their estimate of him. The fact was that he rarely showed more than one aspect of himself to one man. He opened himself to men in different directions. To illustrate the effect of the peculiarity of Mr. Lincoln's intercourse with men it may be said that men who knew him through all his professional and political life offered opinions as diametrically opposite as these, viz.: that he was a very ambitious man, and that he was without a particle of ambition; that he was one of the saddest men that ever lived, and that he was one of the jolliest men that ever lived; that he was very religious, but that he was not a Christian; that he was a Christian, but did not know it; that he was so far from being a religious man or a Christian that "the less said upon that subject the better"; that he was the most cunning man in America, and that he had not a particle of cunning in him; that he had the strongest personal attachments, and that he had no personal attachments at all—only a general good feeling towards everybody; that he was a man of indomitable will, and that he was a man almost without a will; that he was a tyrant, and that he was the softest-hearted, most brotherly man that ever lived; that he was remarkable for his pure-mindedness, and that he was the foulest in his jests and stories of any man in the country; that he was a witty man, and that he was only a retailer of the wit of others; that his apparent candor and fairness were only apparent, and that they were as real

As quoted in William H. Herndon and Jesse William Weik, *Herndon's Lincoln,* 1889.

as his head and his hands; that he was a boor, and that he was in all respects a gentleman; that he was a leader of the people, and that he was always led by the people; that he was cool and impassive, and that he was susceptible of the strongest passions. It is only by tracing these separate streams of impression back to their fountain that we are able to arrive at anything like a competent comprehension of the man, or to learn why he came to be held in such various estimation. Men caught only separate aspects of his character—only the fragments that were called into exhibition by their own qualities.

LINCOLN IN 1860

WILLIAM DEAN HOWELLS

Mr. Lincoln's political room is an apartment in the State House, at the door of which you knock unceremoniously. A sturdy voice calls out, "Come in!" and you find yourself in the presence of a man who rises to the hight [*sic*] of six feet three inches, as you enter. He shakes you with earnest cordiality by the hand—receiving you as in the old days he would have received a friend who called upon him at his farm-work; for those who have always known him, say that, though Lincoln is now more distinguished, he has always been a great man, and his simple and hearty manners have undergone no change. You find him, in physique, thin and wiry, and he has an appearance of standing infirmly upon his feet, which often deceived those who contended with him in the wrestle, in his younger days.

The great feature of the man's face is his brilliant and piercing eye, which has never been dimmed by any vice, great or small. His rude and vigorous early life contributed to

From *Life of Abraham Lincoln*, 1860.

strengthen the robust constitution which he inherited, and he is now, at fifty, in the prime of life, with rugged health, though bearing, in the lines of his face, the trace of severe and earnest thought.

LINCOLN IN 1862

NATHANIEL HAWTHORNE

By and by there was a little stir on the staircase and in the passageway, and in lounged a tall, loose-jointed figure, of an exaggerated Yankee port and demeanor, whom (as being about the homeliest man I ever saw, yet by no means repulsive or disagreeable) it was impossible not to recognize as Uncle Abe.

Unquestionably, Western man though he be, and Kentuckian by birth, President Lincoln is the essential representative of all Yankees, and the veritable specimen, physically, of what the world seems determined to regard as our characteristic qualities. There is no describing his lengthy awkwardness, nor the uncouthness of his movement; and yet it seemed as if I had been in the habit of seeing him daily, and had shaken hands with him a thousand times in some village street; so true was he to the aspect of the pattern American, though with a certain extravagance which, possibly, I exaggerated still further by the delighted eagerness with which I took it in. If put to guess his calling and livelihood, I should have taken him for a country schoolmaster (the Ichabod Crane type) as soon as anything else.

As quoted in Roy P. Basler, *The Lincoln Legend,* 1935. Reprinted by permission of and arrangement with Houghton Mifflin Company, the authorized publishers.

The whole physiognomy is as coarse a one as you would meet anywhere in the length and breadth of the states; but, withal, it is redeemed, illuminated, softened, and brightened by a kindly though serious look out of his eyes, and an expression of homely sagacity, that seems weighted with rich results of village experience. A great deal of native sense; no bookish cultivation, no refinement; honest at heart, and thoroughly so, and yet, in some sort, sly,—at least, endowed with a sort of tact and wisdom that are akin to craft, and would impel him, I think, to take an antagonist in flank, rather than to make a bull-run at him right in front.

His manner toward us was wholly without pretense, but yet had a kind of natural dignity, quite sufficient to keep the forwardest of us from clapping him on the shoulder and asking him for a story.

However, lest the above allusions to President Lincoln's little peculiarities (already well known to the country and to the world) should be misinterpreted, I deem it proper to say a word or two in regard to him, of unfeigned respect and measurable confidence. He is evidently a man of keen faculties, and what is still more to the purpose, of powerful character. As to his integrity, the people have that intuition of it which is never deceived. The President is teachable by events, and has now spent a year in a very arduous course of education; he has a flexible mind, capable of much expansion, and convertible towards far loftier studies and activities than those of his early life; and if he came to Washington a backwoods humorist, he has already transformed himself into as good a statesman (to speak moderately) as his prime-minister.

LINCOLN IN 1863

WALT WHITMAN

I think well of the President. He has a face like a Hoosier
Michael Angelo, so awful ugly it becomes beautiful with its
strange mouth, its deep cut, criss-cross lines, and its doughnut
complexion. My notion is, too, that underneath his outside
smutched mannerism, and stories from third-class county bar-
rooms (it is his humor) Mr. Lincoln keeps a fountain of first-
class practical telling wisdom. I do not dwell on the supposed
failures of his government; he has shown, I sometimes think,
an almost supernatural tact in keeping the ship afloat at all,
with head steady, not only not going down, and now certain
not to, but with proud and resolute spirit, and flag flying in
sight of the world, menacing and high as ever, I say never yet
captain, never ruler, had such a perplexing dangerous task
as his, the past two years. I more and more rely upon his
idiomatic western genius, careless of court dress or court
decorum.

From a letter written by Whitman, March 19, 1863.

PAINTING LINCOLN'S PORTRAIT

ALBAN JASPER CONANT · 1860

Something had to be done, and I began by asking permission
to arrange his hair, which stood out like an oven broom. He
nodded, and with my fingers I brushed it back, disclosing the

splendid lines of the forehead. At least that was something, I thought, as I backed away. But it was not enough. All the other features seemed to me hopeless, as I stood there. His ill repute in my section flooded into my mind; his common origin —born of Kentucky "poor white trash"; his plebeian pursuits, his coarse tastes and low associates. He seemed to me, indeed, the story-telling, whisky-drinking, whisky-selling country grocer who, they said, had been exalted to the exclusion of the astute Seward.

As I sat down again before my easel, I made some flippant remark calculated to appeal to the vulgarian. It was then I got my first hint of the innate dignity of the man. He made some monosyllabic reply, and there came over his face the most marvelously complex expression I have ever seen—a mingling of instant shrewd apprehension of the whole attitude of mind back of my remark, pained disappointment of my misunderstanding of him, and patient tolerance. In a flash, I saw I had made a mistake.

THE PRESIDENT IN 1864

HORACE GREELEY

Mr. Lincoln, if you will, is not a hero—not a genius—not a man of the very highest order of intellect. He has made mistakes as President, some of which it is quite possible that another might have avoided. But is the God-forsaken traitor who reviles him as an ape, a hyena, as a jackass, one whit more absurd than the feeble Northern imitator who prates of him as "a railsplitting buffoon," who has "grown up in uncouth ignorance," etc., etc.? If that is a true characterization of one who

From *The New York Tribune,* June 24, 1864.

has stood such tests, overcome such impediments, and achieved such successes as Abraham Lincoln, then a democracy based on popular suffrage is an impudent fraud—a stupendous hoax —and we ought at once to burn our constitutions, close our schoolhouses, prohibit all future elections, and dispatch a deputation of notables to Louis Napoleon to beg him to send us an Emperor. That's all.

HERNDON'S LINCOLN

WILLIAM H. HERNDON · 1889

Mr. Lincoln was six feet four inches high, and when he left the city of his home for Washington was fifty-one years old, having good health and no gray hairs, or but few, on his head. He was thin, wiry, sinewy, raw-boned; thin through the breast to the back, and narrow across the shoulders; standing he leaned forward—was what may be called stoop-shouldered, inclining to the consumptive by build. His usual weight was one hundred and eighty pounds. His organization—rather his structure and functions—worked slowly. His blood had to run a long distance from his heart to the extremities of his frame, and his nerve force had to travel through dry ground a long distance before his muscles were obedient to his will. His structure was loose and leathery; his body was shrunk and shrivelled; he had dark skin, dark hair, and looked woe-struck. The whole man, body and mind, worked slowly, as if it needed oiling. Physically he was a very powerful man, lifting with ease four hundred, and in one case six hundred, pounds. His mind was like his body, and worked slowly but strongly.

From *Herndon's Lincoln*, 1889.

Hence there was very little bodily or mental wear and tear in him. This peculiarity in his construction gave him great advantage over other men in public life. No man in America —scarcely a man in the world—could have stood what Lincoln did in Washington and survived through more than one term of the Presidency.

Mr. Lincoln's head was long, and tall from the base of the brain and from the eyebrows. His head ran backwards, his forehead rising as it ran back at a low angle, like Clay's, and unlike Webster's, which was almost perpendicular. The size of his hat measured at the hatter's block was seven and one-eighth, his head being, from ear to ear, six and one-half inches, and from the front to the back of the brain eight inches. Thus measured it was not below the medium size. His forehead was narrow but high; his hair was dark, almost black, and lay floating where his fingers or the winds left it, piled up at random. His cheek-bones were high, sharp, and prominent; his jaws were long and upcurved; his nose was large, long, blunt, and a little awry towards the right eye; his chin was sharp and upcurved; his eyebrows cropped out like a huge rock on the brow of a hill; his long, sallow face was wrinkled and dry, with a hair here and there on the surface; his cheeks were leathery; his ears were large, and ran out almost at right angles from his head, caused partly by heavy hats and partly by nature; his lower lip was thick, hanging, and undercurved, while his chin reached for the lip upcurved; his neck was neat and trim, his head being well balanced on it; there was the lone mole on the right cheek, and Adam's apple on his throat.

Thus stood, walked, acted, and looked Abraham Lincoln. He was not a pretty man by any means, nor was he an ugly one; he was a homely man, careless of his looks, plain-looking and plain-acting. He had no pomp, display, or dignity, so-called. He appeared simple in his carriage and bearing. He was a sad-looking man; his melancholy dripped from him as he walked. His apparent gloom impressed his friends, and created sympathy for him—one means of his great success. He was gloomy, abstracted, and joyous—rather, humorous—by turns; but I do not think he knew what real joy was for many years.

His power in the association of ideas was as great as his memory was tenacious and strong. His language indicated oddity and originality of vision as well as expression. Words and language are but the counterparts of the idea—the other half of the idea; they are but the stinging, hot, leaden bullets that drop from the mould; in a rifle, with powder stuffed behind them and fire applied, they are an embodied force resistlessly pursuing their object. In the search for words Mr. Lincoln was often at a loss. He was often perplexed to give proper expression to his ideas; first, because he was not master of the English language; and secondly, because there were, in the vast store of words, so few that contained the exact coloring, power, and shape of his ideas. This will account for the frequent resort by him to the use of stories, maxims, and jokes in which to clothe his ideas, that they might be comprehended. So true was this peculiar mental vision of his that, though mankind has been gathering, arranging, and classifying facts for thousands of years, Lincoln's peculiar standpoint could give him no advantage over other men's labor. Hence he tore down to their deepest foundations all arrangements of facts, and constructed new ones to govern himself. He was compelled from his peculiar mental organization to do this. His labor was great and continuous.

The great predominating elements of Mr. Lincoln's peculiar character were: first, his great capacity and power of reason; second, his conscience and his excellent understanding; third, an exalted idea of the sense of right and equity; fourth, his intense veneration of the true and the good. His conscience, his heart and all the faculties and qualities of his mind bowed submissively to the despotism of his reason. He lived and acted from the standard of reason—that throne of logic, home of principle—the realm of Deity in man.

With the sympathy and love of the people to sustain him, Lincoln had unlimited power over them; he threw an invisible and weightless harness over them, and drove them through disaster and desperation to final victory. The trust and worship by the people of Lincoln were the result of his simple character. He held himself not aloof from the masses. He became one of them. They feared together, they struggled together, they hoped together; thus melted and moulded into one, they became one in thought, one in will, one in action. If Lincoln cautiously awaited the full development of the last fact in the great drama before he acted, when longer waiting would be a crime, he knew that the people were determinedly at his back. Thus, when a blow was struck, it came with the unerring aim and power of a bolt from heaven. A natural king—not ruling men, but leading them along the drifts and trends of their own tendencies, always keeping in mind the consent of the governed, he developed what the future historian will call the sublimest order of conservative statesmanship.

Whatever of life, vigor, force, and power of eloquence his peculiar qualities gave him; whatever there was in a fair, manly, honest, and impartial administration of justice under law to all men at all times; whatever there was in a strong will in the right governed by tenderness and mercy; whatever there was in toil and sublime patience; whatever there was in these things or a wise combination of them, Lincoln is justly entitled to in making up the impartial verdict of history. These limit and define him as a statesman, as an orator, as an executive of the nation, and as a man. They developed in all the walks of his life; they were his law; they were his nature, they were Abraham Lincoln.

CHARNWOOD'S LINCOLN

GODFREY RATHBONE BENSON, LORD CHARNWOOD · 1917

Many great deeds had been done in the war. The greatest was the keeping of the North together in an enterprise so arduous, and an enterprise for objects so confusedly related as the Union and freedom. Abraham Lincoln did this; nobody else could have done it; to do it he bore on his sole shoulders such a weight of care and pain as few other men have borne. When it was over it seemed to the people that he had all along been thinking their real thoughts for them; but they knew that this was because he had fearlessly thought for himself. He had been able to save the nation, partly because he saw that unity was not to be sought by the way of base concession. He had been able to free the slaves, partly because he would not hasten to this object at the sacrifice of what he thought a larger purpose. This most unrelenting enemy to the project of the Confederacy was the one man who had quite purged his heart and mind from hatred or even anger towards his fellow-country-men of the South. That fact came to be seen in the South too, and generations in America are likely to remember it when all other features of his statecraft have grown indistinct. A thousand reminiscences ludicrous or pathetic, passing into myth but enshrining hard fact, will prove to them that this great feature of his policy was a matter of more than policy. They will remember it as adding a peculiar lustre to the renovation of their national existence; as no small part of the glory, surpassing that of former wars, which has become the common heritage of North and South. For per-

haps not many conquerors, and certainly few successful statesmen, have escaped the tendency of power to harden or at
least to narrow their human sympathies; but in this man a
natural wealth of tender compassion became richer and more
tender while in the stress of deadly conflict he developed an
astounding strength.

Beyond his own country some of us recall his name as the
greatest among those associated with the cause of popular
government. He would have liked this tribute, and the element of truth in it is plain enough, yet it demands one final
consideration. He accepted the institutions to which he was
born, and he enjoyed them. His own intense experience of the
weakness of democracy did not sour him, nor would any
similar experience of later times have been likely to do so. Yet
if he reflected much on forms of government it was with a
dominant interest in something beyond them. For he was a
citizen of that far country where there is neither aristocrat
nor democrat. No political theory stands out from his words
or actions; but they show a most unusual sense of the possible
dignity of common men and common things. His humour
rioted in comparisons between potent personages and Jim
Jett's brother or old Judge Brown's drunken coachman, for
the reason for which the rarely jesting Wordsworth found a
hero in the "Leech-Gatherer" or in Nelson and a villain in
Napoleon or in Peter Bell. He could use and respect and pardon
and overrule his far more accomplished ministers because he
stood up to them with no more fear or cringing, with no more
dislike or envy or disrespect than he had felt when he stood up
long before to Jack Armstrong. He faced the difficulties and
terrors of his high office with that same mind with which he
had paid his way as a poor man or navigated a boat in rapids
or in floods. If he had a theory of democracy it was contained
in this condensed note which he wrote, perhaps as an auto-

graph, a year or two before his Presidency: "As I would not be a slave, so I would not be a master. This expresses my idea of democracy. Whatever differs from this, to the extent of the difference, is no democracy.—A. Lincoln."

III
Victorian Setting

❋ ❋ ❋ ❋ ❋ ❋ ❋ ❋ ❋ ❋ ❋ ❋ ❋ ❋ ❋ ❋ ❋ ❋

SETTING, the background or frame for an event or a story or an idea, presents the simplest problem in exposition. It is static, it is factual, it is material. Yet the first sentence of a description of place, as diagrammatic as that from "Scene of the Crime" or as mechanical as that from "Stage Set," introduces suggestions and implications which are not pure fact and are not purely objective.

Description of a room enables an author to present an abundance of revealing detail as highly selective as he wishes to make it and capable of infinite shades of coloring. He furnishes the room with objects chosen for their significance; he modifies the objects with adjectives or phrases of interpretation which contribute to his purpose; finally, he adjusts the light and heat which are the climate of his scene. "Cord," "weapon," "clock," "salt cellar," and "chair cover" are important. "Crimson," "ancient," "gilt," "pot-bellied," "tartan," each makes the object more significant. "Cold winter sunshine," "needlessly dark," "full glare," "the damp on their minds" are further interpretations.

These descriptions of Victorian rooms are arranged to proceed from the most purely factual and objective, through the subjective, to the figurative. Sir Arthur Conan Doyle's room is a clue, Granville-Barker's a social background, Somerset Maugham's an emotion, Lytton Strachey's a composite or montage, and Virginia Woolf's a state of mind.

❋ ❋ ❋ ❋ ❋ ❋ ❋ ❋ ❋ ❋ ❋ ❋ ❋ ❋ ❋ ❋ ❋ ❋

SCENE OF THE CRIME

SIR ARTHUR CONAN DOYLE · 1905

It was a very large and high chamber, with carved oak ceiling, oaken panelling, and a fine array of deers' heads and ancient weapons around the walls. At the farther end from the door was the high French window of which we had heard. Three smaller windows on the right-hand side filled the apartment with cold winter sunshine. On the left was a large, deep fireplace, with a massive overhanging oak mantelpiece. Beside the fireplace was a heavy oaken chair with arms and cross-bars at the bottom. In and out through the open woodwork was woven a crimson cord, which was secured at each side to the crosspiece below. In releasing the lady the cord had been slipped off her, but the knots with which it had been secured still remained. These details only struck our attention afterwards, for our thoughts were entirely absorbed by the terrible object which lay spread upon the tigerskin hearthrug in front of the fire.

Holmes was down on his knees examining with great attention the knots upon the red cord with which the lady had been secured. Then he carefully scrutinized the broken and frayed end where it had snapped off when the burglar had dragged it down.

"When this was pulled down the bell in the kitchen must have rung loudly," he remarked.

"No one could hear it. The kitchen stands right at the back of the house."

From "The Adventure of the Abbey Grange," *The Return of Sherlock Holmes*, by Sir Arthur Conan Doyle. Included in this book by kind permission of the Estate of the late Sir Arthur Conan Doyle.

"How did the burglar know no one would hear it? How dare he pull at a bell-rope in that reckless fashion?"

"Exactly, Mr. Holmes, exactly. You put the very question which I have asked myself again and again. There can be no doubt that this fellow must have known the house and its habits. He must have perfectly understood that the servants would all be in bed at that comparatively early hour, and that no one could possibly hear a bell ring in the kitchen. Therefore he must have been in close league with one of the servants. Surely that is evident. But there are eight servants, and all of good character."

"These three glasses upon the sideboard have been untouched, I suppose?"

"Yes; and the bottle stands as they left it."

The three glasses were grouped together, all of them tinged with wine, and one of them containing some dregs of beeswing. The bottle stood near them, two-thirds full, and beside it lay a long, deeply stained cork. Its appearance and the dust upon the bottle showed that it was no common vintage which the murderers had enjoyed.

STAGE SET

HARLEY GRANVILLE GRANVILLE-BARKER · 1911

The Huxtables live at Denmark Hill, for Mr. Huxtable is the surviving partner in the well-known Peckham drapery establishment of Roberts & Huxtable, and the situation, besides being salubrious, is therefore convenient. It is a new house.

From *The Madras House*, 1911. Reprinted with the kind permission of Ben Abramson, for the Estate of the Author.

Mr. Huxtable bought it half finished, so that the interior might be to his liking; its exterior the builder said one might describe as of a Free Queen Anne Treatment; to which Mr. Huxtable rejoined, after blinking at the red brick spotted with stone ornament, that after all it was inside they were going to live, you know.

Through the stained, grained front door, rattling with colored glass, one reaches the hall, needlessly narrow, needlessly dark, but with its black-and-white tessellated pavement making for cleanliness. On the left is the stained and grained staircase, with its Brussels carpet and twisted brass stair rods, on the right the drawing-room. The drawing-room can hardly be said to express the personality of Mr. Huxtable. The foundations of its furnishings are in the taste of Mrs. Huxtable. For fifteen years or so additions to this family museum have been disputed into their place by the six Miss Huxtables: Laura (aged thirty-nine), Minnie, Clara, Julia, Emma, Jane (aged twenty-six). The rosewood cabinets, the picture from some Academy of the early Seventies, entitled In Ye Olden Time (this was a wedding present, most likely), the gilt clock, which is a Shakespeare, narrow-headed, but with a masterly pair of legs, propped pensively against a dial and enshrined beneath a dome of glass, another wedding present. These were the treasures of Mrs. Huxtable's first drawing-room, her solace in the dull post-honeymoon days. She was the daughter of a city merchant, wholesale as against her husband's retail; but even in the Seventies retail was lifting its head.

THE LAPHAM DRAWING-ROOM

WILLIAM DEAN HOWELLS · 1884

The Lapham drawing-room in Nankeen Square was in the parti-coloured paint which the Colonel had hoped to repeat in his new house: the trim of the doors and windows was in light green and the panels in salmon; the walls were a plain tint of French grey paper, divided by gilt mouldings into broad panels with a wide stripe of red velvet paper running up the corners; the chandelier was of massive imitation bronze; the mirror over the mantel rested on a fringed mantel-cover of green reps, and heavy curtains of that stuff hung from gilt lambrequin frames at the window; the carpet was of a small pattern in crude green, which, at the time Mrs. Lapham bought it, covered half the new floors in Boston. In the panelled spaces on the walls were some stone-coloured landscapes, representing the mountains and cañons of the West, which the Colonel and his wife had visited on one of the early official railroad excursions. In front of the long windows looking into the Square were statues, kneeling figures which turned their backs upon the company within-doors, and represented allegories of Faith and Prayer to people without. A white marble group of several figures, expressing an Italian conception of Lincoln Freeing the Slaves—a Latin negro and his wife—with our Eagle flapping his wings in approval, at Lincoln's feet, occupied one corner, and balanced the what-not of an earlier period in another. These phantasms added their chill to that imparted by the tone of the walls, the landscapes, and the carpets, and contributed to the violence of the contrast when the chandelier was lighted up full glare, and the heat of the whole furnace welled up from the registers into the quivering

From *The Rise of Silas Lapham*, 1884.

atmosphere on one of the rare occasions when the Laphams invited company.

MRS. CAREY'S ROOM

W. SOMERSET MAUGHAM · 1915

Philip went downstairs slowly and found the door open. Mr. Carey had left the room. Philip walked slowly round. They had been in the house so short a time that there was little in it that had a particular interest to him. It was a stranger's room, and Philip saw nothing that struck his fancy. But he knew which were his mother's things and which belonged to the landlord, and presently fixed on a little clock that he had once heard his mother say she liked. With this he walked again rather disconsolately upstairs. Outside the door of his mother's bed-room he stopped and listened. Though no one had told him not to go in, he had a feeling that it would be wrong to do so; he was a little frightened, and his heart beat uncomfortably; but at the same time something impelled him to turn the handle. He turned it very gently, as if to prevent anyone within from hearing, and then slowly pushed the door open. He stood on the threshold for a moment before he had the courage to enter. He was not frightened now, but it seemed strange. He closed the door behind him. The blinds were drawn, and the room, in the cold light of a January afternoon, was dark. On the dressing-table were Mrs. Carey's brushes and the hand mirror. In a little tray were hairpins. There was a photograph of himself on the chimney-piece and one of his father. He had often been in the room when his mother was not in it, but now it seemed different. There was something curious in the look of the chairs. The bed was made as though someone were going to sleep in it that night, and in a case on the pillow was a night-dress.

Philip opened a large cupboard filled with dresses and, stepping in, took as many of them as he could in his arms and buried his face in them. They smelt of the scent his mother used. Then he pulled open the drawers, filled with his mother's things, and looked at them: there were lavender bags among the linen, and their scent was fresh and pleasant. The strangeness of the room left it, and it seemed to him that his mother had just gone out for a walk. She would be in presently and would come upstairs to have nursery tea with him. And he seemed to feel her kiss on his lips.

It was not true that he would never see her again. It was not true simply because it was impossible. He climbed up on the bed and put his head on the pillow. He lay there quite still.

THE PODSNAP ESTABLISHMENT

CHARLES DICKENS · 1864–1865

Mr. and Mrs. Veneering, and Mr. and Mrs. Veneering's brannew bride and bridegroom, were of the dinner company; but the Podsnap establishment had nothing else in common with the Veneerings. Mr. Podsnap could tolerate taste in a mushroom man who stood in need of that sort of thing, but was far above it himself. Hideous solidity was the characteristic of the Podsnap plate. Everything was made to look as heavy as

From *Our Mutual Friend*, 1864–1865.

it could, and to take up as much room as possible. Everything said boastfully, "Here you have as much of me in my ugliness as if I were only lead; but I am so many ounces of precious metal worth so much an ounce;—wouldn't you like to melt me down?" A corpulent straddling epergne, blotched all over as if it had broken out in an eruption rather than been ornamented, delivered this address from an unsightly silver platform in the centre of the table. Four silver wine-coolers, each furnished with four staring heads, each head obtrusively carrying a big silver ring in each of its ears, conveyed the sentiment up and down the table, and handed it on to the pot-bellied silver salt-cellars. All the big silver spoons and forks widened the mouths of the company expressly for the purpose of thrusting the sentiment down their throats with every morsel they ate. The majority of the guests were like the plate, and included several heavy articles weighing ever so much.

Certain big, heavy vehicles, built on the model of the Podsnap plate, took away the heavy articles of guests weighing ever so much; and the less valuable articles got away after their various manners; and the Podsnap plate was put to bed. As Mr. Podsnap stood with his back to the drawing-room fire, pulling up his shirt-collar, like a veritable cock of the walk literally pluming himself in the midst of his possessions, nothing would have astonished him more than an intimation that Miss Podsnap, or any other young person properly born and bred, could not be exactly put away like the plate, brought out like the plate, polished like the plate, counted, weighed, and valued like the plate. That such a young person could possibly have a morbid vacancy in the heart for anything younger than the plate, or less monotonous than the plate; or that such a young person's thoughts could try to scale the region bounded on the north, south, east, and west, by the plate; was a monstrous imagination which he would on the spot have flourished into space.

BALMORAL CASTLE

LYTTON STRACHEY · 1921

Spacious, built of granite in the Scotch baronial style, with a tower 100 feet high, and minor turrets and castellated gables, the castle was skilfully arranged to command the finest views of the surrounding mountains and of the neighbouring river Dee. Upon the interior decorations Albert and Victoria lavished all their care. The wall and the floors were of pitch-pine, and covered with specially manufactured tartans. The Balmoral tartan, in red and grey, designed by the Prince, and the Victoria tartan, with a white stripe, designed by the Queen, were to be seen in every room: there were tartan curtains, and tartan chair-covers, and even tartan linoleums. Occasionally the Royal Stuart tartan appeared, for Her Majesty always maintained that she was an ardent Jacobite. Water-colour sketches by Victoria hung upon the walls, together with innumerable stags' antlers, and the head of a boar, which had been shot by Albert in Germany. In an alcove in the hall, stood a life-sized statue of Albert in Highland dress.

Victoria declared that it was perfection. "Every year," she wrote, "my heart becomes more fixed in this dear paradise, and so much more so now, that *all* has become my dear Albert's *own* creation, own work, own building, own lay-out; . . . and his great taste, and the impress of his dear hand, have been stamped everywhere."

THE EMPIRE

VIRGINIA WOOLF · 1928

Thus, stealthily, and imperceptibly, none marking the exact
day or hour of the change, the constitution of England was
altered and nobody knew it. Everywhere the effects were
felt. The hardy country gentleman, who had sat down gladly
to a meal of ale and beef in a room designed, perhaps by the
brothers Adam, with classic dignity, now felt chilly. Rugs
appeared, beards were grown and trousers fastened tight
under the instep. The chill which he felt in his legs he soon
transferred to his house; furniture was muffled; walls and
tables were covered too. Then a change of diet became essential. The muffin was invented and the crumpet. Coffee
supplanted the after-dinner port, and, as coffee led to a
drawing-room in which to drink it, and a drawing-room to
glass cases, and glass cases to artificial flowers, and artificial
flowers to mantelpieces, and mantelpieces to pianofortes, and
pianofortes to drawing-room ballads, and drawing-room ballads (skipping a stage or two) to innumerable little dogs,
mats, and antimacassars, the home—which had become extremely important—was completely altered.

But the change did not stop at outward things. The damp
struck within. Men felt the chill in their hearts; the damp in
their minds. In a desperate effort to snuggle their feelings into
some sort of warmth one subterfuge was tried after another.
Love, birth, and death were all swaddled in a variety of fine
phrases. The sexes drew further and further apart. No open
conversation was tolerated. Evasions and concealments were
sedulously practised on both sides. And just as the ivy and the
evergreen rioted in the damp earth outside, so did the same

fertility show itself within. The life of the average woman was a succession of childbirths. She married at nineteen and had fifteen or eighteen children by the time she was thirty; for twins abounded. Thus the British Empire came into existence; and thus—for there is no stopping damp; it gets into the inkpot as it gets into the woodwork—sentences swelled, adjectives multiplied, lyrics became epics, and little trifles that had been essays a column long were now encyclopaedias in ten or twenty volumes.

While this went on in every part of England, it was all very well for Orlando to mew herself in her house at Blackfriars and pretend that the climate was the same; that one could still say what one liked and wear knee-breeches or skirts as the fancy took one. Even she, at length, was forced to acknowledge that times were changed. One afternoon in the early part of the century she was driving through St. James' Park in her old panelled coach when one of those sunbeams, which occasionally, though not often, managed to come to earth, struggled through, marbling the clouds with strange prismatic colours as it passed. But what was her surprise when, as it struck the earth, the sunbeam seemed to call forth, or to light up, a pyramid, hecatomb, or trophy (for it had something of a banquet-table air)—a conglomeration at any rate of the most heterogeneous and ill-assorted objects, piled higgledy-piggledy in a vast mound where the statue of Queen Victoria now stands! Draped about a vast cross of fretted and floriated gold were widow's weeds and bridal veils; hooked on to other excrescences were crystal palaces, bassinettes, military helmets, memorial wreaths, trousers, whiskers, wedding cakes, cannon, Christmas trees, telescopes, extinct monsters, globes, maps, elephants and mathematical-instruments—the whole supported like a gigantic coat of arms on the right side by a female figure clothed in flowing white; on the left, by a portly gentleman wearing a frock-coat and sponge-bag trousers. The incongruity of the objects, the association of the fully clothed and the partly draped, the garishness of the different colours and their plaid-like juxtapositions afflicted Orlando with the most profound dismay. She had never, in all her life, seen anything at once so indecent, so hideous, and so monumental.

IV
Small Town, U.S.A.

❋ ❋ ❋ ❋ ❋ ❋ ❋ ❋ ❋ ❋ ❋ ❋ ❋ ❋ ❋ ❋ ❋ ❋ ❋

THE SMALL TOWN is so useful as a circumscribed epitome of life that it has become an almost universal setting, not for fiction only but also for the sociological and political study, the patriotic discourse, and the artistic or satiric representation. The variety of its uses testifies to the rich and intricate complexity of admiration, detraction, interpretation, dissection, devotion, and confusion with which different authors have treated the subject. It is all things to all people, and many things to many authors.

The most interesting aspect of these readings, and the most difficult, is therefore the recognition of the tone of the description and its relation to the author's intention. Tarkington's "matronly hen" and "itinerant pigs," Lewis's "brass cuspidors" and "pink arm-garters," Gunther's "overhead lights" and "chain stores," Kate Douglas Wiggin's "purple clover-fields" and "palm leaf fans," Marquand's Johnson Street, and Bliven's Anglo-Saxons are clues to the attitudes of their authors. "Jails," says Faulkner, are "the true record of . . . history." The endless chain of meaning in each detail of small-town geography is a challenge to repeated and thoughtful reading.

❋ ❋ ❋ ❋ ❋ ❋ ❋ ❋ ❋ ❋ ❋ ❋ ❋ ❋ ❋ ❋ ❋ ❋ ❋

PLATTVILLE

BOOTH TARKINGTON · 1899

The social and business energy of Plattville concentrates on
the Square. Here, in summer-time, the gentlemen are wont
to lounge from store to store in their shirt sleeves; and here
stood the old, red-brick court-house, loosely fenced in a
shady grove of maple and elm—"slipp'ry ellum"—called the
"Court-House Yard." When the sun grew too hot for the
dry-goods box whittlers in front of the stores around the
Square and the occupants of the chairs in front of the Palace
Hotel on the corner, they would go across and drape themselves over the court-house fence, under the trees, and leisurely
carve their initials on the top board. The farmers hitched their
teams to the fence, for there were usually loafers energetic
enough to shout "Whoa!" if the flies worried the horses beyond patience. In the yard, amongst the weeds and tall, unkept
grass, chickens foraged all day long; the fence was so low
that the most matronly hen flew over with propriety; and
there were gaps that accommodated the passage of itinerant
pigs. Most of the latter, however, preferred the cool wallows
of the less important street corners. Here and there a big
dog lay asleep in the middle of the road, knowing well that
the easy-going Samaritan, in his case, would pass by on the
other side.

Only one street attained to the dignity of a name—Main
Street, which formed the north side of the Square. In Carlow
County, descriptive location is usually accomplished by des-
ignating the adjacent, as, "Up at Bardlocks'," "Down by
Schofields'," "Right where Hibbards live," "Acrost from
Sol Tibbs's," or, "Other side of Jones's field." In winter, Main
Street was a series of frozen gorges and hummocks; in fall

From *The Gentleman from Indiana*, 1899.

and spring, a river of mud; in summer, a continuing dust heap; it was the best street in Plattville.

The people lived happily; and, while the world whirled on outside, they were content with their own. It would have moved their surprise as much as their indignation to hear themselves spoken of as a "secluded community"; for they sat up all night to hear the vote of New York, every campaign. Once when the President visited Rouen, seventy miles away, there were only a few bankrupts (and not a baby amongst them) left in the deserted homes of Carlow County. Everybody had adventures; almost everybody saw the great man; and everybody was glad to get back home again. It was the longest journey some of them ever set upon, and these, elated as they were over their travels, determined to think twice ere they went that far from home another time.

On Saturdays, the farmers enlivened the commercial atmosphere of Plattville; and Miss Tibbs, the postmaster's sister and clerk, used to make a point of walking up and down Main Street as often as possible, to get a thrill in the realization of some poetical expressions that haunted her pleasingly; phrases she had employed frequently in her poems for the "Carlow County Herald." When thirty or forty country people were scattered along the sidewalks in front of the stores on Main Street, she would walk at nicely calculated angles to the different groups so as to leave as few gaps as possible between the figures, making them appear as near a solid phalanx as she could. Then she would murmur to herself, with the accent of soulful revel, "The throngèd city streets," and, "Within the throngèd city," or, "Where the thronging crowds were swarming and the great cathedral rose." Although she had never been beyond Carlow and the bordering counties in her life, all her poems were of city streets and bustling multitudes. She was one of those who had been unable to join the excursion to Rouen when the President was there; but she had listened avidly to her friends' descriptions of the crowds. Before that time her muse had been sylvan, speaking of "Flow'rs of May," and hinting at thoughts that o'ercame her when she roved the woodlands thro'; but now the inspiration was become decidedly municipal and urban, evidently reluctant to depart beyond the retail portions of a metropolis. Her verses beginning, "O, my native city, bride of Hibbard's winding stream," —Hibbard's Creek runs west of Plattville, except in time of drought—"When thy myriad lights are shining, and thy faces, like a dream, Go flitting down thy sidewalks when their daily toil is done," were pronounced, at the time of their publication, the best poem that had ever appeared in the "Herald."

GOPHER PRAIRIE

SINCLAIR LEWIS · 1920

I

She saw that Gopher Prairie was merely an enlargement of all the hamlets which they had been passing. Only to the eyes of a Kennicott was it exceptional. The huddled low wooden houses broke the plains scarcely more than would a hazel thicket. The fields swept up to it, past it. It was unprotected and unprotecting; there was no dignity in it nor any hope of greatness. Only the tall red grain-elevator and a few tinny church-steeples rose from the mass. It was a frontier camp. It was not a place to live in, not possibly, not conceivably.

The people—they'd be as drab as their houses, as flat as

their fields. She couldn't stay here. She would have to wrench loose from this man, and flee. She peeped at him. She was at once helpless before his mature fixity, and touched by his excitement as he sent his magazine skittering along the aisle, stooped for their bags, came up with flushed face, and gloated, "Here we are!"

She smiled loyally, and looked away. The train was entering town. The houses on the outskirts were dusky old red mansions with wooden frills, or gaunt frame shelters like grocery boxes, or new bungalows with concrete foundations imitating stone. Now the train was passing the elevator, the grim storage-tanks for oil, a creamery, a lumber-yard, a stock-yard muddy and trampled and stinking. Now they were stopping at a squat red frame station, the platform crowded with unshaven farmers and with loafers—unadventurous people with dead eyes. She was here. She could not go on. It was the end—the end of the world. She sat with closed eyes, longing to push past Kennicott, hide somewhere in the train, flee on toward the Pacific.

II

When Carol had walked for thirty-two minutes she had completely covered the town, east and west, north and south; and she stood at the corner of Main Street and Washington Avenue and despaired. Main Street with its two-story brick shops, its story-and-a-half wooden residences, its muddy expanse from concrete walk to walk, its huddle of Fords and lumber-wagons, was too small to absorb her. The broad, straight, unenticing gashes of the streets let in the grasping prairie on every side. She realized the vastness and the emptiness of the land. The skeleton iron windmill on the farm a few blocks away, at the north end of Main Street, was like the ribs of a dead cow. She thought of the coming of the Northern winter, when the unprotected houses would crouch together in terror of storms galloping out of that wild waste. They were so small and weak, the little brown houses. They were shelters for sparrows, not homes for warm laughing people. She told herself that down the street the leaves were a splendor. The maples were orange; the oaks a solid tint of raspberry. And the lawns had been nursed with love. But the thought would not hold. At best the trees resembled a thinned wood-lot. There was no park to rest the eyes. And since not Gopher Prairie but Wakamin was the county-seat, there was no court-house with its grounds.

She glanced through the fly-specked windows of the most pretentious building in sight, the one place which welcomed strangers and determined their opinion of the charm and luxury of Gopher Prairie—the Minniemashie House. It was a tall lean shabby structure, three stories of yellow-streaked wood, the corners covered with sanded pine slabs purporting to symbolize stone. In the hotel office she could see a stretch of bare unclean floor, a line of rickety chairs with brass cuspidors between, a writing-desk with advertisements in mother-of-pearl letters upon the glass-covered back. The dining-room beyond was a jungle of stained table-cloths and catsup bottles. She looked no more at the Minniemashie House.

A man in cuffless shirt-sleeves with pink arm-garters, wearing a linen collar but no tie, yawned his way from Dyer's Drug Store across to the hotel. He leaned against the wall, scratched a while, sighed, and in a bored way gossiped with a man tilted back in a chair. A lumber-wagon, its long green box filled with large spools of barbed-wire fencing, creaked down the block. A Ford, in reverse, sounded as though it were shaking to pieces, then recovered and rattled away. In the Greek candy-store was the whine of a peanut-roaster, and the oily smell of nuts. There was no other sound nor sign of life. She wanted to run, fleeing from the encroaching prairie, demanding the security of a great city. Her dreams of creating a beautiful town were ludicrous. Oozing out from every drab wall, she felt a forbidding spirit which she could never conquer.

She trailed down the street on one side, back on the other, glancing into the cross streets. It was a private Seeing Main Street tour. She was within ten minutes beholding not only the heart of a place called Gopher Prairie, but ten thousand towns from Albany to San Diego:

Dyer's Drug Store, a corner building of regular and unreal blocks of artificial stone. Inside the store, a greasy marble soda-fountain with an electric lamp of red and green and curdled-yellow mosaic shade. Pawed-over heaps of toothbrushes and combs and packages of shaving-soap. Shelves of soap-cartons, teething-rings, garden-seeds, and patent medicines in yellow packages—nostrums for consumption, for "women's diseases"—notorious mixtures of opium and alcohol, in the very shop to which her husband sent patients for the filling of prescriptions.

From a second-story window the sign "W. P. Kennicott, Phys. & Surgeon," gilt on black sand.

A small wooden motion-picture theater called "The Rosebud Movie Palace." Lithographs announcing a film called "Fatty in Love."

Howland & Gould's Grocery. In the display window, black, overripe bananas and lettuce on which a cat was sleeping. Shelves lined with red crêpe paper which was now faded and torn and concentrically spotted. Flat against the wall of the second story the signs of lodges—the Knights of Pythias, the Maccabees, the Woodmen, the Masons.

Dahl & Oleson's Meat Market—a reek of blood.

A jewelry shop with tinny-looking wrist-watches for women. In front of it, at the curb, a huge wooden clock which did not go.

A fly-buzzing saloon with a brilliant gold and enamel whisky sign across the front. Other saloons down the block. From them a stink of stale beer, and thick voices bellowing pidgin German or trolling out dirty songs—vice gone feeble and unenterprising and dull—the delicacy of a mining-camp minus its vigor. In front of the saloons, farm-wives sitting on the seats of wagons, waiting for their husbands to become drunk and ready to start home.

A tobacco shop called "The Smoke House," filled with young

men shaking dice for cigarettes. Racks of magazines, and pictures of coy fat prostitutes in striped bathing-suits.

A clothing store with a display of "ox-blood-shade Oxfords with bull-dog toes." Suits which looked worn and glossless while they were still new, flabbily draped on dummies like corpses with painted cheeks.

The Bon Ton Store—Haydock & Simons'—the largest shop in town. The first-story front of clear glass, the plates cleverly bound at the edges with brass. The second story of pleasant tapestry brick. One window of excellent clothes for men, interspersed with collars of floral piqué which showed mauve daisies on a saffron ground. Newness and an obvious notion of neatness and service. Haydock & Simons. Haydock. She had met a Haydock at the station; Harry Haydock; an active person of thirty-five. He seemed great to her, now, and very like a saint. His shop was clean!

Axel Egge's General Store, frequented by Scandinavian farmers. In the shallow dark window-space heaps of sleazy sateens, badly woven galateas, canvas shoes designed for women with bulging ankles, steel and red glass buttons upon cards with broken edges, a cottony blanket, a granite-ware frying-pan reposing on a sun-faded crêpe blouse.

Sam Clark's Hardware Store. An air of frankly metallic enterprise. Guns and churns and barrels of nails and beautiful shiny butcher knives.

Chester Dashaway's House Furnishing Emporium. A vista of heavy oak rockers with leather seats, asleep in a dismal row.

Billy's Lunch. Thick handleless cups on the wet oilcloth-covered counter. An odor of onions and the smoke of hot lard. In the doorway a young man audibly sucking a toothpick.

The warehouse of the buyer of cream and potatoes. The sour smell of a dairy.

The Ford Garage and the Buick Garage, competent one-story brick and cement buildings opposite each other. Old and new cars on grease-blackened concrete floors. Tire advertisements. The roaring of a tested motor; a racket which beat at the nerves. Surly young men in khaki union-overalls. The most energetic and vital places in town.

A large warehouse for agricultural implements. An impressive barricade of green and gold wheels, of shafts and sulky seats, belonging to machinery of which Carol knew nothing—potato-planters, manure-spreaders, silage-cutters, disk-harrows, breaking-plows.

A feed store, its windows opaque with the dust of bran, a patent medicine advertisement painted on its roof.

Ye Art Shoppe, Prop. Mrs. Mary Ellen Wilks, Christian Science Library open daily free. A touching fumble at beauty. A one-room shanty of boards recently covered with rough stucco. A show-window delicately rich in error: vases starting out to imitate tree-trunks but running off into blobs of gilt—an aluminum ash-tray labeled "Greetings from Gopher Prairie"—a Christian Science magazine—a stamped sofa-cushion portraying a large ribbon tied to a small poppy, the correct skeins of embroidery-silk lying on the pillow. Inside the shop, a glimpse of bad carbon prints of bad and famous pictures, shelves of phonograph records and camera films, wooden toys, and in the midst an anxious small woman sitting in a padded rocking chair.

A barber shop and pool room. A man in shirt sleeves, presumably Del Snafflin the proprietor, shaving a man who had a large Adam's apple.

Nat Hicks's Tailor Shop, on a side street off Main. A one-story building. A fashion-plate showing human pitchforks in garments which looked as hard as steel plate.

On another side street a raw red-brick Catholic Church with a varnished yellow door.

The post-office—merely a partition of glass and brass shutting off the rear of a mildewed room which must once have been a shop. A tilted writing-shelf against a wall rubbed black and scattered with official notices and army recruiting-posters.

The damp, yellow-brick schoolbuilding in its cindery grounds.

The State Bank, stucco masking wood.

The Farmers' National Bank. An Ionic temple of marble. Pure, exquisite, solitary. A brass plate with "Ezra Stowbody, Pres't."

A score of similar shops and establishments. Behind them and mixed with them, the houses, meek cottages or large, comfortable, soundly uninteresting symbols of prosperity. In all the town not one building save the Ionic bank which gave pleasure to Carol's eyes; not a dozen buildings which suggested that, in the fifty years of Gopher Prairie's existence, the citizens had realized that it was either desirable or possible to make this, their common home, amusing or attractive.

It was not only the unsparing unapologetic ugliness and the rigid straightness which overwhelmed her. It was the planlessness, the flimsy temporariness of the buildings, their faded unpleasant colors. The street was cluttered with electric-light poles, telephone poles, gasoline pumps for motor cars, boxes of goods. Each man had built with the most valiant disregard of all the others. Between a large new "block" of two-story brick shops on one side, and the fire-brick Overland garage on the other side, was a one-story cottage turned into a millinery shop. The white temple of the Farmers' Bank was elbowed back by a grocery of glaring yellow brick. One store-building had a patchy galvanized iron cornice; the building beside it was crowned with battlements and pyramids of brick capped with blocks of red sandstone.

GOPHER PRAIRIE REVISITED

JOHN GUNTHER · 1946

How has Main Street—the street, not the book—changed in a quarter of a century? What would Dr. Will Kennicott and Carol find if they walked today in Gopher Prairie? *Main Street* was published in 1920, and a whole generation of Americans has grown up since the phrase imbedded itself into the language. The model for Gopher Prairie was of course Lewis's own birthplace, Sauk Centre. The house where Lewis was born is still in good shape and is lived in today by a mail carrier; the one to which he moved later is now the residence

of the local manager of Swift & Co. I talked with a dozen
of his oldest friends, and tried to find out how, if at all, the
community has changed. Does the tawdry provincialism and
vulgarity that shocked Carol still exist? Do the good qualities
symbolized by the stout Kennicott—devotion to hard work,
neighborliness, frugality, deep roots in sound native soil—still
play their role?

First, the population has scarcely risen; it is still about 3,000
—3,016 to be exact. ("3,000 swell folks—and 16 skunks!" is
the way I heard this subdivided.) The railway station is as it
was, but the bus service is new, and, wonder of wonders,
Sauk Centre is soon to have its own airfield, with a half-mile
landing strip! The lines of elms have grown twenty-five
years older, and Kennicott would marvel at the overhead
lights on the road leading into town. The post office is new;
the library is a vast improvement on what it was. How proud
Carol—who saw that indecent author, Balzac, driven from
the shelves—would be to learn that it now has the largest
per capita circulation of books of any community in Minnesota!

Remember the barbed and glittering description of the shops
on Main Street, as Carol took her first walk downtown?
Today she would see few buildings that existed twenty-five
years ago; the old frame structures have given way to brick.
She might look for Hedine's, where Kennicott had his shoes
resoled; now it's a Ben Franklin store. Of all the buildings on
the west side of Main Street between Third and Fourth, she
would remember only three: a bank, Hanson's Home Brand
Foods, and the corner drugstore, drugstores being imperish-
able. On the east side every shop but one would be new to
Carol, including a Chevrolet agency, a neat mortuary, and a
movie.

Take a trip from Sauk Centre to the lush dairy farms surrounding it. The standard of living has jumped to a level that
would leave Kennicott incredulous. Remember how he

charged one of his country patients $11.00 for an operation, and told him he could wait till next year to pay up—if his crop was good enough? Today the mortgages and "barnyard loans" are largely paid off.

There are several reasons for this prosperity; one is the phenomenal growth of co-operatives, in everything from telephones to coal, and another is rural electrification, which began on a substantial scale in the late thirties. Not all farms are electrified, by any means; but the good ones are. A family with rural electrification is at one jump removed from peasanthood, because not only does electric power bring "luxuries" like telephones and running water; it means cream separators, milking machines, and twice as many pigs per litter.

Three other main elements have contributed to the development of Sauk Centre—and a thousand other middle western Main Streets—since Lewis wrote his book.

(1) Enormous advance in the use of the automobile. No one who has read *Main Street* will easily forget its arduous winter journeys on horse-drawn sleighs. Today, these have virtually vanished. Automobiles did, of course, exist in Carol's time, but they couldn't be used in winter. As motoring became universal, more and better highways cut across the land, and the whole picture of rural society was altered irremediably. The automobile—plus good roads—changed Sauk Centre from a village into a metropolis; instead of being an outpost, it became a pivot. On the other hand, the automobile came near to killing the near-by hamlets, with populations of two hundred to five hundred, because their people could drive into bigger towns to market. This phenomenon we have already observed in Colorado and the West.

(2) Chain stores. These were of course unknown in Kennicott's day. I heard two contrary points of view about them. The chain store obviously makes it easier, more economical, for Main Street to shop. In 1920, a shopping tour for outright

necessities could be a day's work; now, it takes half an hour. The other attitude is that the chain store undermines civic spirit; it has made small business migratory, and thus destroyed the town's homogeneity. The manager of a chain store will stay in Sauk Centre, say, for six months to a year; then he moves on, never having become a real ingredient in the life of the community.

(3) Movies and radio. It is almost unthinkable, but neither Will nor Carol ever saw a newsreel. Nor could they have ever heard a radio show. Main Street itself may not have moved very much; but the world itself has moved to Main Street's door, and people have become broadened, willy-nilly.

These factors have helped to modify another aspect of the former life of Main Street—it does not have to hibernate in winter. Winters in Minnesota are still bitterly long and trying, but no longer does the citizen have to dig in and insulate himself from the outside world for five or six solid months. The roads are open, and he can even keep warm at home. (An incidental point is that the relative comfort of modern living has given rise to the illusion that "Minnesota's climate is getting milder!")

The automobile has contributed, so Sauk Centre admits, to juvenile delinquency. Sixteen-year-old girls wander down Main Street nowadays in red slacks, or even shorts! Other social patterns have changed too. In 1920, the town's bar was a refuge for the healthy male seeking to get away from home for an hour or so; today, it is no longer a masculine inner sanctum—the youngsters, boys and girls both, swarm all over it. Again, in Kennicott's time, an important and distinctive role was played by the lodges and fraternal organizations, not only at business meetings but on picnics and excursions. Now the social functions of the lodge have been largely usurped by the movies, luncheon clubs, automobile drives, and golf.

One Sauk Centre veteran lamented what he called a decline in the "pioneer spirit." In the old days, he told me, two men who quarreled would go into the back yard and slug it out. Then, like as not, they would be arrested—briefly—for disturbance of the peace. But in the last few years, only one fist fight and consequent arrest has taken place in the whole town!

The gist of *Main Street*, the book, was Carol's revolt against the iron-clad taboos of her environment. Has Main Street, the town, grown up at all in this respect? Yes. Carol would certainly be talked about, today as in 1920, but the criticism would probably be more diffuse, more tolerant. A suggestive confirmation of this is that Lewis himself was, of course, reviled and calumniated when his book appeared. Today he is something of a hero, and is considered by all to be the most distinguished citizen the community has ever produced. There was even a movement to change the actual name of Sauk Centre to Gopher Prairie! Some years ago Lewis returned for a visit. He wrote a brief inscription for the new movie theater, which the town proudly cast in bronze, and which adorns the wall today:

THESE ARE THE PORTALS OF IMAGINATION.
RECOVER HOPE, ALL YE WHO ENTER HERE.

EDGEWOOD

KATE DOUGLAS WIGGIN · 1905

We all remember the dusty uphill road that leads to the green church common. We remember the white spire pointing up-

From *The Old Peabody Pew*, by Kate Douglas Wiggin. Copyright, 1905. Reprinted by kind permission of and arrangement with Houghton Mifflin Company, the authorized publishers.

ward against a background of blue sky and feathery elms. We remember the sound of the bell that falls on the Sabbath morning stillness, calling us across the daisy-sprinkled meadows of June, the golden hayfields of July, or the dazzling whiteness and deep snowdrifts of December days. The little cabinet-organ that plays the Doxology, the hymn-books from which we sing "Praise God from whom all blessings flow," the sweet freshness of the old meeting-house, within and without,—how we have toiled to secure and preserve these humble mercies for ourselves and our children!

As you have sat there on open-windowed Sundays, looking across purple clover-fields to blue distant mountains, watching the palm-leaf fans swaying to and fro in the warm stillness before sermon time, did not the place seem full of memories, for has not the life of two villages ebbed and flowed beneath that ancient roof? You heard the hum of droning bees and followed the airy wings of butterflies fluttering over the gravestones in the old churchyard, and underneath almost every moss-grown tablet some humble romance lies buried and all but forgotten.

CLYDE, MASSACHUSETTS

JOHN P. MARQUAND · 1947

1. CLYDE

The way to learn about Clyde was to be brought up there. One learned who the Lovells were imperceptibly by a word here and there, and one grew up knowing that the Lovells could say what they wanted and do what they wanted and that they would always be right no matter what they said or did. One learned that there was a living plan in Clyde, without ever learning exactly what the plan was, for it kept growing as one grew, starting with Spruce Street and one's own back yard and spreading up to Johnson Street and down to Dock Street.

Everyone had a place in that plan and everyone instinctively seemed to know where he belonged. Its completeness reminded Charles of what his Aunt Jane said once when she was arranging the flat silver in the sideboard of her dining room —everything in its place and a place for everything. The Irish, for instance, had their place, and so had the French-Canadians and the new immigrants, like the Italians and the Poles, who naturally belonged close to the Wright-Sherwin factory and the shoeshops. There was a place for the North Enders, too. They lived in the North End and went to the North End Congregational Church and even if they lived in other parts of Clyde they were still North Enders.

The same sorts of people, he learned, usually lived in the same sections of Clyde; but you began to learn quite early, without ever knowing how, that certain people who lived on Johnson Street were not Johnson Street people, and hence, because you knew, their living on Johnson Street did not disturb the plan. For example, the Stanleys lived on Johnson Street. They had bought the old Holt house, and it was still called the Holt house though the Stanleys lived in it. Mr. Stanley, everyone knew, was richer than the Lovells or the Thomases or old Miss Sarah Hewitt. You could tell this from his new greenhouse and from the number of men who worked on the garden and the lawns; and Mr. Stanley had a Cadillac automobile, driven by old Arthur Stevens, who had worked for the Holts and whose brother was a clam digger. Yet the Stanleys' prosperity was without the same face value as that of others. They lived on Johnson Street but they did not belong there.

You came to understand that the Holts, who had sold their house to the Stanleys and had moved to the North End, still belonged on Johnson Street. Miss Sarah Hewitt's house needed painting and Mr. Fogarty, who worked for her and for the Lovells too, only gave her one day a week, but Miss Sarah Hewitt belonged on Johnson Street. The same was true with the Lovells. They had always been on Johnson Street. You understood that Mr. Lovell was not very rich but his money somehow had the dignity of age. You heard it spoken of as the Lovell money. He was a director of the Dock Street Savings Bank and a trustee of the West India Insurance Company, which were both partially founded on Lovell money. He was a trustee of the public library, also partially founded on Lovell money. You came to understand that Mr. Stanley could do more generous things because he was richer, and anyone who was richer could do these things of course, but his contribution did not have the same value as a Lovell or a Hewitt contribution. You seemed to know these things implicitly.

The same was true with Spruce Street. The Grays belonged on Spruce Street and so, too, did the Masons, who lived next door; but when Vincent Sullivan, who was in the contracting business and who had the contract for the addition to the Wright-Sherwin plant, bought the house on the corner of Spruce and Chestnut, he still did not belong on Spruce Street. Everyone knew that Mr. Sullivan's father had been the Lovells' gardener and that Mr. Sullivan had driven a truck for the Bronson Shoeshop until he had invested his father's savings in the old livery stable on South Street. You could not get away from your past in Clyde and few wanted to get away from it, perhaps because it was not worth trying.

Malcolm Bryant, who had come to Clyde as a complete

stranger with a scientific preoccupation and only his boyhood in a small Midwestern town as a basis for comparison,
had called Clyde a ghost town, as though it were like an
abandoned Colorado mining settlement. It was true that Clyde
had not changed much since the sailing days, because its harbor was now useless for heavy shipping. It had no water power
as the mill towns further up the river had and it had little to
attract summer tourists. It was a place to be born in and a
place to leave, but it was not a ghost town.

There was a curtain, translucent but not transparent, between the present and the past. When you were young you
did not bother in the least about it because there was too much
present, and thus you accepted the older people and you accepted their deaths very easily, because you were so occupied
with living. They disappeared behind that translucent curtain,
which moved forward a little every year to cover up the year
before. Charles knew, for instance, that Aunt Mathilda was
going to die and when she did everyone said it was a mercy
and so much easier for her poor sister Jane. She was gone and
life went on, and she was hard to remember. Dorothea was too
worried about Frank Setchell to remember much, and Sam
was too occupied with problems of revolt, and Charles still
had too much to learn.

He had to learn the new steps at dancing school and new
jokes from the Meader boys and *The Bells* by Edgar Allan
Poe for the declamation contest in the seventh grade. He had
to learn why certain people thought the Catholic Church
was a political menace, and what was difficult about the
Irish, and why the boys on Johnson Street, the Thomases
and the Stanleys, went away to boarding school when he and
his friends did not. He had to learn why couples sat in back
of the courthouse at night. He had to learn why Washington
Irving's *Sketch Book* was worth reading, and he had to learn

the dates and facts in the school history of the United States.

One's ideas about everything underwent perpetual change while one was growing up, such as ideas of God and immortality and of wealth and poverty, and even one's family was not a constant quantity. You knew them better than anyone else, but suddenly something would happen and they were not the people you had thought they were. This experience was like seeing the back of a house for the first time when you had always been familiar with its front. You knew the lawn and the front windows, but in back were the clothes yard, the garbage pail, the woodshed, and the weedy garden. Nevertheless, it was still the same house. That was the way it was with the family, Charles used to think. Sometimes they turned their fronts to you and sometimes they turned their backs.

II. YANKEE PERSEPOLIS

"*Yankee Persepolis*," Charles read, "appears as the final and considered summation of part of a study made some years ago of a typical New England town, its culture, and its social implications. This volume has been written by Malcolm Bryant, in general charge of the survey. Mr. Bryant, fresh from the study of the Zambesis of Central Africa, has applied, in broad principle, the methods of research which he developed and perfected there. The result of this, his concluding volume, is a brilliant and exhaustive case history which can serve as an adequate text . . ."

The first chapter was entitled "Yankee Persepolis, Its Geography and Population" and the second "Social Structure," with a number of charts and drawings which Charles could not understand. Turning the pages hastily, Charles could see the names of streets and neighborhoods and buildings, thin and inartistic parodies of real names. Johnson Street was called Mason Street, the North End was called Hill Town, Dock

Street was called River Street, and so it went, down to the names of families. The Lovells were obviously called the Johnsons and the Thomases were called the Hopewells, in a chapter entitled "Family Sketches." It was not difficult to perceive, in spite of these clumsy concealments, that Clyde was Yankee Persepolis. It was like looking at Clyde through a distorted lens or seeing Clyde through rippling water, with small things assuming portentous shapes.

"For the purposes of distinction," Charles read, "it will be well arbitrarily to define the very definite and crystallized social strata of Yankee Persepolis as upper, middle, and lower. These will be subdivided into upper-upper, middle-upper, and lower-upper, and the same subdivisions will be used for middle and lower classes."

Charles turned to the middle of the book. Even that quick perusal brought him back to the time when Malcolm Bryant had been studying Yankee Persepolis. He could remember Malcolm's voice and Malcolm's alien figure on the main street, but it was curiously shocking to find that period preserved in print. He remembered Malcolm Bryant and his team examining Clyde and occasionally descending to taste of its life, like minor gods and nymphs sporting with mortals.

"Let's think of Clyde," Malcolm said, "as a big aquarium, and, by God, it's a wonderful aquarium, and I scooped you out and put you in a globe to show the team."

"I hope the team likes it," Charles said, and again everyone laughed.

"Now, Charley, here, lives on Spruce Street. Spruce Street runs into Johnson Street and yet Charley is not a side streeter, in the broader sense of the term. He has an upward and downward mobility that is very interesting. He is able to touch, without belonging to, the cliques on Johnson Street, and yet at the same time he can move downward. His societal mobility is emphasized because he was brought up in the Clyde public

school system. He has rubbed shoulders with all the group-
ings. He may not have the middle class mobility but he has
mobility, the downward trend of which has been checked
somewhat by a college education. The first time I laid eyes
on him I knew he was a beautifully conditioned type."

"It's a wonderful town because its structural cleavages are
so distinct and undisturbed and so unconsciously accepted.
You see, it goes this way"—Malcolm Bryant raised his hand
and began counting on his fingers: "there are three distinct
social groups, the upper class, the middle class and the lower
class, but each of these can be divided into thirds—the upper-
upper, the middle-upper, and the lower-upper; the same way
with the middle class—the upper-middle, the middle-middle,
and the lower-middle; and the same way with the lower class
—the same three categories. Everyone in Clyde falls into one
of them. That's the procedural pattern."

"Well, I don't see why it's so remarkable. I could have told
you that myself," Charles said, and then Malcolm Bryant
became a kindly instructor in a lecture hall.

"Of course it doesn't seem remarkable to you, because
you're integrated in the group. Look at yourself, Charley
—not that you can possibly see. You have a suitable education,
you understand your taboos and your rituals, you're working
happily under an almost immobile system, and the beauty
of it is you're perfectly happy."

III. CLYDE REVISITED

He was standing on the platform holding his suitcase, an
outlander now, a stranger, but at the same time nothing was
strange to him at all. There was the same smell of coal smoke
from the train, the same damp in the air, the same chill of
frost in the ground and the same dull, forbidding April sky
that he had known. It had been raining and the roofs were
wet and the wind made tiny ripples in the puddles in the

street and the clouds still hung sullenly over the town. It was going to rain again. The cars were parked about the station in the old disorderly way and a single car was waiting for passengers in the taxi space but everyone was walking home. The driver, a gangling boy of about seventeen, reminded Charles of Earl Wilkins but of course he was not Earl because he was too young to be.

"Taxi, sir?" he asked, and his voice sounded like Earl's.

It never occurred to Charles until he heard the driver's voice that he would not be walking home to Spruce Street, now that he was off the train. He had been thinking of himself and Clyde without ever planning what he would do when he arrived there. Now he did not know where to go and he did not want to go anywhere. He wanted to be alone but he could not stand there holding the suitcase. It was not at all like those stories he had read of persons returning to the scenes of their childhood. He was not Rip van Winkle after a twenty-year sleep. He was simply back in Clyde on an earlier train than usual.

There were a few places that he did not want to see—the part of Johnson Street where the Lovell home stood, the Judge's house on Gow Street, and Spruce Street; so he walked up Fillmore Street from the station, not along Chestnut, as he would have if he had been going to Dock Street and then home. First there were the shabby rooming houses near the station, where the workers in the shoeshops and Wright-Sherwin lived, and then came the larger houses as Fillmore approached the northern end of Johnson Street, but he was not thinking of the street. The wind and the dampness of the air were so characteristic of reluctant spring that he might have been waiting in front of the courthouse again for Jessica to come by, just by accident, in her Dodge car. It was too late for snowdrops already but in a flower bed with a southern exposure blue grape hyacinths and a few crocuses might be blooming, flaming orange, white and blue. He saw none and he did not look for them but he was as certain that they would be there as that there would be robins in the budding branches of the lilacs. The willow branches would be turning yellow and on some wooded slope beneath fallen oak leaves there might even be hepaticas. Spring was like autumn, except that everything was coming to life instead of dying. In the country the peeper frogs would be singing in the puddles that could not yet soak through the sodden, frosty ground. Clyde, unhindered by its ghosts, was approaching its annual resurrection.

OUR VILLAGE, SEPTEMBER, 1921

BRUCE BLIVEN · 1921

If you live in a large city—New York for instance—it is readily noticeable that, what with Bolshevism and profiteering and the Ku Klux and the post-war psychosis, the world is speedily going all to smash. After all, though, this will not happen until Our Village notices it too. What has Our Village to report on the State of Things in General?

Perhaps before you ask that question you had better be introduced; for while our manners are rustic, we are the very soul of punctilio. . . . Our Village, then, is on the coast of Maine. Broad ocean breaks on the rocks at its feet; a bright blue, boulder-strewn river flows past on one side (but it moves both ways with the tide and is salty to its source). On the other side is a huge deep arm of the sea, sprinkled with islands and fringed with coves, bays, and here and there a

From *The New Republic*, xxviii, Oct. 9, 1921. Copyright, 1921. Used by permission of *The New Republic*.

gut (which as all true Norsemen know, is a small body of water with exits fore and aft). It is a bad coast for the mariner; even the children in Our Village must accumulate a great store of sea-knowledge. They must know how much water there is on the reef north of Angel Island at half-tide, and how to avoid the big black rock off Nigger Point which is never revealed except once or twice a year when sun and moon combine in a mighty effort to haul the waters off his glistening bulk. Also, how to watch the horizon when off shore, to turn and scud for home when the gray sou'easter comes roaring up.

With the children, as with all of us, it is a case of learn or drown, for the whole village goes afloat some part, at least, of every day. Our occupation is the sea. When our men are not fishing far out upon the banks, they are tending the in-shore lobster pots. In the summer, of course, we take in boarders from the city, and despise them because they make loud noises when excited and become ill on boats in thick weather.

Though our men are so marine, they do not dress in sailor-ish toggery. The saltiest old captain of us all, as he stands at the wheel of his sloop and shakes the spray from his eyebrows, wears the thoroughly nautical costume of a plain blue serge coat and trousers, a felt hat and white shirt and collar— unless he is fishing, when his shirt may be of black sateen. The only time our men seem nautical is when they are ashore, driving their automobiles—for every village family has a Ford. There is an irresistible deep-water touch about these cars which is quite lacking in our boats. They are apt to be fes-tooned with rope and when the hood is lifted you need never be surprised to see a useful bit of oakum here and there about the engine. Our men swing aboard with easy grace over the closed side-doors; there are no doors in a yawl.

If you were to "date" Our Village, 1880 would be about right. Preserved by the invigorating sea breezes, here mid-

Victorianism is still in full flower. Our furniture is of golden oak, full of curves. On our walls hang colored enlargements of the photographs of our families. We feel that there is no carpet like good Brussels, with plenty of pink and green and brown, and roses the size of mature cabbages. Not long ago wires were strung in from Smithton Harbor, where the shipyards are, for electric light; but after all, there's comfort in a good kerosene lamp with a china shade, its brass work kept shining by those remorseless housekeepers, our wives. As for architecture—our cottages are square and white with little porches and handsome scrollwork railings. Down by the stores there is quite a piece of sidewalk, but for the rest a deeply worn path is ample, with whitewashed stones on both sides where it turns in toward the porch.

Now that you know us, ask us anything you like. Would you care, for instance, to know about our politics?

By heredity we are, of course, Republicans. Our politics is like our religion; it is taken for granted, and it would be as improper to start an argument in the back of the general store after supper about the grand old party as to question the virgin birth. Specifically, however, we like this man Harding. He seems sort of friendly, and we guess he wants to do the right thing. True, he plays this highfalutin' golf; but we understand that his doctor makes him.

It's probably just as well that America didn't go into that League of Nations. At the time we were inclined to think it was a good thing, but now all the men at Washington seem to be sort of against it, and they likely know best. These foreigners are a tricky lot.

About Prohibition? Well, Prohibition is probably a good thing. Maine has had it for half a century and it hasn't hurt Maine none. There is some bootlegging, of course; always has been a little. But the boys of the village grow up without seeing a saloon, and there is no wife who needs to look forward with terror to a husband reeling home every Saturday night.

Another problem which hardly exists for Our Village is the Labor Question. In part, this is because our men work for themselves, or son works for father. In Our Village, industry is still in the handicraft stage. Every man's effort is directly productive day by day. If he is building a boat, as nearly all of us do in the winter, there it is, you see; so many planks laid over the ribs since Friday. The lobster potman brings home his catch of twenty or two hundred after each circuit of his pots. Under such conditions, enormous quantities of work can be accomplished without fatigue. To be sure, a few of us are shiftless, lazy; but Our Village regards these as pathological cases. There's somethin' wrong with a man that don't like to work. We read about these labor unions and strikes in the Portland papers, and though we all work with our hands, our sympathies as a whole are with the employer.

The high cost of living has not meant so much to us as to the city dweller, since we take a great part of our sustenance from the sea. Lobsters may still be caught on the old terms. The village has a few vegetable gardens, and we sell the produce to our neighbors pretty much at pre-war prices. The things which we sell to the outside markets, however, bring far greater sums than before. Some families have been pinched a little by the post-war problem, but there has been no real suffering.

As for the war itself, it is as though it had never been. The village did its part; it sent its sons, and one of them died of influenza at Camp Devens, and is the village hero now. We were in the war with all our might, but with one exception it has left no slightest mark upon our souls. The exception is that we still believe that the Germans are a malignant subhuman race; we believe in all the atrocities, but we are no longer excited about them.

The problem of reckless wild youth, of the cocktail flapper and the automobile boy, does not exist for us. Our growing girls wear their hair down their backs and help Ma with the supper dishes as of yore. To be sure, once a decade or so there is a horrid scandal among the adolescents; but no more frequent, nor worse, than they have been any time this past hundred and fifty years. We are not complacent, not even cynical about these scandals. Our Village is still firm in the grip of the dying Puritan tradition. Our elders are eternally unreconciled to the weakness of the flesh which leads fullblooded youth astray. Each new disclosure of Sin comes with as great a shock as though it were the first in centuries.

For the most part, of course, we inhibit our impulses toward wrong. Even the young do so. A psycho-analyst would find as much pleasure in seeking to smooth out our cramped and knotted souls as a laundress in ironing a basketfull of crumpled garments. Everywhere among us you find the bright, self-conscious eye of New England, the face which is an alert, defensive mask (and therefore so often makes its possessor seem more intelligent than he is).

This Puritanism does not prevent us from doing brave and unique things when circumstance falls that way. In fact, once our emotions have flowed out along the line of nonconformity and hardened there, we are as immovable as macadam. In a village not far from ours there is an old man who is a woodcarver. Many years ago, he happened to carve a life-sized butterfly, paper-thin wings and all, painted in its natural colors. For some obscure psychological reason, since then butterflies have been his métier. He carves nothing else; hundreds of them; thousands of them, and sells them to the squawking female summer visitors for a few cents.

Somewhat further away there is an island off the coast which does not recognize the sovereignty of the United States. In local tradition the reason goes back to the Civil War and the drafts of '63. After years of parley the inhabitants were persuaded not long ago to pay a school tax and have a teacher from the mainland. But the school tax is too heavy, they say, and the islanders are chafing to be free even from that light bond of loyalty. A stranger landing on that shore tomorrow would stand a chance of rough handling, under suspicion of being a representative of the obnoxious government. Yet these magnificent rebels are good Methodists and Baptists, Anglo-Saxons and sober fishermen. Rebellion is simply the form in which their Puritanism happened to come out on them.

As Anglo-Saxons the islanders are no novelty on the Maine coast. There is not a person in Our Village who does not claim to come of the undiluted breed of the British Isles. If we can judge by faces and names, there are no south Europeans, nor Jews in the village. Only northern stock seems to thrive on these cold and rugged shores. The community is consanguineous in two senses: by race and by intermarriage. Three or four families control the village, and the ramifications of their cousinship are astonishing. Nearly everybody has married into, or out of, the McPhersons, and the first group is as loyal to the clan as the second. Once we got a new school teacher in, a stranger, practically a foreigner, since he came all the way from Smithton Harbor. In his first week he had the unparalleled audacity to spank a McPherson child. At once he discovered that the town was a nest of outraged relatives. They raised a quiet New England uproar, and at the end of the term he was glad to flee for his life, to a community less closely inbred.

Perhaps because we are of one blood, we view our monetary relations with a cheerful serenity which astonishes the visitor, and most of all if he be from New York, where every man's hand is against your purse. Captain Robertson will bring you over from the railroad in his Ford and charge you two dollars for a twenty mile trip; but he won't ask you for the money as you alight. You must remember it yourself and press it upon him. Otherwise he will let the matter drop for a week or a month. He takes it for granted that you are honest and wish to pay. Anyone who has been in town as much as forty-eight hours can get credit at the village store; defalcations occur almost never.

The remarkable honesty of Our Village is the more interesting because, so far as the outward eye can see, at least, we are not notably religious. There is a church, and services are held on Sunday. Most of the time the service is so arranged as to be a sort of greatest common divisor of the varieties of Protestantism, though sometimes we import a minister of one of the specific faiths. The old churchgoing zeal of our Puritan ancestors has quite departed. It is pleasant to put on clean clothes on Sunday and have a place to go and hear Miss Petrie play the organ and the Gummel girls sing "Come Heavenly Love." But the real religious mania is entirely lacking. Our forefathers would say that the services are disgracefully short and the pews disgracefully comfortable. The Bible is still read in some of the cottages, but with a certain furtiveness, as though we had been told it was no longer quite the right thing.

Perhaps the only aspect of our religious life which remains with its old-time color undimmed, is the playing of church politics. From time to time the village is rent in twain by a fearful feud over church affairs. It may be McPherson against the field, or, most terrible of all, McPherson vs. McPherson. When one of these cataclysms is at its height, our minister is hard put to it to frame his discourse so that it shall not be interpreted as an allegorical taking sides. Since his sermons must always be, as it were, composite photographs of many creeds and therefore slightly blurred about the edges, the poor man knows the pangs of authorship in an aggravated form.

I have said that Our Village "dates" at 1880; but in one respect this is not true. We have become modern as regards a matter which may perhaps be explained with due delicacy by illustrating its obverse. The village postmaster and his wife have been married ten years; and have scandalized Our Village by producing ten children, of whom (as the statisticians would say) ninety per cent are living. With the rest of us, two or at the most three children are regarded as sufficient; and for that matter, the couple who are surrounded by this rising tide of progeny feel the same way about it. The difference is that they have been somehow unable to orientate themselves in the New Sophistication. When you note that forty years ago eight or nine children were the rule, and that with us, the economic value of the child has hardly depreciated, you can discern progress here, and can roughly determine its rate, as a train traveller estimates velocity, by the rapidity with which the postmaster's offspring whizz past.

At this point I can well imagine an indignant reader—if any—rising to complain. The only usefulness of any study of the American scene, he might argue, is to help one to understand the American problem. These people in Maine are all very well, in their way; but they are out of the current of many real and vital things—things which the rest of America has to be concerned about, whether it will or not.

True enough; or rather, half-true enough. It is no secret that America consists of the cities and the country. In the cities, as I have already said, it is easy to see that the world is coming to an end forthwith. In the country, they do not believe that this is so; and that is a bond between the divergent types of culture in the East, the South and West. If you can understand the Americanism of Our Village, you can understand the Americanism of the country people of other places, even though their surface manifestations are so fascinatingly different. . . . I wonder (as O. Henry might have said) what they are thinking today in Emmetsburg and San Bernardino!

JEFFERSON, MISSISSIPPI

WILLIAM FAULKNER · 1948

I. SUNDAY NIGHT

But tonight the street was empty. The very houses themselves looked close and watchful and tense as though the people who lived in them, who on this soft May night (those who had not gone to church) would have been sitting on the dark galleries for a little while after supper in rocking chairs or porch-swings, talking quietly among themselves or perhaps talking from gallery to gallery when the houses were close enough. But tonight they passed only one man and he was not walking but standing just inside the front gate to a small neat shoebox of a house built last year between two other houses already close enough together to hear one another's toilets flush (his uncle had explained that: "When you were born and raised and lived all your life where you can't hear anything but owls at night and roosters at dawn and on damp days when sound carries your nearest neighbor chopping wood two miles away, you like to live where you can hear and smell people on either side of you every time they flush a drain or open a can of salmon or of soup."), himself darker than shadow and certainly stiller—a country man who had moved to town a year ago and now owned a small shabby side street grocery whose customers were mostly Negroes.

Now they could see the Square, empty too—the amphi-
theatric lightless stores, the slender white pencil of the Confederate monument against the mass of the courthouse looming
in columned upsoar to the dim quadruple face of the clock
lighted each by a single faint bulb with a quality as intran-
sigeant against their four fixed mechanical shouts of adjuration
and warning as the glow of a firefly. Then the jail and at that
moment, with a flash and glare and wheel of lights and a roar
of engine at once puny against the vast night and the empty
town yet insolent too, a car rushed from nowhere and circled
the Square; a voice, a young man's voice squalled from it
—no words, not even a shout: a squall significant and meaningless—and the car rushed on around the Square, completing
the circle back to nowhere and died away. They turned in at
the jail.

It was of brick, square, proportioned, with four brick
columns in shallow basrelief across the front and even a
brick cornice under the eaves because it was old, built in a
time when people took time to build even jails with grace
and care and he remembered how his uncle had said once that
not courthouses nor even churches but jails were the true
record of a county's, a community's history, since not only
the cryptic forgotten initials and words and even phrases
cries of defiance and indictment scratched into the walls but
the very bricks and stones themselves held, not in solution
but in suspension, intact and biding and potent and indestruc-
tible, the agonies and shames and griefs with which hearts
long since unmarked and unremembered dust had strained
and perhaps burst. Which was certainly true of this one because it and one of the churches were the oldest buildings in
the town, the courthouse and everything else on or in the
Square having been burned to rubble by Federal occupation
forces after a battle in 1864. Because scratched into one of
the panes of the fanlight beside the door was a young girl's

single name, written by her own hand into the glass with a diamond in that same year and sometimes two or three times a year he would go up onto the gallery to look at it, it cryptic now in reverse, not for a sense of the past but to realise again the eternality, the deathlessness and changelessness of youth—the name of one of the daughters of the jailer of that time (and his uncle who had for everything an explanation not in facts but long since beyond dry statistics into something far more moving because it was truth: which moved the heart and had nothing whatever to do with what mere provable information said, had told him this too: how this part of Mississippi was new then, as a town a settlement a community less than fifty years old, and all the men who had come into it less long ago almost than even the oldest's lifetime were working together to secure it, doing the base jobs along with the splendid ones not for pay or politics but to shape a land for their posterity, so that a man could be the jailer then or the innkeeper or farrier or vegetable peddler yet still be what the lawyer and planter and doctor and parson called a gentleman) who stood at that window that afternoon and watched the battered remnant of a Confederate brigade retreat through the town, meeting suddenly across that space the eyes of a ragged unshaven lieutenant who led one of the broken companies scratching into the glass not his name also, not only because a young girl of that time would never have done that but because she didn't know his name then, let alone that six months later he would be her husband.

In fact it still looked like a residence with its balustraded wooden gallery stretching across the front of the lower floor. But above that the brick wall was windowless except for the single tall crossbarred rectangle and he thought again of the Sunday nights which seemed now to belong to a time as dead as Nineveh when from suppertime until the jailer turned the lights out and yelled up the stairs for them to shut up, the dark limber hands would lie in the grimed interstices while the mellow untroubled repentless voices would shout down to the women in the aprons of cooks or nurses and the girls in their flash cheap clothes from the mail order houses or the other young men who had not been caught yet or had been caught and freed yesterday, gathered along the street. But not tonight and even the room behind it was dark though it was not yet eight oclock and he could see, imagine them not huddled perhaps but certainly all together, within elbow's touch whether they were actually touching or not and certainly quiet, not laughing tonight nor talking either, sitting in the dark and watching the top of the stairs because this would not be the first time when to mobs of white men not only all black cats were gray but they didn't always bother to count them either.

II. MONDAY MORNING

It was after eight now; one of the county schoolbusses passed as he prepared to drive Miss Habersham's truck away from the curb and the street would be full of children too fresh for Monday morning with books and paper bags of recess-time lunches and behind the schoolbus was a string of cars and trucks stained with country mud and dust so constant and unbroken that his uncle and his mother would already have reached the jail before he ever managed to cut into it because Monday was stock-auction day at the sales barns behind the Square and he could see them, the empty cars and trucks rank on dense rank along the courthouse curb like shoats at a feed-trough and the men with their stock-trader walking-sticks not even stopping but gone straight across the Square and along the alley to the sales barns to chew tobacco and unlighted cigars from pen to pen amid the ammonia-reek of manure and liniment and the bawling of calves and the stamp and sneeze of horses and mules and the secondhand wagons and plow gear and guns and harness and watches and only the women (what few of them that is since stock-sale day unlike Saturday was a man's time) remained about the Square and the stores so that the Square itself would be empty except for the parked cars and trucks until the men would come back for an hour at noon to meet them at the cafes and restaurants.

III. SATURDAY

Finally he even got up and went to one of the front windows looking down into the Square because if Monday was stock-auction and trade day then Saturday was certainly radio and automobile day; on Monday they were mostly men and they drove in and parked the cars and trucks around the Square and went straight to the sales barns and stayed there until time to come back to the Square and eat dinner and then went back to the sales barns and stayed there until time to come and get in the cars and trucks and drive home before full dark. But not Saturday; they were men and women and children too then and the old people and the babies and the young couples to buy the licenses for the weddings in the country churches tomorrow, come in to do a week's shopping for staples and delicacies like bananas and twenty-five-cent sardines and machine-made cakes and pies and clothes and stockings and feed and fertilizer and plow-gear: which didn't take long for any of them and no time at all for some of them so that some of the cars never really became permanently stationary at all and within an hour or so many of the others had joined them moving steadily processional and quite often in second gear because of their own density round and round the Square then out to the end of the tree-dense residential streets to turn and come back and circle round and round the Square again as if they had come all the way in from the distant circumambient settlements and crossroads stores and isolate farms for that one purpose of enjoying the populous coming and going and motion and recognising one another and the zephyr-like smoothness of the paved streets and alleys themselves as well as looking at the neat new painted small houses among their minute neat yards and flowerbeds and garden ornaments which in the last few years had come to line them as dense as sardines or bananas; as a result of which the radios had to play louder than ever through their super-charged amplifiers to be heard above the mutter of exhausts and swish of tires and the grind of gears and the constant horns, so that long before you even reached the Square you not only couldn't tell where one began and another left off but you didn't even have to try to distinguish what any of them were playing or trying to sell you.

V
Waterloo

❀ ❀ ❀ ❀ ❀ ❀ ❀ ❀ ❀ ❀ ❀ ❀ ❀ ❀ ❀ ❀ ❀ ❀ ❀

THE VERY NAME, Waterloo, has come to have several distinctly different meanings: the place, the battle, a defeat or a nemesis, the symbol of an ironic contrast between a military ball and a battle. The authors who reconstruct the great battle in these pages are dealing with several difficult and controversial aspects of the event which shook the century. For the historian and the biographer the task of describing the terrain and the movement of troops, no small challenge in itself, is further complicated by the duty to interpret the strategy of the battle and to assess Napoleon and Wellington. The author whose vision extends beyond the first principles of the forces and the succession of events must deal with French and British loyalties, the delusion and the glory, the sham and the courage and the waste of war.

The attitudes of biography, history, fiction, romance, and satire are represented here; sometimes they are mingled in the same work. The battle is seen from above, from the British point of view, from the French lines, from Pauline's kitchen well away from the field. It is seen as a letter A, as a series of tremendous charges, as a crushing last hour, as a glorious national triumph, as a travesty of courage, and as an ironic fate.

❀ ❀ ❀ ❀ ❀ ❀ ❀ ❀ ❀ ❀ ❀ ❀ ❀ ❀ ❀ ❀ ❀ ❀ ❀

THE BATTLEFIELD OF WATERLOO

VICTOR HUGO · 1862

Those who wish to form a clear idea of the battle of Waterloo need only imagine a capital A laid on the ground. The left stroke of the A is the Nivelles road, the right one the Genappe road, while the cross of the A is the sunken road from Ohain to Braine l'Alleud. The top of the A is Mont-Saint-Jean; Wellington is there; the left-hand lower point is Hougomont; Reille is there with Jerome Bonaparte; the right-hand lower point is La Belle Alliance; Napoleon is there. A little below the point where the cross of the A meets the right stroke, is La Haye Sainte; in the center of this cross is the precise point where the final battle-word was spoken. It is here that the lion is placed, the involuntary symbol of the supreme heroism of the Imperial Guard.

The triangle contained at the top of the A between the two strokes and the cross is the plateau of Mont-Saint-Jean. The dispute for this plateau was the whole battle.

From *Les Misérables*, 1862.

THE FRENCH ATTACK AT WATERLOO

HERBERT FISHER · 1912

In bare outline the battle of Waterloo takes the form of a series of tremendous charges delivered at the left and right centre of the British position supported by a concentrated fire from the guns, and repelled by the steadiness of the Eng-

From *Napoleon*, by H. A. L. Fisher. London: Oxford University Press, 1912. Used by permission.

lish and German troops. In the execution of these famous attacks there appear to have been two important faults from which Napoleon may with some probability be absolved. The great charge of d'Erlon's division which opened the central attack at one o'clock was made in four columns each of so narrow a front and great a depth (seeing that the column was composed of eight battalions ranged one behind another), that while offering an admirable target to the British infantry, it possessed an altogether inadequate power of reply. It was, however, Napoleon's custom to leave the minor tactics to the discretion of his subordinates; and the vicious formation of d'Erlon's charge may be classed as one of those mistakes for which the lieutenant is more properly responsible than his chief. The other error was even more serious, for it conditioned all subsequent stages of the fight. At 3.30 p.m., when the British infantry was still unshaken, Ney dashed across the valley, if the shallow depression between these two ridges can so be called, at the head of an immense body of horse, to attack it. Then began a long succession of furious cavalry charges, which spent themselves in vain against the solid valour of the British and German squares. That the first charge was premature and insufficiently supported is certain, and those for whom Napoleon's word is as impeccable as his tactics, believe that it was undertaken without the Emperor's authority.

The battle was won by the skill and courage of Wellington, by the imperturbable steadiness of his English and German troops, and finally by the advance of the Prussians who began to affect Napoleon's dispositions soon after four p.m., and in the last hour of daylight converted a repulse into a rout. With greater activity Grouchy might have delayed but could not have arrested the Prussian advance. Blücher could have contained him and yet had two divisions to spare for Wellington. If a handful of cavalry had been told off to follow the retreat from Ligny instead of a whole division, or if the Old Guard had been sent in earlier and at full strength at Waterloo, would the result have been otherwise?

THE LAST HOUR AT WATERLOO

HILAIRE BELLOC · 1932

Somewhat after seven in the evening of Sunday, June 18, 1815, the French troops which had faced Wellington's line east of the highroad were looking westward, for there had fallen a half silence. The main attack upon the centre had ceased; the defending line was not replying and all fire for the moment was held.

It was the last hour of daylight. In the low broad dip of land across which the great Brussels highway runs in its straight line north and south, all was obscured with smoke; the battered remnant of La Haye Sainte, the farm buildings and walls, had been cleared of Baring's men long before; over the endless rolls of land to the west there was a band of bright light through which the sun could be seen under the large storm-clouds which had now thus much lifted. Through that smoke as it rose could be seen, slowly breasting the low, long even rise, the four columns of the Guard. Their tall figures —the taller for the bearskins they wore and for the lines of their cloaks—cast long shadows over the trampled wheat; and behind them the Emperor, who had accompanied the first of their advance, rode back to the position he had held during all that day, upon the opposing height, nearly a mile away, by the farm of the Belle Alliance.

The position had long been desperate, but the French

troops in line to the east of the highway, though they had sus-
pected the peril, could not know. There had run through the
army much talk of Grouchy with his 40,000, and how he
might appear at the last moment and change the face of fate
and the great day. But Grouchy was far off; there was no
reinforcement at hand, and all was lost—long lost.

Since mid-afternoon they had heard without wavering that
most ominous of sounds—fire over the right shoulder, guns
and the rattle of musketry, not far off upon the flank, but
near and almost behind them. For Blücher's first men had
already, so early in the action, arrived on the French right
flank at Plancenoit, and more and more and more were coming
up on that right flank of the French, closing in upon the battle.
The superiority in numbers had grown from half as much
again of Napoleon's command to three-quarters—it would
be double his soon. With Blücher's Prussians lying thus, in
greater and greater strength upon the eastern side, coming
with greater and greater pressure towards the only line of
retirement, it was certain that the army was doomed. The
Guard now going forward in its four columns was to attempt
the impossible. As it marched forward solemnly over the
trodden grain, still damp with the heavy rains of the night
before, it was going to death without respite. Yet such was
the remaining strength of legend and of inherited glory that
this solemn advance gave the illusion, the cheat, almost the
vision of a possible victory in the balance. But still the Prussian
forces came onward from the east in flank and still that line
extended and its numbers grew. The net had all but closed.

Wellington's batteries upon the ridge, those batteries which,
within the squares, had so withstood and for so many hours
the early, too impetuous charges of Ney, had orders not to
reply to the French guns but to hold their fire until they could
break with their grape the four advancing columns of the
Guard.

These four dense lines struck successively, not all their

fronts at once but from east to west in order, the easternmost
first, the west last. The first the Dutch guns caught as it came
on, breaking the head of its advance. The long dense line
filled the gaps and still went forward, but more slowly as the
men fell and were replaced—at last the extreme of the column
no longer advanced.

The second—the men watching upon the east of the road,
held their breaths to see the second column almost succeed
as it struck Halkett's Brigade; but the 33rd and 69th, their
standing recovered, rallied and held the enemy.

The third column, striking just after the second, came upon
the Brigade of Guards, and these, reserving their fire until
the French Grenadiers were just upon them, threw them into
confusion, charged—drove their opponents down the slope
—and were then themselves driven back to the ridge. But
their line held.

The fourth, the westernmost column, had still to deliver
its blow against the right of the British line. Here stood Adam's
Brigade, and on the extremity of it, next against the Guards,
the 52nd with Colbourne in command. Colbourne, just as
this final attack of the Old Guard approached the summit of
the slope, took the hazard which has rendered him famous.
He swung round the 52nd right out of the line—careless of
the gap there left—and took that fourth column of the French
in flank. The perilous move was successful; the attack was
stayed, all the head of the column wavered. It began to break.

Even at that moment, while the last rays of the sun showed
the more fiercely over the horizon from below the heavy
clouds which overhung the belt of remaining light, that
light caught the steel of new thousands approaching—the
last gap left of the net which was pressing upon the victims.
It was Zeithen's corps, the last Prussian body, coming in from
the north-east. Of those men now standing to the east of the
road, now wavering, some—as they saw this dense fresh mass

coming forward from the only space in the field still free—raised cries which began the confusion. Others, who had been fixed upon the great scene playing to their left beyond the road—the advance of the Guard—seeing the fourth and last column not only shaken in its turn but wavering and beginning to break, raised the cry which ran throughout the army at last—"The Guard is breaking!" The forward units began to fall into disarray, the Allied line advanced, and while the sun was setting the confusion gained upon the French within the crushed and breaking crescent they still held. The contagion spread, the general confusion turned, as dusk fell, into a rout; in the torrent of men only the squares of the Guard here and there stood firm, retiring still in formation while about them all was dissolving. All the highroad and the fields about it became, under the gathering night, a flood of broken and flying men, and all through the darkness as that rout poured down the highroad, the Allied cavalry followed, sabring at will, with the moon still showing until after midnight through the rifts of the clouds.

THE STORY OF WATERLOO

WILLIAM HAMILTON MAXWELL · 1834

When morning broke, the rival armies were visible to each other. It was said that Napoleon betrayed a mixed feeling of surprise and pleasure when it was announced to him that the British army were on the same ground they had occupied the preceding evening. "*Ah! Je les tiens donc, ces Anglais!*" was his observation; for he believed that Wellington would have retreated, and waited for the advance of the Prussians,

Condensed from *Stories of Waterloo*, 1834.

rather than hazard a decisive battle, assisted only by the small portion of the allies who fought with the British troops at Waterloo. Little did the French emperor know the man opposed to him; and still less, the *matériel* of the gallant army which the English duke commanded.

The British soon recovered from the chill cast over them by the inclemency of the weather; and from the ridge of their position calmly observed the enemy's masses coming up in long succession, and forming their numerous columns on the heights in front of La Belle Alliance.

The bearing of the French was very opposite to the steady and cool determination which marked the feelings of the British soldiery: with the former, all was exultation and arrogant display.

The place from which Buonaparte viewed the field was a gentle rising ground beside the farm-house of La Belle Alliance. There he remained for a considerable part of the day, dismounted, pacing to and fro with his hands behind him, receiving communications from his aides-de-camp, and issuing orders to his officers. As the battle became more doubtful, he approached nearer the scene of action, and betrayed increased impatience to his staff by violent gesticulation, and using immense quantities of snuff. At three o'clock he was on horseback in front of La Belle Alliance; and in the evening, just before he made his last attempt with the guard, he had reached a hollow close to La Haye Sainte.

Wellington, at the opening of the engagement, stood upon a ridge immediately behind La Haye; but as the conflict thickened, where difficulties arose, and dangers threatened, *there* the Duke was found. He traversed the field exposed to a storm of balls, and passed from point to point uninjured; and more than on one occasion, when the French cavalry charged the British squares, the Duke was there for shelter.

There was a terrible sameness in the battle of the 18th of June, which distinguishes it in the history of modern slaughter. Although designated by Napoleon "a day of false manoeuvres," in reality there was less display of military tactics at Waterloo than in any general action we have on record. Buonaparte's favourite plan was perseveringly followed. To turn a wing or separate a position was his customary system, and both were tried—at Hougomont to turn the right, and at La Haye Sainte to break through the left centre. Hence the French operations were confined to fierce and incessant onsets with masses of cavalry and infantry, supported by a numerous and destructive artillery.

Knowing that to repel these desperate and sustained attacks a tremendous sacrifice of human life must occur, Napoleon, reckless of their acknowledged bravery, calculated on wearying the British into defeat. But when he saw his columns driven back in confusion—when his cavalry receded from the squares they could not penetrate—when battalions were reduced to companies by the fire of his cannon, and still that "feeble few" showed a perfect front, and held the ground they had originally taken, no wonder his admiration was expressed to Soult—"How beautifully these English fight! but they must give way!"

And well did British bravery merit the proud encomium which their enduring courage elicited from Napoleon. For hours, with uniform and unflinching gallantry, had they repulsed the attacks of troops who had proved their superiority over the soldiers of every other nation in Europe.

But the situation of Wellington momently became more critical: though masses of the enemy had fallen, thousands came on anew. With desperate attachment, the French army pressed forward at Napoleon's command, and while each advance terminated in defeat and slaughter, fresh battalions crossed the valley, and, mounting the ridge with cries of "Vive l'Empereur!" exhibited a devotion which never has been equalled. Wellington's reserves had gradually been brought into action; and the left, though but partially engaged, dared not, weakened, to send assistance to the right and centre. Many battalions were miserably reduced. The 5th division, already cut up at Quatre-Bras, on the evening of the 18th, presented but skeletons of what these beautiful brigades had been when they left Brussels two days before.

No wonder that Wellington almost despaired; he calculated, and justly, that he had an army who would perish where they stood. But when he saw the devastation caused by the incessant attacks of an enemy, who appeared determined to succeed, is it surprising that his watch was frequently consulted, and that he prayed for night or Blücher?

Then came the hour of British triumph. The magic word was spoken—"Up, Guards, and at them!" In a moment they were on their feet: then waiting till the French closed, they delivered a tremendous volley, cheered, and rushed forward with the bayonet. Wellington in person directed the attack. With the 42d and 95th he threw himself on Ney's flank, and rout and destruction succeeded. In vain their gallant leader attempted to rally the recoiling column: driven down the hill, they were intermingled with the old Guard, who were formed at the bottom in reserve.

In their unfortunate *mêlée*, the British cavalry seized on the moment of confusion, and plunging into the mass, cut down and disorganised the regiments which had hitherto been unbroken. The artillery ceased firing, and those who had escaped the iron shower of the guns fell beneath sabre and bayonet.

The irremediable disorder consequent on this decisive repulse, and the confusion in the French rear, where Bülow had fiercely attacked them, did not escape the eagle glance of Wellington. "The hour is come!" he is said to have exclaimed, as, closing his telescope, he commanded the whole line to advance. The order was exultingly obeyed, and, forming four deep, on came the British. Wounds, and fatigue, and hunger, were all forgotten! With their customary steadiness they crossed the ridge; but when they saw the French, and began to move down the hill, a cheer that seemed to rend the heavens pealed from their proud array, and with levelled bayonets they pressed on to meet the enemy.

But, panic-struck and disorganised, the French resistance was short and feeble. The Prussian cannon thundered in their rear; the British bayonet was flashing in their front; and, unable to stand the terror of the charge, they broke and fled. A dreadful and indiscriminate carnage ensued. The great road was choked with the equipage, and cumbered with the dead and dying; while the fields, as far as the eye could reach, were covered with a host of helpless fugitives. Courage and discipline were forgotten. Napoleon's army of yesterday was now a splendid wreck. His own words best describe it—"It was a total rout!"

WATERLOO

WILLIAM MAKEPEACE THACKERAY · 1847

As far as his regiment was concerned, this campaign was over now. They had formed a part of the division under the command of his sovereign-apparent, the Prince of Orange; and as respected length of swords and mustachios, and the

From *Vanity Fair*, 1847–1848.

richness of uniform and equipments, Regulus and his comrades looked to be as gallant a body of men as ever trumpet sounded for.

When Ney dashed upon the advance of the allied troops, carrying one position after the other, until the arrival of the great body of the British army from Brussels changed the aspect of the combat of Quatre Bras, the squadrons among which Regulus rode showed the greatest activity in retreating before the French, and were dislodged from one post and another, which they occupied with perfect alacrity on their part. Their movements were only checked by the advance of the British in their rear. Thus forced to halt, the enemy's cavalry (whose bloodthirsty obstinacy cannot be too severely reprehended) had at length an opportunity of coming to close quarters with the brave Belgians before them; who preferred to encounter the British rather than the French, and at once turning tail rode through the English regiments that were behind them, and scattered in all directions. The regiment in fact did not exist any more; it was nowhere; it had no headquarters. Regulus found himself galloping many miles from the field of action, entirely alone; and whither should he fly for refuge so naturally as to that kitchen and those faithful arms in which Pauline had so often welcomed him?

The hussar showed he was no ghost by the prodigious quantity of flesh and beer which he devoured—and during the mouthfuls he told his tale of disaster.

His regiment had performed prodigies of courage, and had withstood for a while the onset of the whole French army. But they were overwhelmed at last, as was the whole British army by this time. Ney destroyed each regiment as it came up. The Belgians in vain interposed to prevent the butchery of the English. The Brunswickers were routed and had fled —their Duke was killed. It was a general *débâcle*. He sought to drown his sorrow for the defeat in floods of beer.

All that day, from morning until past sunset, the cannon never ceased to roar. It was dark when the cannonading stopped all of a sudden.

All of us have read of what occurred during that interval. The tale is in every Englishman's mouth; and you and I, who were children when the great battle was won and lost, are never tired of hearing and recounting the history of that famous action. Its remembrance rankles still in the bosoms of millions of the countrymen of those brave men who lost the day. They pant for an opportunity of revenging that humiliation; and if a contest, ending in a victory on their part, should ensue, elating them in their turn, and leaving its cursed legacy of hatred and rage behind to us, there is no end to the so-called glory and shame, and to the alternations of successful and unsuccessful murder, in which two high-spirited nations might engage. Centuries hence, we Frenchmen and Englishmen might be boasting and killing each other still, carrying out bravely the Devil's code of honour.

All our friends took their share and fought like men in the great field. All day long, whilst the women were praying ten miles away, the lines of the dauntless English infantry were receiving and repelling the furious charges of the French horsemen. Guns which were heard at Brussels were ploughing up their ranks, and comrades falling, and the resolute survivors closing in. Towards evening, the attack of the French, repeated and resisted so bravely, slackened in its fury. They had other foes besides the British to engage, or were preparing for a final onset. It came at last: the columns of the Imperial Guard marched up the hill of Saint Jean, at length and at once to sweep the English from the height which they had maintained all day, and spite of all. Unscared by the thunder of the artillery, which hurled death from the English line, the dark rolling column pressed on and up the hill. It seemed almost to crest the eminence, when it began to wave and falter. Then it stopped, still facing the shot. Then at last the English troops rushed from the post from which no enemy had been able to dislodge them, and the Guard turned and fled.

No more firing was heard at Brussels—the pursuit rolled miles away. Darkness came down on the field and city; and Amelia was praying for George, who was lying on his face, dead, with a bullet through his heart.

VI
Dunkirk

❋ ❋ ❋ ❋ ❋ ❋ ❋ ❋ ❋ ❋ ❋ ❋ ❋ ❋ ❋ ❋ ❋ ❋ ❋ ❋

ALL THESE ACCOUNTS of the retreat from Dunkirk were written by Englishmen; all of them were written within hours or at most weeks of an event so miraculous and so little hoped for that it remains even today clothed in an aura of human courage and divine deliverance. This is war which is the antithesis of the romantic, but, paradoxically, war idealized, triumphant in defeat.

The most characteristic element in these reports is the laconic, unadorned statement, said to be traditionally British. The proportions of the events themselves make superlatives and even descriptive coloring both unnecessary and excessive. The immediacy of the events, related by eyewitnesses, prompts the authors to a restraint which suggests fear of emotion, fatigue, and inability to believe in the reality of their own experiences. Even Churchill's ringing challenge, which will go down in history as one of the great orations of all time, is a simple statement of purpose, though it moves with the rhythms and the force of an ocean.

❋ ❋ ❋ ❋ ❋ ❋ ❋ ❋ ❋ ❋ ❋ ❋ ❋ ❋ ❋ ❋ ❋ ❋ ❋ ❋

THE RETREAT

A BRITISH SOLDIER · 1940

A British soldier, returned to London, describes the retreat through Belgium, started on May 11, and his landing in England a few days ago. His story follows:

"On May 11, the second day of the invasion of Belgium, we continued our retreat with remnants of a Belgian division which had seen heavy fighting the previous day. We had been bombarded and machine-gunned from the air continuously from dawn, with as many as thirty or forty planes being over us at a time. In the evening we were being bombed by sixteen Dorniers when suddenly four Spitfires appeared. They engaged the enemy and within six minutes brought down four Dorniers. The others broke and dispersed.

"One of the Dorniers fell within a few yards of our column. The pilot and crew were burned before we could reach them. One of their machine guns was intact. My sergeant dismounted it and took about 700 rounds of ammunition in drums from the plane. We continued on our journey and eventually camped in a woods for the night, where one of our fitters mounted the German machine gun on a side-car.

"Two days after this we were found at dawn by a Heinkel. We had with us a trooper who is a deadly shot. Using the German machine gun, he brought it down. When we went over to the wrecked plane, which had fallen about a mile off, we got another machine gun out of it, but this was damaged. But what was even more precious, we got another 700 rounds of ammunition which could be used, we hoped, in a subsequent encounter.

"When we were about to embark the enemy had been bombing the quayside trying to get our small boat all day.

From *The New York Times*, June 1, 1940. By permission.

Just at dusk a last German plane brought down one of our fighters. The British pilot jumped in his parachute and was in the air coming down when the German plane circled low over sheds where we were sheltering. We got in a burst of machine-gun fire and brought him down as well.

"The German plane crashed; the pilot in his parachute came down at about the same time. We sent out a motorcycle to pick up the British pilot whom we took on board and brought back to England that night."

YOUNG BRITONS IN FLANDERS

SIR PHILIP GIBBS · 1940

Paris, May 31—All the world awaits with suspense the fate of the British and French troops fighting with their backs to the sea around Dunquerque. Some of them, as announced officially, have been embarked and have reached England with the help of the Royal Navy and Air Force.

This morning I had an account of the heroic fighting of the B.E.F. from a general, who belonged to general headquarters. In the last crisis, due to the defection of the Belgian king, he took command of a force in the field. It is a terrible story, relieved only by the superhuman valor of men who knew that they were making a last stand against overwhelming odds. After fighting back from Brussels and Louvain, they were surrounded on three sides. The enemy had cut them off from the south by driving through the gap to Boulogne. They were striking at them from the east across the old battlefields of the Ypres salient.

The young pilots of the R.A.F. did marvelously and were

From *The New York Times*, June 1, 1940. By permission.

reckless in their attack against the German bombers, whom they destroyed in odds of one to ten, but the superior numbers of the German planes could not be broken and their bombing was constant and horrible. Nevertheless the B.E.F. fell back to shorten their line in good order and, despite heavy casualties, in such good shape and spirit that more than once they counter-attacked and drove the enemy back. When one knows that many of these young men had never faced fire before and that until a few months ago they were ordinary civilians doing their jobs in peace-time ways, it is a proof of fine courage and noble discipline that they withstood the tragic ordeal with such steadiness and unflinching spirit. Germany's best troops were sent against them.

By the capitulation of the Belgians, the British were isolated and outflanked. German artillery had them as targets. German tanks tried to smash them up. They were under slashing machine-gun fire and storms of steel. Many officers and men fell on those old fields on which their fathers fought and died in the last war. It was difficult and dreadful to get away the wounded, who were not safe even on the hospital ships, which were deliberately bombed by enemy planes.

The old regular divisions were magnificent. Their non-commissioned officers were very steady. The younger men, recruited since the war—clerks and shop assistants and boys from English farms and Scottish villages—behaved like veterans after the first shock of war in all its horror. In spite of the abomination of rear-guard fighting, this stubborn retreat of the B.E.F. will live in history as an epic of human valor, whatever losses in men and material may be the final account in the enemy's reckoning. They are bound to be very heavy. The Germans may capture many guns and great stores. But they will not have captured or annihilated the spirit of those comrades in arms, who were forced into this retreat by the Belgian king's defection.

On their way and behind them now lie many ruined cities. Ypres is in ruins again. Arras is in ruins. The military grave-yards of the last war have been ravaged. The war memorials are down. Hundreds of villages rebuilt after the wreckage of twenty-five years ago have been bombed into new ruin or set on fire by incendiary shells. Meanwhile, south of the Somme, the situation remains without change, and that in itself is a proof that the first German push has been checked and weakened. The French Army is wonderfully confident that all is well and that General Maxime Weygand is master of the game.

Tank officers who have been in many actions, doing deadly work among the enemy, say the quality of the German troops is very mixed and unequal. The best troops are formidable, but after fighting with them, they come up against untrained boys, who have no idea of war and whom they almost pity, so that they dislike killing them. The French heavy tanks are invulnerable against infantry, and with their fast-firing guns, inflict terrific casualties upon battalions. From all the stories which come back it is certain that German losses are enormous.

They have only one superior weapon, and that is in the air. It is by their air power that they have gone so fast and so far. It is by aerial bombing far behind the lines that they destroy the beauty of France and make war upon women and children. They have no respect or pity even for the wounded. From a young American ambulance driver I heard yesterday a horrible tale of the way in which his ambulance convoy has been deliberately bombed with its loads of mutilated men.

THE DELIVERANCE OF DUNKIRK

WINSTON CHURCHILL · 1949

May 26 to June 4, 1940

There was a short service of intercession and prayer in Westminster Abbey on May 26. The English are loth to expose their feelings, but in my stall in the choir I could feel the pent-up, passionate emotion, and also the fear of the congregation, not of death or wounds or material loss, but of the defeat and the final ruin of Britain.

On the evening of the 26th (6.57 P.M.) an Admiralty signal put "Operation Dynamo" into play, and the first troops were brought home that night. After the loss of Boulogne and Calais only the remains of the port of Dunkirk and the open beaches next to the Belgian frontier were in our hands. At this time it was thought that the most we could rescue was about 45,000 men in two days. Early the next morning, May 27, emergency measures were taken to find additional small craft "for a special requirement." This was no less than the full evacuation of the British Expeditionary Force. It was plain that large numbers of such craft would be required for work on the beaches, in addition to bigger ships which could load in Dunkirk Harbour. On the suggestion of Mr. H. C. Riggs, of the Ministry of Shipping, the various boatyards, from Teddington to Brightlingsea, were searched by Admiralty officers, and yielded upwards of forty serviceable motor-boats or launches, which were assembled at Sheerness on the following day. At the same time lifeboats from liners in the London docks, tugs from the Thames, yachts, fishing-craft, lighters, barges, and pleasure-boats—anything that could be of use

From *Their Finest Hour*, by Winston Churchill. Reprinted by permission of and arrangement with Houghton Mifflin Company, the authorized publishers.

along the beaches—were called into service. By the night of
the 27th a great tide of small vessels began to flow towards
the sea, first to our Channel ports, and thence to the beaches
of Dunkirk and the beloved Army.

Once the need for secrecy was relaxed, the Admiralty did
not hesitate to give full rein to the spontaneous movement
which swept the seafaring population of our south and south-
eastern shores. Everyone who had a boat of any kind, steam
or sail, put out for Dunkirk, and the preparations, fortunately
begun a week earlier, were now aided by the brilliant impro-
visation of volunteers on an amazing scale. The numbers arriving on the 29th were small, but they were the forerunners
of nearly four hundred small craft which from the 31st were
destined to play a vital part by ferrying from the beaches to
the off-lying ships almost a hundred thousand men. In these
days I missed the head of my Admiralty map room, Captain
Pim, and one or two other familiar faces. They had got hold
of a Dutch *schuit* which in four days brought off eight hundred soldiers. Altogether there came to the rescue of the Army
under the ceaseless air bombardment of the enemy about 860
vessels, of which nearly seven hundred were British and the
rest Allied.

Meanwhile ashore around Dunkirk the occupation of the
perimeter was effected with precision. The troops arrived out
of chaos and were formed in order along the defences, which
even in two days had grown. Those men who were in best
shape turned about to form the line. Divisions like the 2d
and 5th, which had suffered most, were held in reserve on the
beaches and were then embarked early. In the first instance
there were to be three corps on the front, but by the 29th
we shortened it so that two sufficed. The enemy had closely
followed the withdrawal, and hard fighting was incessant,
especially on the flanks near Nieuport and Bergeus. As the
evacuation went on, the steady decrease in the number of

troops, both British and French, was accompanied by a corresponding contraction of the defence. On the beaches among the sand dunes, for three, four, or five days scores of thousands of men dwelt under unrelenting air attack. Hitler's belief that the German Air Force would render escape impossible, and that therefore he should keep his armoured formations for the final stroke of the campaign, was a mistaken but not unreasonable view.

Three factors falsified his expectations. First, the incessant air-bombing of the masses of troops along the seashore did them very little harm. The bombs plunged into the soft sand which muffled their explosions. In the early stages, after a crashing air raid, the troops were astonished to find that hardly anybody had been killed or wounded. Everywhere there had been explosions, but scarcely anyone was the worse. A rocky shore would have produced far more deadly results. Presently the soldiers regarded the air attacks with contempt. They crouched in the sand dunes with composure and growing hope. Before them lay the gray but not unfriendly sea. Beyond, the rescuing ships and—Home.

The second factor which Hitler had not foreseen was the slaughter of his airmen. Wherever German aircraft were encountered, sometimes in forties and fifties, they were instantly attacked, often by single squadrons or less, and shot down in scores, which presently added up into hundreds. The whole Metropolitan Air Force, our last sacred reserve, was used. Sometimes the fighter pilots made four sorties a day. A clear result was obtained. The superior enemy were beaten or killed, and for all their bravery mastered, or even cowed. This was a decisive clash.

But all the aid of the sand and all the prowess in the air would have been vain without the sea. The instructions given ten or twelve days before had under the pressure and emotion of events borne amazing fruit. Perfect discipline prevailed ashore and afloat. The sea was calm. To and fro between the shore and the ships plied the little boats, gathering the men from the beaches as they waded out or picking them from the water, with total indifference to the air bombardment, which often claimed its victims. Their numbers alone defied air attack. The Mosquito Armada as a whole was unsinkable. In the midst of our defeat glory came to the island people, united and unconquerable; and the tale of the Dunkirk beaches will shine in whatever records are preserved of our affairs.

May 31 and June 1 saw the climax though not the end at Dunkirk. On these two days over 132,000 men were safely landed in England, nearly one-third of them having been brought from the beaches in small craft under fierce air attack and shell fire. On June 1 from early dawn onward the enemy bombers made their greatest efforts, often timed when our own fighters had withdrawn to refuel. These attacks took heavy toll of the crowded shipping, which suffered almost as much as in all the previous week. On this single day our losses by air attack, by mines, E-boats, or other misadventure were thirty-one ships sunk and eleven damaged.

The final phase was carried through with much skill and precision. For the first time it became possible to plan ahead instead of being forced to rely on hourly improvisations. At dawn on June 2, about four thousand British with seven anti-aircraft guns and twelve anti-tank guns remained with the considerable French forces holding the contracting perimeter of Dunkirk. Evacuation was now possible only in darkness, and Admiral Ramsay determined to make a massed descent on the harbour that night with all his available resources. Besides tugs and small craft, forty-four ships were sent that evening from England, including eleven destroyers and fourteen mine-sweepers. Forty French and Belgian vessels also participated. Before midnight the British rearguard was embarked.

Parliament assembled on June 4, and it was my duty to lay the story fully before them both in public and later in secret session. The narrative requires only a few extracts from my speech, which is extant. It was imperative to explain not only to our own people but to the world that our resolve to fight on was based on serious grounds, and was no mere despairing effort. It was also right to lay bare my own reasons for confidence:

Even though large tracts of Europe and many old and famous States have fallen or may fall into the grip of the Gestapo and all the odious apparatus of Nazi rule, we shall not flag or fail. We shall go on to the end, we shall fight in France, we shall fight in the seas and oceans, we shall fight with growing confidence and growing strength in the air, we shall defend our island, whatever the cost may be, we shall fight on the beaches, we shall fight on the landing-grounds, we shall fight in the fields and in the streets, we shall fight in the hills; we shall never surrender, and even if, which I do not for a moment believe, this island or a large part of it were subjugated and starving, then our Empire beyond the seas, armed and guarded by the British Fleet, would carry on the struggle, until, in God's good time, the New World, with all its power and might, steps forth to the rescue and the liberation of the Old.

THE BEACHES OF DUNKIRK

"BARTIMEUS" · 1940

The chalk cliffs of Dover made a curiously tranquil background in the early morning sunlight, with jackdaws cawing and circling, and the faint echoes of gunfire across the Channel whispering about the escarpment.

Abridged from *The Atlantic Monthly*, clxvi, August, 1940. By permission of Paul R. Reynolds & Son, agents for the author.

Away to the Westward, alongside the pier reaching out from what was once the Lord Warden Hotel, were the funnels and smoke of transports and a hospital ship. They were pouring ashore their khaki-clad cargoes and stretcher cases, fruits of a night's desperate garnering, and long trains crammed with men were sliding along the foreshore into the haze. But that was far away; one imagined rather than saw what was going on there. Here in the shadow of the cliffs were actualities —a destroyer limping in with a heavy list, spattered with splinter holes, making fast alongside to disembark hundreds of weary *poilus*, an armed trawler going out with a defiant toot of her siren, followed by a motor yacht painted gray. The owner-skipper, in the uniform of the Volunteer Reserve, was cleaning a revolver with a silk bandanna handkerchief. He hailed the crippled destroyer's bridge. "What's it like over there this morning?" he shouted. It was his first trip. A bandaged figure replied with an impotent movement of his hand to his ears. He was probably deaf with gunfire and bomb explosions. "Not so funny!" replied a man busy about a wire aft. "Not so bloody funny." The haze swallowed them.

There was another destroyer alongside. Her captain came out of his bridge cabin yawning. He was hollow-eyed and unshaven, but he had had nearly two hours' sleep while they patched some splinter holes in his funnel and filled up with ammunition. Two hours in four days.

The lookout to port yelled the first air alarm as they neared the Dunkirk beaches. "Here they come," said the navigator grimly. The foremost guns opened fire; the hot blast from their muzzles swept over the bridge; the multiple pompom joined in. The captain had his glasses leveled on the beaches. They looked like a holiday resort thronged by a vast dun-colored motionless crowd. Fires were burning in the background under a pall of smoke.

He ignored the causes that made his own guns open fire.

His immediate concern was the navigation of his ship in the treacherous shallows. There were a sudden bright yellow flash and a cloud of smoke among the packed throngs ashore. Another bomb. The water was dark with men wading out waist-deep. He counted the ships inshore: three destroyers, their boats coming and going laden to the gunwales, and their guns blazing skyward; six trawlers, motor launches, motorboats . . . he lost count of them. The army had contrived to drive some lorries into the sea during the night and to build a sort of pier. There was a trawler sinking to the westward in a cloud of steam and smoke. Well, they'd have to fend for themselves. He glanced skyward, where there was a dogfight going on between some Spitfires and Heinkels. His guns ceased firing.

The captain watched the boats toiling shoreward. God, the men were tired! He began calculating the number of trips they would have to make. A motor barge swung away from the improvised pier and came towards them, crowded with troops. That was better; now they could get on with it.

The yacht-club telephone rang, and the elderly steward, unaccustomed to the sound of it, laid down his paper, removed his spectacles, and picked up the receiver. A man's voice spoke authoritatively for about a minute.

The steward said nothing. He was an old Navy man and had been a pensioner for a quarter of a century, but he recognized the note in the speaker's voice. He waited till the end of the message.

"Aye, aye, sir," he said, and then added, "There's only the one yacht here now, sir. The *Wanderer*. Motor yacht, forty feet long. There's no crew, sir. Owner's fighting in France. There's a young lady on board at this moment—"

The voice interrupted him. He listened, turning the spectacles over in his knotted fingers, staring into vacancy.

"Aye, aye, sir. I'll do what I can. Old Navy man my-self. . . ."

The *Wanderer* was lying at her buoy and there was no sign of the girl. He untied the dinghy lying at the jetty and rowed alongside. At the sound of the oars as he boated them the girl's head and shoulders appeared above the companion-way. She was flushed and had a scrubbing brush in her hand.

"They want her, miss," he said simply. "They rung up from the Admiralty. Proceed to Ramsgate for orders. They're tak-ing every craft on the south coast."

She brushed a lock of hair back from her damp forehead with her forearm. "I'm single-handed," she said. "Can you run the engine if I steer?"

"You, miss?" He hadn't thought of that.

"She's full up with petrol. There's water, too, and some stuff in tins to eat. Bring some bread."

"You know what it's for, don't you, miss? They won't let a woman—"

"They needn't know," was the girl's answer. She stood motionless, thinking. The ebb tide running past the strakes of the dinghy made a little chuckling noise in the stillness.

"Bring a couple of shrapnel helmets. Get them from the A.R.P. people. What about Johnnie?"

"Johnnie?" He turned that over in his mind. Johnnie was simple, but he was useful in a boat.

The sky line was like the edge of the Pit. To the westward the oil tanks of Dunkirk were a sullen blaze that every now and again leaped upwards like the eruption of a volcano as a shell burst in the flaming inferno. Fires glowed dully along the coast, and shore batteries blinked white flashes that reached the ear as dull reverberations like distant thunder. The search-lights wheeled about the low-lying clouds into which tracer shells were soaring.

They had solved the problem of navigating to La Panne by

following a paddle steamer that had half a dozen lifeboats
in tow. The whole night was full of the sound of motorboats'
exhausts. There was a young moon peeping in and out of the
drifting clouds, and it revealed the indistinct lines of little
craft far and wide, heading in the same direction.

The dawn came slowly, revealing the small craft of the
south coast of England covering the Channel like water beetles
on the surface of a pool. Pleasure steamers and yachts, barges,
scoots, wherries, lifeboats, motorboats, rowing boats, and
canoes. Fishermen, yachtsmen, longshoremen, men who had
never been afloat in their lives, millionaires and the very poor,
elderly men and lads in their teens, answering in a headlong
rush the appeal for boats. Boats for the beaches and the last
of the Expeditionary Force.

Somehow she hadn't thought about the dead. Her thoughts
were entirely occupied with the living. It wasn't till Johnnie
began making queer noises of distress and pointing down into
the shallow water that she saw them—the men who had been
machine-gunned in the shallows, wading out into the water
to reach security. They were still there, some floating, some
submerged; in an odd way they seemed to convey resentment
at the disturbance of their oblivion by the passing keels.

She crept inshore. The beach was pitted with shell craters
out of which men came running, wading out into the water
to meet them. From the sand dunes more men stumbled, helping the wounded. The whole foreshore was alive with men
and boats, and the smoke from the Dunkirk fires flowed over
them like a dark river.

At three and a half feet she would stop. It was the least
they could float in. She listened to the strange cries Johnnie
emitted as he hauled in the dripping lead line, understanding
them perfectly.

Presently, her mouth to the voice pipe, she gave the order
to stop. Tanner was having trouble with the Bren gun and

swearing in a ceaseless flow of incomprehensible blasphemy. Old Ferris, complete in shrapnel helmet and life belt, climbed out of his hatch and came towards her, lighting his pipe.

She searched every face as they came splashing and gasping towards her and somehow contrived to hoist each other inboard. She took sixty or seventy at a trip and transferred them to the nearest vessel lying out in the deep water; she had hitherto believed that the utmost capacity of the *Wanderer* was a dozen. Backwards and forwards they went under exploding bombs, under machine-gun fire and whining shells. Tanner ran out of ammunition and they went alongside a destroyer, where he got another case and a spare barrel for the Bren gun. She lost all count of time, all fear, all feeling. Sometimes she interrogated weary men: Had they seen his unit? Had they ever heard his name? They shook their heads and begged for water. She had none left.

Then suddenly it seemed that the beaches were empty. She didn't know that the men were being marched westward to Dunkirk, where the French and British destroyers were crowding alongside the mole and embarking troops in thousands under the shellfire. Except for a few scattered units moving west, the beaches were empty. The task was done; but where was he—Oh Christ, where was he?

The Bren gun had been silent for a long time, but she hadn't noticed. Now, turning to look seaward, she saw Tanner lying beside it with his knees screwed up into his belly. She ran aft and knelt beside him.

His eyes sought hers out of his gray face. "I bought it, Skipper. Sorry. Got a drop of water?"

They followed a big gray coaster back to Dover. Old Ferris got a spare red ensign out of the locker and tucked Tanner up in it. He didn't mind Tanner's being killed, having been disposed to regard him jealously as an intruder into a nice little family party. Moreover, he disapproved of his language.

He walked forward to the wheel-house. She was moving the spokes of the wheel slowly between her blistered hands. Her shrapnel helmet lay on the chart beside the valiant briar pipe. She was aware of the old man beside her and of having reached the end of her tether at one and the same moment.

Old Ferris kicked Johnnie, asleep at her feet, into wakefulness. "Take the wheel," he said gruffly, and held her as she pitched, sobbing and exhausted, into his arms.

They berthed alongside the Admiralty pier and she climbed ashore to find someone who could give them fuel and water. The quays were thronged with troops in thousands, being fed and sorted out into units and entrained. A hospital ship was evacuating wounded into fleets of ambulances. She stepped aside to give room to the bearers of a stretcher and glanced at the face on the pillow.

He had a bandage round his head and opened his eyes suddenly on her face.

"I've been looking for you," she announced in a calm matter-of-fact tone. She felt no emotion whatever.

He smiled. "Well, here I am," he said.

VII
London Fire

❀ ❀ ❀ ❀ ❀ ❀ ❀ ❀ ❀ ❀ ❀ ❀ ❀ ❀ ❀ ❀ ❀ ❀

THE CLASSIC descriptions of London's destruction in 1666 are those of the practical Mr. Pepys and of John Evelyn, the friend whom he admired for his philosophical turn of mind. The eyewitness of a complicated event may choose one of two ways to present his experience: the immediate cumulative development, detail by detail, or the panoramic survey in logical perspective of selected detail. By a beneficent chance, Pepys the practical was in the middle of London during the fire, burying cheeses and carrying movables. The more philosophical Mr. Evelyn watched the flames from the Bankside in Southwark, separated from them by the Thames. Pepys's account builds up by an accumulation of vivid small details and experiences: the pigeons, the singed cat, the neighbors, street names, and cold meat with Sir W. Penn. His scheme of organization follows the chronological pattern of his days. Evelyn begins with a panoramic description of the fire, geographically located, and continues in a logical development of the subject: the shock to the people, the spectacle of displaced households, the light of the flames, the sound. On September 5 he moves into Whitehall and Fetter Lane, but he still sees the calamity in perspective, his observations directed by a central idea or colored by a persistent impression.

The modern descriptions of the fire bombs of 1940 illustrate the same two points of view. Tomlinson, like Evelyn, looks across the river, and, like Evelyn, he meditates upon destiny and the panorama of time. White, like Pepys, is in the thick

of firefighters, and like Pepys's account, his follows the natural
course of the night's adventure. But he is more detached than
Pepys. It is not his own goods which are burning, and the
event takes on some of the quality of a grand spectacle, par-
ticularized, however, by the central figure of Marguerite,
human and destructible, around whom he gathers the poignant
mortal reminders that this is a city not only of buildings and
of history but of men and women.

❀ ❀ ❀ ❀ ❀ ❀ ❀ ❀ ❀ ❀ ❀ ❀ ❀ ❀ ❀ ❀ ❀ ❀

THE GREAT FIRE

JOHN EVELYN · 1666

September 2, 1666. This fatal night, about ten, began the deplorable fire near Fish Street in London.

September 3. I had public prayers at home. The fire continuing, after dinner I took coach with my wife and son and
went to the Bankside in Southwark, where we beheld that
dismal spectacle, the whole city in dreadful flames near the
water-side; all the houses from the Bridge, all Thomas Street,
and upwards towards Cheapside, down to the Three Cranes,
were now consumed; and so returned exceeding astonished
what would become of the rest.

The fire having continued all this night—if I may call that
night which was light as day for ten miles round about after
a dreadful manner—when conspiring with a fierce eastern
wind in a very dry season, I went on foot to the same place;
and saw the whole south part of the city burning from
Cheapside to the Thames and all along Cornhill—for it likewise kindled back against the wind as well as forward—

From *The Diary of John Evelyn*, first published 1818.

Tower Street, Fenchurch Street, Gracious Street, and so along to Baynard's Castle, and was now taking hold of St. Paul's Church, to which the scaffolds contributed exceedingly. The conflagration was so universal and the people so astonished that from the beginning, I know not by what despondency or fate, they hardly stirred to quench it; so that there was nothing heard or seen but crying out and lamentation, running about like distracted creatures without at all attempting to save even their goods, such a strange consternation there was upon them; so as it burned both in breadth and length the churches, public halls, Exchange, hospitals, monuments, and ornaments, leaping after a prodigious manner from house to house and street to street at great distances one from the other. For the heat, with a long set of fair and warm weather, had even ignited the air and prepared the materials to conceive the fire, which devoured after an incredible manner, houses, furniture and everything. Here we saw the Thames covered with goods floating, all the barges and boats laden with what some had time and courage to save, as on the other side the carts, etc., carrying out to the fields, which for many miles were strewed with movables of all sorts, and tents erecting to shelter both people and what goods they could get away. Oh, the miserable and calamitous spectacle! such as haply the world had not seen since the foundation of it! nor can be outdone till the universal conflagration thereof. All the sky was of a fiery aspect, like the top of a burning oven, and the light seen above forty miles round about for many nights. God grant mine eyes may never behold the like, who now saw above 10,000 houses all in one flame! The noise and cracking and thunder of the impetuous flames, the shrieking of women and children, the hurry of people, the fall of towers, houses, and churches was like a hideous storm; and the air all about so hot and inflamed that at the last one was not able to approach it, so that they were forced to stand still and let the flames burn on, which they did, for near two miles in length and one in breadth. The clouds also of smoke were dismal and reached, upon computation, near fifty miles in length. Thus I left it this afternoon burning, a resemblance of Sodom, or the last day. It forcibly called to my mind that passage—*non enim hic habemus stabilem civitatem*, the ruins resembling the picture of Troy, London was, but is no more! Thus I returned.

September 4. The burning still rages, and it is now gotten as far as the Inner Temple. All Fleet Street, the Old Bailey, Ludgate Hill, Warwick Lane, Newgate, Paul's Chain, Watling Street now flaming and most of it reduced to ashes; the stones of Paul's flew like grenados, the melting lead running down the streets in a stream, and the very pavements glowing with fiery redness, so as no horse nor man was able to tread on them, and the demolition had stopped all the passages, so that no help could be applied. The eastern wind still more impetuously driving the flames forward. Nothing but the almighty power of God was able to stop them; for vain was the help of man.

September 5. It crossed towards Whitehall; but oh! the confusion there was then at that court! It pleased his Majesty to command me, among the rest, to look after the quenching of Fetter Lane end, to preserve, if possible, that part of Holborn, whilst the rest of the gentlemen took their several posts, some at one part, and some at another; for now they began to bestir themselves, and not till now, who hitherto had stood as men intoxicated with their hands across, and began to consider that nothing was likely to put a stop but the blowing up of so many houses as might make a wider gap than any had yet been made by the ordinary method of pulling them down with engines. This some stout seamen proposed early enough to have saved near the whole city, but this some tenacious and avaricious men, aldermen, etc., would not permit because their houses must have been of the first. It was, therefore, now commanded to be practised; and my concern being particularly for the Hospital of St. Bartholomew near Smithfield, where I had many wounded and sick men, made me the more diligent to promote it; nor was my care for the Savoy less. It now pleased God by abating the wind and by the industry of the people, when almost all was lost infusing a new spirit into them, that the fury of it began sensibly to abate about noon, so as it came no farther than the Temple westward nor than the entrance of Smithfield north. But continued all this day and night so impetuous toward Cripplegate and the Tower as made us all despair. It also broke out again in the Temple; but the courage of the multitude persisting and many houses being blown up, such gaps and desolations were soon made as, with the former three days' consumption, the back fire did not so vehemently urge upon the rest as formerly. There was yet no standing near the burning and glowing ruins by near a furlong's space.

September 7. I was infinitely concerned to find that goodly church, St. Paul's, now a sad ruin and that beautiful portico, for structure comparable to any in Europe, as not long before repaired by the late King, now rent in pieces, flakes of vast stones split asunder, and nothing remaining entire but the inscription in the architrave showing by whom it was built, which had not one letter defaced! It was astonishing to see what immense stones the heat had in a manner calcined, so that all the ornaments, columns, friezes, capitals, and projectures of massy Portland stone flew off even to the very roof, where a sheet of lead covering a great space, no less than six acres by measure, was totally melted. The ruins of the vaulted roof falling broke into St. Faith's, which being filled with the magazine of books belonging to the stationers and carried thither for safety they were all consumed, burning for a week following. It is also observable that the lead over the altar at the east end was untouched, and among the divers monuments the body of one bishop remained entire. Thus lay in ashes that most venerable church, one of the most ancient pieces of early piety in the Christian world, besides near one hundred more. The lead, iron-work, bells, plate, etc., melted, the exquisitely wrought Mercers' Chapel, the sumptuous Exchange, the august fabric of Christ Church, all the rest of the companies' halls, splendid buildings, arches, entries, all in dust; the fountains dried up and ruined, whilst the very waters remained boiling; the voragos of subterranean cellars, wells, and dungeons, formerly warehouses, still burning in stench and dark clouds of smoke; so that in five or six miles traversing about I did not see one load of timber unconsumed, nor many stones but were calcined white as snow.

The people who now walked about the ruins appeared like men in some dismal desert, or rather in some great city laid waste by a cruel enemy; to which was added the stench that came from some poor creatures' bodies, beds, and other combustible goods. Sir Thomas Gresham's statue, though fallen from its niche in the Royal Exchange, remained entire, when all those of the kings since the Conquest were broken to pieces. Also the standard in Cornhill and Queen Elizabeth's effigies, with some arms on Ludgate, continued with but little detriment, whilst the vast iron chains of the city streets, hinges, bars, and gates of prisons were many of them melted and reduced to cinders by the vehement heat. Nor was I yet able to pass through any of the narrow streets, but kept the widest; the ground and air, smoke and fiery vapor, continued so intense that my hair was almost singed and my feet insufferably surbated. The bye-lanes and narrow streets were quite filled up with rubbish; nor could one have possibly known where he was but by the ruins of some church or hall that had some remarkable tower or pinnacle remaining.

I then went towards Islington and Highgate, where one

might have seen 200,000 people of all ranks and degrees dispersed and lying along by their heaps of what they could save from the fire, deploring their loss and, though ready to perish for hunger and destitution, yet not asking one penny for relief, which appeared to me a stranger sight than any I had yet beheld. His Majesty and council indeed took all imaginable care for their relief by proclamation for the country to come in and refresh them with provisions.

LONDON FIRE, 1666

SAMUEL PEPYS · 1666

2nd [*September*]. (*Lord's day*) Some of our maids sitting up late last night to get things ready against our feast today, Jane called us up about three in the morning to tell us of a great fire they saw in the city. So I rose and slipped on my nightgown and went to her window; and thought it to be on the back-side of Mark Lane at the farthest; but, being unused to such fires as followed, I thought it far enough off; and so went to bed again and to sleep. About seven rose again to dress myself, and there looked out at the window and saw the fire not so much as it was, and further off. So to my closet to set things to rights, after yesterday's cleaning. By and by Jane comes and tells me that she hears that above 300 houses have been burned down tonight by the fire we saw and that it is now burning down all Fish Street by London Bridge. So I made myself ready presently, and walked to the Tower; and there got upon one of the high places, Sir J. Robinson's little son going up with me; and there I did see the houses at that end of the bridge all on fire and an infinite great fire on this

From *The Diary of Samuel Pepys*, first published 1825.

and the other side the end of the bridge; which, among other people, did trouble me for poor little Michell and our Sarah on the bridge. So down, with my heart full of trouble, to the lieutenant of the Tower, who tells me that it begun this morning in the King's baker's house in Pudding Lane and that it had burned down St. Magnus' Church and most part of Fish Street already. So I down to the water-side, and there got a boat, and through bridge, and there saw a lamentable fire. Poor Michell's house, as far as the Old Swan, already burned that way, and the fire running further, that in a very little time it got as far as the Steel-yard, while I was there. Everybody endeavoring to remove their goods, and flinging into the river or bringing them into lighters that lay off; poor people staying in their houses as long as till the very fire touched them, and then running into boats or clambering from one pair of stairs, by the water-side, to another. And among other things, the poor pigeons, I perceive, were loth to leave their houses, but hovered about the windows and balconies, till they burned their wings and fell down. Having stayed and in an hour's time seen the fire rage every way, and nobody, to my sight, endeavoring to quench it, but to remove their goods and leave all to the fire, and having seen it get as far as the Steel-yard, and the wind mighty high and driving it into the city; and everything, after so long a drought, proving combustible, even the very stones of churches; . . . I to Whitehall, with a gentleman with me, who desired to go off from the Tower, to see the fire, in my boat; and there up to the King's closet in the chapel, where people came about me, and I did give them an account dismayed them all, and word was carried in to the King. So I was called for, and did tell the King and Duke of York what I saw; and that, unless his Majesty did command houses to be pulled down, nothing could stop the fire. They seemed much troubled, and the King commanded me to go to my Lord Mayor from him and command him to spare no houses, but to pull down before the fire every way. The Duke of York bid me tell him that if he would have any more soldiers, he shall; and so did my Lord Arlington afterwards, as a great secret. Here meeting with Captain Cocke, I in his coach, which he lent me, and Creed with me to Paul's; and there walked along Watling Street, as well as I could, every creature coming away laden with goods to save, and, here and there, sick people carried away in beds. Extraordinary good goods carried in carts and on backs. At last met my Lord Mayor in Canning Street, like a man spent, with handkercher about his neck. To the King's message he cried, like a fainting woman, "Lord! what can I do? I am spent! people will not obey me. I have been pulling down houses; but the fire overtakes us faster than we can do it." That he needed no more soldiers and that, for himself, he must go and refresh himself, having been up all night. So he left me, and I him, and walked home; seeing people all almost distracted, and no manner of means used to quench the fire. The houses, too, so very thick thereabouts, and full of matter for burning, as pitch and tar, in Thames Street; and warehouses of oil and wines and brandy and other things. . . . Met with the King and Duke of York in their barge, and with them to Queenhithe, and there called Sir Richard Browne to them. Their order was only to pull down houses apace, and so below bridge at the water-side; but this little was or could be done, the fire coming upon them so fast. Good hopes there was of stopping it at the Three Cranes above and at Buttulph's Wharf below bridge, if care be used; but the wind carries it into the city so as we know not, by the water-side, what it do there. River full of lighters and boats taking in goods, and good goods swimming in the water; and only I observed that hardly one lighter or boat in three that had the goods of a house in but there was a pair of virginals in it. Having seen as much as I could now, I away to Whitehall by appointment, and there walked to St. James's Park; and there met my wife and Creed and Wood, and his wife, and walked to my boat; and there upon the water again, and to the fire up and down, it still increasing and the wind great. So near the fire as we could for smoke; and all over the Thames, with one's faces in the wind you were almost burned with a shower of fire-drops. This is very true, so as houses were burned by these drops and flakes of fire three or four, nay, five or six houses one from another. When we could endure no more upon the water, we to a little ale-house on the Bankside over against the Three Cranes, and there stayed till it was dark almost, and saw the fire grow; and, as it grew darker, appeared more and more; and in corners and upon steeples and between churches and houses, as far as we could see up the hill of the city, in a most horrid, malicious, bloody flame, not like the fine flame of an ordinary fire. Barbary and her husband away before us. We stayed till, it being dark-ish, we saw the fire as only one entire arch of fire from this to the other side of the bridge and in a bow up the hill for an arch of above a mile long. It made me weep to see it. The churches, houses, and all on fire and flaming at once; and a horrid noise the flames made, and the cracking of houses at their ruin. So home with a sad heart, and there find everybody discoursing and lamenting the fire; and poor Tom Hater come with some few of his goods saved out of his house, which was burned upon Fish Street Hill. I invited him to lie at my house, and did receive his goods; but was deceived in his lying there, the news coming every moment of the growth of the fire; so as we were forced to begin to pack up our own goods and prepare for their removal; and did by moonshine, it being brave, dry, and moonshine and warm weather, carry much of my goods into the garden; and Mr. Hater and I did remove my money and iron chests into my cellar, as thinking that the

safest place. And got my bags of gold into my office, ready
to carry away, and my chief papers of accounts also there,
and my tallies into a box by themselves.

4th. Sir W. Batten not knowing how to remove his wine,
did dig a pit in the garden, and laid it in there; and I took
the opportunity of laying all the papers of my office that I
could not otherwise dispose of. And in the evening Sir W.
Penn and I did dig another, and put our wine in it; and I
my parmesan cheese as well as my wine and some other things.
. . . This night, Mrs. Turner, who, poor woman, was removing her goods all this day, good goods, into the garden,
and knows not how to dispose of them, and her husband
supped with my wife and me at night in the office upon a
shoulder of mutton from the cook's without any napkin or
anything in a sad manner, but were merry. Only now and
then, walking into the garden, saw how horribly the sky
looks, all on a fire in the night, was enough to put us out
of our wits; and, indeed, it was extremely dreadful, for it
looks just as if it was at us, and the whole heaven on fire. I
after supper walked in the dark down to Tower Street, and
there saw it all on fire, at the Trinity House on that side and the
Dolphin Tavern on this side, which was very near us; and
the fire with extraordinary vehemence. Now begins the practice of blowing up of houses in Tower Street, those next the
Tower, which at first did frighten people more than anything; but it stopped the fire where it was done, it bringing
down the houses to the ground in the same places they stood,
and then it was easy to quench what little fire was in it,
though it kindled nothing almost. W. Hewer this day went
to see how his mother did, and comes late home, telling us
how he hath been forced to remove her to Islington, her
house in Pye Corner being burned; so that the fire is got
so far that way and to the Old Bailey, and was running down

to Fleet Street; and Paul's is burned and all Cheapside. I wrote
to my father this night, but the post-house being burned, the
letter could not go.

5th. I lay down in the office again upon W. Hewer's quilt,
being mighty weary and sore in my feet with going till I
was hardly able to stand. About two in the morning my wife
calls me up and tells me of new cries of fire, it being come to
Barking Church, which is the bottom of our lane. I up; and
finding it so, resolved presently to take her away, and did,
and took my gold, which was about £2,350, W. Hewer
and Jane down by Proundy's boat to Woolwich. But, Lord!
what a sad sight it was by moonlight to see the whole city
almost on fire that you might see it as plain at Woolwich as
if you were by it. There, when I come, I find the gates shut,
but no guard kept at all; which troubled me, because of dis-
courses now begun that there is a plot in it and that the French
had done it. I got the gates open, and to Mr. Shelden's, where
I locked up my gold and charged my wife and W. Hewer
never to leave the room without one of them in it night or day.
So back again, by the way seeing my goods well in the
lighters at Deptford and watched well by people. Home,
and whereas I expected to have seen our house on fire, it being
now about seven o'clock, it was not. But to the fire, and there
find greater hopes than I expected; for my confidence of
finding our office on fire was such that I durst not ask anybody how it was with us till I come and saw it was not burned.
But going to the fire, I find, by the blowing up of houses
and the great help given by the workmen out of the King's
yards, sent up by Sir W. Penn, there is a good stop given
to it, as well at Mark Lane end as ours; it having only burned
the dial of Barking Church and part of the porch, and was
there quenched. I up to the top of Barking steeple, and there
saw the saddest sight of desolation that I ever saw; everywhere great fires, oil-cellars and brimstone and other things

burning. I became afraid to stay there long, and therefore down again as fast as I could, the fire being spread as far as I could see it; and to Sir W. Penn's, and there eat a piece of cold meat, having eaten nothing since Sunday, but the remains of Sunday's dinner. Here I met with Mr. Young and Whistler; and, having removed all my things and received good hopes that the fire at our end is stopped, they and I walked into the town, and find Fenchurch Street, Gracious Street, and Lombard Street all in dust. The Exchange a sad sight, nothing standing there of all the statues or pillars but Sir Thomas Gresham's picture in the corner. Into Moorfields, our feet ready to burn walking through the town among the hot coals, and find that full of people and poor wretches carrying their goods there and everybody keeping his goods together by themselves; and a great blessing it is to them that it is fair weather for them to keep abroad night and day; drunk there, and paid two-pence for a plain penny loaf. Thence homeward, having passed through Cheapside and Newgate market, all burned; and seen Anthony Joyce's house in fire; and took up, which I keep by me, a piece of glass of the Mercers' Chapel in the street, where much more was, so melted and buckled with the heat of the fire like parchment. I also did see a poor cat taken out of a hole in a chimney, joining to the wall of the Exchange, with the hair all burnt off the body, and yet alive. So home at night, and find there good hopes of saving our office; but great endeavors of watching all night and having men ready; and so we lodged them in the office, and had drink and bread and cheese for them. And I lay down and slept a good night about midnight, though, when I rose, I heard that there had been a great alarm of French and Dutch being risen, which proved nothing.

LONDON FIRE, 1940

WILLIAM L. WHITE · 1941

The night the Nazis tried to burn London I was at a matinee of the Charlie Chaplin movie with Marguerite, who is 25 and very good-looking. She is half English and half French and speaks both languages with just a trace of accent. She used to work for the *Matin* but got out of Paris just ahead of the Nazis and came to London where she now holds a newspaper job.

The show was over at seven and we stepped out into the weirdest city I had ever seen. London looked like a technicolor production of *The Burning of Rome* by Cecil B. De Mille. The whole sky was pink, with splotches of bright orange on the horizon. It was so garish as to be a little bit overdramatized and in bad taste. Though long after dark, there was enough light from the sky for me to tell the tone of Marguerite's lipstick. People along the streets were a little nervous, and at times someone would break into a trot or a run when there was a good bomb whistle nearby. Marguerite made a point of not running. Because of this crazy Cecil B. De Mille pink over everything you could see the faces of the people, see which ones were scared and just how scared. A few of them weren't liking it at all.

There was so much pink in the sky by this time that we both knew this was a big night for London and maybe was going to get bigger. So Marguerite suggested we walk over by the Embankment to see just how big it already was. When we got there we found the Thames was the same kind of baby ribbon pink as the sky, except for yellow flames from

From *Journey for Margaret,* by W. L. White, *Reader's Digest,* xxxviii, March, 1941. Used by kind permission of the author and of *The Reader's Digest.*

a barge that had caught fire and high yellow flames in two patches from what might have been warehouses. But most of the trouble was apparently on our side of the river.

There wasn't a taxi in sight. Most of the people were off the streets now, except for policemen and air-raid wardens. Suddenly stuff began bouncing all around us on the pavement. At first I thought it was shrapnel, but when each piece as it struck burst into a ball of flame about the size of a cat and the greenish color of a mercury vapor lamp, we knew they were incendiaries. Two landed within three yards of us. They were bouncing all up and down the street, and we could see air-raid wardens running to put them out, and hear the watchers on the roofs calling for help. It was those immediately around us, burning harmlessly on the sidewalk, which infuriated Marguerite's sense of tidiness, and I turned around just in time to see her give one of them a healthy kick which sent it spinning into the gutter. It had fallen close to some glass set into the sidewalk, and the glass was still bubbling. As I glanced at it Marguerite was holding one foot in her hands and hopping around on the other. We took off her shoe. The leather was burned through, but the stocking beneath was only scorched. She said it probably would only raise a blister, and anyway, she said, it was worth it.

Then we went across the street to a bank which had a lot of sandbags around it protecting people's investments, and took half a dozen of the bags, one at a time, and dumped the contents over the rest of the burning incendiary bombs around us. The contents turned out to be ashes and clinkers instead of sand but it was almost as good. On both sides of the street we could see roof fires starting. First there would be a curl of smoke above the eaves, then a flickering orange-yellow glow would appear behind the top-story windows. Because this was the downtown commercial and financial district of London, most of the houses were vacant and there were few roof watchers. So the air-raid wardens in the street below had no way of knowing where the fires were until these lights appeared. Then I remembered something I had picked up in Berlin a year ago and forgotten until now. A Nazi newspaperman, blowing off in front of a bunch of us after a foreign office press conference, was bragging that large areas of London—the docks and the older parts of the City district—could be burned off like weed patches from the air any time they decided to do it.

Then suddenly we saw a taxi coming lickety-brindle down the street from the direction of the pinkest glow in the sky. We hailed him and he pulled up. He was a very scared, rat-faced young man with flaring ears. His taxi was splattered with water from fire hoses. He was very shaky and excited, and when we said we wanted to go to the fire he told us that he would not go back there for anything in the world. He said the entire city was alight and out of control and would burn to the ground tonight and he was getting out. Marguerite said she didn't want a frightened man around anyway, so we started out to walk. About 10 o'clock we found a young taxi driver with thick black hair slicked down with grease who said he would like very much to see the fire himself and would go for whatever we thought it was worth. He had heard the flames were moving onto St. Paul's and that the Guildhall was going and maybe would be gone before we got there. We told him to drive toward where the sky was reddest and when he got into the thick of it to steer for St. Paul's. We rolled down the rear windows to hang out and watch the sky. We smelled the first whiff of fire as we rounded a corner. The smell of a city fire is usually strong with the stench of rubber or the odor of scorched tar roofing. There was none of these in this smell, which was even rather pleasant.

Soon we found police lines blocking off a street. The driver pulled up and we held our press passes out through the window. The policeman touched his hand to the brim of his blue steel helmet and waved us through. This impressed the driver greatly. He said he thought we were only a couple of crazy sightseers and had not guessed we were reporters. After that every time we came to a police line he would lean out and say, importantly, "We are the press," but presently we found the street way blocked with fire engines so we told the driver to park his car and we would walk. We were a little surprised to find the fire was in a building we both knew—a six-story affair which housed a newspaper and a press association. The top story was ablaze and we could tell the roof had fallen by the way the sparks rose. We had both been in that building half a dozen times, sitting on desks piled with copy, talking to newspapermen we knew. The bottom windows were dark, and it was silent now except for the hissing of the nozzles and the frying noise as water hit the red-hot roof timbers.

The firemen told us the worst fires were further into the City and that half a dozen churches were burning. Marguerite suggested we walk to see if her favorite church was all right—a beautiful little Christopher Wren structure nestled among ratty old office buildings. As we got near, it looked like a Christmas card picture of a church at night, a black silhouette with a holy light streaming from its windows. But this light flickered uneasily; someone, probably firemen, had left the front doors open and light streamed out of them too. Standing as close to the doors as the heat would let us we looked into a great furnace. The roof had come down and glowing beams were sprawled over the red embers that had once been pews. As we watched the work of Christopher Wren crumbling away, we thought that after the war people with money would give lavishly so that architects would restore the church even better than it had been before. And

yet, as Marguerite pointed out, it was sad to stand here and
see it go, because it had been such a sweet little soot-stained
church with perfectly balanced classical lines like a minuet
in stone.

The smell of fire was all around us now, and Marguerite
remarked how curious it was. This was not the ordinary
smell of fresh wood smoke. It was almost like incense, spiced
with the odor of mellowed oak beams put into place 250
years ago, after London's first great fire. And with this haunting odor was blended the charred smell of the ancient records
of business firms whose columns of figures have supported
the British Empire for centuries. Surely no attar of roses
could ever be so expensive as this scent you got by burning
the city of London. It clung to our clothes as we walked
back to the car.

Trying again to reach St. Paul's, we went bouncing along
a street over fire hose coiled like giant strands of gray spaghetti.
We drove cautiously, with frequent stops, through a traffic
jam the like of which I hope I will never see again. With the
exception of our taxi, all of it was fire engines—hose carts,
pumps, hook and ladder trucks—slowly oozing into the fire
zone ahead. The firemen were looking at Marguerite, but
Marguerite was looking down the flaming street into that
beautiful snowstorm of sparks. "But it's magnificent," she
said. "It's Wagnerian. It's a blizzard of fire. I want to run
through it."

"That's not sensible," I said.

"It's not sensible to be a fireman," said Marguerite. "It's
not sensible to be out at all tonight. It's not even sensible for
less than fifty million English to be fighting almost a hundred
million Nazis. All the sensible people in London are down
under the Savoy Hotel tonight. Are you coming?"

"Yes," I said.

"I'm coming with you," said the taxi driver suddenly. "This

is my town and I'll never see anything like this again." He didn't say "sir" and we were both glad he didn't. So we started running down that flaming street. I put Marguerite on the side of me opposite the crackling buildings and took hold of her arm to steady her as we ran over the piles of hot bricks. The driver, instead of walking two paces behind, came up and took her other arm.

The fire was terribly hot; I could feel it roasting the oil out of my right cheek. I turned up the collar of my trench coat, and with my free hand turned up the collar of Marguerite's tweed coat. The driver turned it up on his side. He was looking after her too. The burned-out shop doors were like openings into blast furnaces. They were a shimmering bluish red inside, which it hurt you to look at. Sparks began coming down—bits of burning wood about the size of your thumbnail. We had to brush them off quickly or they would have burned holes in our coats. All at once a cracking sound behind us swelled into a clattering roar. We glanced back to see that the entire five-story front of the building we had just passed had collapsed and lay piled several feet deep over both sidewalks. We were cut off, and had to go forward into the blizzard of fiery snowflakes before another building collapsed in front of us and trapped us for good.

Then we passed the last burning building and came out into the darkness of the little square where the big sparks were showering down. But we could hardly see them, because of the acrid smoke that burned our streaming eyes. The sparks were so thick I was afraid Marguerite's hair would catch fire so I clapped my hat on her head. Both her eyes were closed and so were the driver's. I could keep one eye open by propping it with my forefinger and thumb, so I led them across the square, telling them when we came to curbs. At last we found a dark street where there was no fire and from there we made our way back to the car. It was four o'clock in the

morning and Marguerite decided she had better go home as
she had to get to work at seven-thirty. So we took her home
and then the driver took me home. When I paid him he
said quite solemnly that he wouldn't have missed it for anything. And he didn't say "sir."

THE BATTLE OF LONDON

H. M. TOMLINSON · 1941

If, when the man who was to write *Moby Dick* looked down
Thames from London Bridge, it had been as late as the night
of September 7, 1940, he would have seen something out of
reach of words. It was the night of doomsday, and not only
the earth but the firmament was blazing. He would have seen
he was present at the final act, the culmination of the long
conflict between good and evil; and there are no words for
that known to men. His fear for human destiny, should pride
in folly continue to challenge powers unknown, would have
told him that he was the last man, the lone watcher of the
sacrifice of mankind's effort to Abaddon. The story was
ending. Others appeared to be beside him at the parapet, but
they were only phantoms, gaping, as he was himself, at the
scene in which human aspirations were going up in smoke.
Phantoms they were; their day was over; and the smoke of
all they had done in their lives was worthy of their unfortunate
yet heroic ways, billowing and passionate volumes of smoke,
—scarlet, orange, gold, purple, and silver,—the mounting in-
flammables of ambition and pride. These figures beside him,
watching with him, were only masks lacquered red by the

From *The Atlantic Monthly*, clxvii, January, 1941. Reprinted by permission
of the Society of Authors for Mr. Tomlinson.

flames of the hot gulf along the gloomy verge of which they floated.

Could that be London? This was its old place. Those wavering shapes were of the Pool, and there the Norman battlements of the Tower were also, as ever, but all shook and pulsed, as if resolving into their incandescent elements, and would pass with everything, with the smoke. The Thames moved below as a river of blood. That dreadful wail he heard was the uprising of man's universal anguish.

No, not quite. One of the phantoms beside him moved abruptly, and spoke. "Hey, out of it, you! Down below. Here the blighters come again." The wraith was off, as a galaxy of sparks exploded in the distance, followed by a blast. There were, that night, watchers on the hills in the suburbs who feared that London was done for, and who were heartened, next morning, when there it was the same as ever, but for patching smoke. They took their trains and buses, not without more difficulty than usual, found the old place veritably was standing, and they did what work they could in it. Ruins were fewer than they expected to find, though there were more than enough; but when the stories from their friends in the eastern parishes began to arrive, they understood well that something had happened which could never be overlooked, for it marked a turning point in the history of civilization. Beyond a peradventure, they knew what must be done. Not for nothing is there a London tradition, though in easy days it can be forgotten.

So we go on. There are nights in London, moonlighted, and altogether new to the old city, which are as beautiful and strange as in a space apart from tribulation. A street in the city, abandoned to only that pale light, is as eerie as the palace Kubla Khan decreed. It is waiting. One keeps to the shadow of a wall, as though in wary desecration of a place not meant for footfalls. For the warning has sounded. There is a whistle and a crash, it is hard to say where, and across a turning in the light of the moon goes a group of helmeted figures at the double. It looks theatrical. It might be of the films, but it is wiser to accept it as present reality and dive underground, if you have time for it and refuge is at hand.

It should be said now, for this is the place, that but for one fact not even the stout hearts of Londoners could have saved their city from destruction. Their courage would have been unavailing. Faith saved them, as they cut off roaring gas mains, stopped the cataracts from fractured conduits, doused the volcanoes, got out the dead and dying. For citizens, though they heard the battle continuous in the clouds, and on certain days saw the gigantic hieroglyphics written on the heavens by the exhaust vapors of invisible engines, could rarely make out anything of it. It was in the heights. They knew their young gallants were aloft; navies were grappling in the central blue. Yet all they could do was to pray that all went well up there.

It went well. And though we had faith in our aerial fleet, as in that other fleet, we were dumbfounded when we heard the measure of victory. Nelson himself could not have asked for more. The enemy had been showered down. He is cruel, that enemy, for chivalry is expunged from his code, yet his fall is a dreadful sight. One day, during the affair, I was trying in vain to glimpse the battle in the sky. Sombre cumulus clouds poised in a brooding air were themselves sufficiently awful with the rays of a declining sun pouring through apertures. The unseen war was among them. Three vast fountains uprose on the calm waters, and stood strangely, as long as while we wondered whether they were planes or bombs. A livid ball appeared, and zigzagged down the bulge of a thundercloud, as if it were phenomenally slow lightning. That was a plane, and it was dying. A sharper rattle of machine guns took our eyes to a cloud right overhead. We shrank within ourselves. A Messerschmitt was diving at us. There was no time to move. It enlarged from a bright toy to a dire meteor, falling headfirst, body alight, arms helplessly outspread, and plunged. One is not likely to forget it. We stood, for another unseen plane seemed to be following immediately and directly at us, with an increasing drone which shuddered one's bones with its power. Only when that sound had passed did we realize that it was the dying cry of the Messerschmitt following its body down. The cloud from which the German had fallen moved on. It uncovered, in an area of blue, a fleet of Hurricanes and Spitfires, bright and tiny as white moths, in leisurely evolutions, heading east, on easy duty bent, driving the enemy out of England.

VIII
Flight

❋ ❋ ❋ ❋ ❋ ❋ ❋ ❋ ❋ ❋ ❋ ❋ ❋ ❋ ❋ ❋ ❋ ❋

MANY readers will remember the popular excitement and the
suspense which surrounded the first trans-Atlantic flights. All
the romance and adventure surrounding ships and sailing was
transferred, in a burst of enthusiasm, to the explorers of space.
Public acclaim rose from climax to superclimax as feats of
aviation crowded one another in weeks or days rather than
years. Fortunately the transocean flights so stimulated the
imagination that the barest record of the flight was a sufficient,
and is still an effective, evocation of the risks, the impulsion,
the reckless courage of the venture. For aviators are only in
rare cases, like that of Saint-Exupéry, also writers. Moreover,
the first books on flights were hastily written against time;
the story of an achievement in aviation which was not published within a month or two was already outdated by a newer
triumph. The books written by Fife and Amelia Earhart and
Commander Byrd are distinguished chiefly for their immediacy and for the accuracy and unadorned truth of statements
which are associated in our minds with such danger that the
venture assumes the dignity of destiny. Their narratives are
of the simplest kind: the organization is chronological; the
vocabulary is small and overworked; the sentences are short
declarations, too many of them beginning with "I." There
is little concern with transitions; phrases and words are tiresomely repeated, but the vitality of suspense, the conviction
of truth, and the intensity of a shared experience are there.

The first narratives provide a sharp contrast to the skillful essays of Mrs. Lindbergh and Saint-Exupéry, who enlarge and enrich the story of a flight until it becomes a discourse upon freedom or fear or faith, a symbol of man in his relation to the universe. The first selections are reporting; the later ones are meditation. The first depend upon circumstance and present simply an action. Mrs. Lindbergh and Saint-Exupéry relate an incident, but to it they add its meaning and beyond that its significance until the experience becomes important as an event, as an idea, as a revelation of truth, and as an aesthetic impression.

Fear, expressed or unexpressed, is the subject of all these essays. In some of them it is not only fear but awe and wonder. The selections measure the range from the purely factual to the mysterious, from technology to philosophy.

❀ ❀ ❀ ❀ ❀ ❀ ❀ ❀ ❀ ❀ ❀ ❀ ❀ ❀ ❀ ❀ ❀ ❀

HOW TO FLY

AMELIA EARHART · 1932

Piloting differs from driving a car in that there is an added necessity for lateral control. An automobile runs up and down hill, and turns left or right. A plane climbs or dives, or turns, and in addition tips from one side to another. There is no worry in a car about whether the two left wheels are on the road or not; but a pilot must normally keep his wings level. Of course, doing so becomes as automatic as driving straight, but is nevertheless dependent upon senses ever alert.

One of the first things a student learns in flying is that he turns by pushing a rudder bar *the way he wants to go*. (The

little wagons most children have turn opposite the push.)
When he turns, he must bank or tip the wings at the same
time. Why? Because, if he doesn't, the plane will skid in
exactly the same way a car does when it whirls too fast around
a level corner.

Perhaps you have noticed that the inside of an automobile
race track is like a bowl with the sides growing steeper and
steeper at the top. The cars climb toward the outer edge in
proportion to their speed, and it is quite impossible to force
a slow car up the steep side of the bowl. The faster the car goes,
the steeper the bank must be and the sharper the turn.

A pilot must make his own "bowl" and learn to tip his
plane to the right degree relative to the sharpness of his turn
and his speed. A bad skid means lack of control, for a while,
either on the ground or in the air, and of course is to be
avoided. By the way, compensating for skidding is the same
with a car or plane—one turns either craft in the direction
of the skid.

The stick—as its name implies—extends up from the floor
of the cockpit. It is a lever by means of which the pilot can
push the nose of the plane up or down. It also tips the wings.
By pushing it to the left, the left wing is depressed, and vice
versa.

The rudder bar, upon which one's feet rest, simply turns
the nose of the ship left or right, a movement to be coordinated
with the action of the stick. Today, by the way, especially
in larger planes, a wheel much like the steering wheel of a car
is used instead of the simple stick.

In addition to the stick and the rudder, the novice must become familiar with certain instruments placed before his
eyes, much as does a driver with a speedometer, gas gauge,
etc., installed on the dashboard of his automobile. These
instruments include a compass for direction, as well as others

which show speed through the air, height above ground, revolutions per minute of the motor, and pressure and temperature of the oil. On planes equipped for all weather flying, several more are necessary.

If a plane is stalled, the motor doesn't stop nor does the vehicle slide backwards. Instead, it begins to drop nose first and the pilot has to wait until enough speed is attained to make the rudder and ailerons effective. Of course, with airplanes there is little or no control at slow speeds any more than there is with a motorboat when it is barely moving.

At several thousand feet, a simple plane stall should not be hazardous. However, if it occurs so close to the earth that there isn't time to recover control, a hard landing, sometimes resulting in considerable damage, may be the outcome.

But in the air, as with automobiles, many accidents are due to the human equation. The careful driver, either below or aloft, barring the hard luck of mechanical failure, has remarkably little trouble, considering what he has to contend with.

Airplanes are equipped with air speed indicators which tell the pilot how fast a stream of air is passing the wing of the ship. If there is little or no wind, it may read approximately true for ground speed. It reads the same whether the plane is flying with the wind or against it. A plane which travels 100 miles in still air would be going only eighty miles an hour over the ground if a twenty-mile wind blew against it, head on. But the air speed indicator doesn't know the difference and gives its hundred m.p.h. reading just the same. Conversely, if the twenty-mile wind were blowing in the *same* direction as the airplane was flying, the speed of the plane would be increased to 120 miles per hour. So there must be other means of determining actual ground speed. Over a mapped territory the pilot without much trouble can clock his speed with the landmarks he can recognize. Where landmarks aren't available, different types of indicators are used to make the calculation.

INSTRUMENT FLYING

A minute later I was headed out to sea.

For several hours there was fair weather with a lingering sunset. And then the moon came up over a low bank of clouds. For those first hours I was flying about 12,000 feet. And then something happened that has never occurred in my twelve years of flying. The altimeter, the instrument which records height above ground, failed. Suddenly the hands swung around the dial uselessly and I knew the instrument was out of commission for the rest of the flight.

About 11:30, the moon disappeared behind some clouds, and I ran into rather a severe storm with lightning, and I was considerably buffeted about, and with difficulty held my course. In fact, I probably got off my course at this point to some extent because it was very rough. This lasted for at least an hour. Then I flew on in calmer weather though in the midst of clouds. Once I saw the moon for a fleeting instant and thought I could pull out on top of the clouds, so I climbed for half an hour when suddenly I realized I was picking up ice. I knew by the climb of the ship which was not as fast as usual that it was accumulating a weight of ice. Then I saw slush on the windowpane. In addition, ice began to coat my air speed indicator so that it refused to register accurately on the panel before me.

In such a situation one has to get into warmer air, so I went down hoping the ice would melt. I descended until I could see the waves breaking although I could not tell exactly how far I was above them. I kept flying here until fog came down so low that I dared not keep on at such an altitude.

Instrument flying cannot be done safely very near the surface with the equipment we have today. There was nothing left but to seek a middle ground, that is, to fly under the altitude at which I picked up ice and over the water by a sufficient margin. This would have been much easier to do had I been able to know my height.

Later, I tried going up again with the same result. So I gave up, just plowing through the "soup" and not looking out of the cockpit again until morning came. I depended on the instruments there to tell me the position of the plane in space, as under these conditions human faculties fail. Had I not been equipped with the best I could never have succeeded. The directional gyro, which is freest of all from fluctuations if set every 15 minutes, was a real life-saver.

About four hours out of Newfoundland, I noticed a small blue flame licking through a broken weld in the manifold ring. I knew that it would grow worse as the night wore on. However, the metal was very heavy and I hoped it would last until I reached land. I was indeed sorry that I had looked at the break at all because the flames appeared so much worse at night than they did in the daytime.

As daylight dawned, I found myself between two layers of clouds, the first very high, probably twenty thousand feet, the lower ones little fluffy white clouds near the water. This was the first sight of the sea in daylight. I noticed from the white caps that there was a northwest wind. The little white clouds soon grew packed and resembled a vast snow field. I could see on the leading edge of my wings particles of ice which had not yet melted. Soon I went a little higher and ran into another bank of clouds. I was in these for at least an hour and then came out in a clear space again over the white snow fields. By this time, the upper layer was thin enough for the sun to come through, and it was as dazzling as on real snow. I had dark glasses but it was too much for me even so, and I came down through the lower layer to fly in the shade, as it were.

Anyway, ten hours had passed, and I wished to see the water lest I was passing a boat. I had seen one vessel shortly after I left Harbor Grace. I blinked my navigation lights but apparently no one saw me as I was flying high. Then I picked up either a fishing vessel or an oil tanker off the coast of Ireland, but those were the only two I saw until I met a fleet near the coast. From then on I met sunshine and low hanging clouds, most of which I kept under even though they were very near the water.

By the way, I didn't bother much about food for myself. The really important thing was fuel for the engine. It drank more than 300 gallons of gasoline. My own trans-Atlantic rations consisted of one can of tomato juice which I punctured and sipped through a straw.

Of course, the last two hours were the hardest. My exhaust manifold was vibrating very badly, and then I turned on the reserve tanks and found the gauge leaking. I decided I should come down at the very nearest place, wherever it was. I had flown a set compass course all night. Now I changed to due east and decided to head for Ireland. I did not wish to miss the tip of Ireland and the weather was such I couldn't see very far. I thought I must be south of the course, for I had been told by the weather man in New York that I might find rain in that direction. When I ran into the storm I thought therefore I probably was in this "weather" he anticipated. Then when breaking white caps below disclosed a wind from the northwest I was sure I must be south. As it happened, I probably was exactly on my course, and I think I hit Ireland about the middle.

I started down the coast and found thunderstorms lower

in the hills. Not having the altimeter and not knowing the country, I was afraid to plow through those lest I hit one of the mountains, so I turned north where the weather seemed to be better and soon came across a railroad which I followed hoping it would lead me to a city, where there might be an airport.

The first place I encountered was Londonderry, and I circled it hoping to locate a landing field but found lovely pastures instead. I succeeded in frightening all the cattle in the county, I think, as I came down low several times before finally landing in a long, sloping meadow. I couldn't have asked for better landing facilities, as far as that is concerned.

There ended the flight and my happy adventure.

THE ATLANTIC FLIGHT

GEORGE BUCHANAN FIFE · 1927

While the feat of Captain Charles A. Lindbergh is imperishably enrolled in the chronicle of the daring ones of the human race, it will be a long, long day before millions on both sides of the Atlantic shall cease to remember, with something akin to the old thrill, the eagerness and anxiety with which they awaited news of the youth and his faithful plane after he had once soared into the air above Roosevelt Field.

It was at 7:52 o'clock on that Friday morning, May 20, 1927, that he took off. Those who watched the start from the field noted with much apprehension that he seemed so long in rising to safe cruising height. There was a reasonable mis-

From *Lindbergh, The Lone Eagle: His Life and Achievements*, copyright, 1927, by World Syndicate, Inc.

giving, because the "Spirit of St. Louis" was bearing the heaviest burden an engine of her horsepower had ever before been called upon to bear.

In the minutes that followed after the plane disappeared from view, vague reports came that it had been seen here, there, several places. But the first authentic word of "Slim" and his ship came from East Greenwich, Rhode Island. They passed over that community at 9:05 o'clock. Thence the course lay over Middleboro, Massachusetts, and at 9:40 o'clock the news was flashed to the world that plane and pilot had been sighted at Halifax, Mass.

The latter was not a wholly encouraging report, because observers said that his plane seemed to be wabbling as if struggling with a great load. It was reported, also, that his elevation was not more than 150 feet, that he appeared to brush the treetops. To add to the seeming uncertainty of flight, watchers and listeners sent out word that his motor was missing.

After the word from Halifax, Mass., there was a prolonged interval of complete silence. Not a word of "Slim" and his ship. As a matter of fact he was roaring along the New England coast, having taken a seaward course at Scituate, Mass., for his first over-water flight on the 200-mile journey to the coast of Nova Scotia.

It was not until he soared over Meteghan, N.S., that the suspense was ended for a time at least. He passed over that city at 12:25 P.M.

Watchers were everywhere posted to seek out the plane in the sky and, at 1:50 o'clock, sharp eyes caught "Slim" over Milford, N.S., which is forty miles north of Halifax. Then came another interval until the good folk of Mulgrave sighted him at 3:05 o'clock, passing over that town and the Straits of Canso, winging toward Cape Breton.

At 5 o'clock, "Slim's" ship cleared Main-a-Dieu, the easternmost tip of Nova Scotia, at Cape Breton. Now there lay between him and Newfoundland a stretch of 200 miles of gray sea. But the weather was clear and "Slim" had driven his plane to a high altitude. The number, 211, painted on her wings could be read with strong glasses.

Then came the last report of the dare-all youth for that day, Friday. It was word which was flashed from St. John's, Newfoundland, at 7:15 in the evening. He was passing there, headed out over the Atlantic.

Now came succeeding flashes by cable and wireless, all hopeful, some seeming incontrovertible, some still arousing doubt in multitudes which were afraid to hope too much.

A radio message reached Cape Race, Newfoundland, from a Dutch ship at 8:10 o'clock Saturday morning that "Slim" and his plane were 500 miles off the Irish coast. On the heels of this came, at 9:50 a dispatch from London that the plane had been sighted 100 miles off Ireland. Whether this was "Slim" or not, it was at least a plane, and that was something.

The suspense which held two continents was relieved measurably at 10 o'clock when the Radio Corporation reported that its Paris office announced the "Spirit of St. Louis" to be then over Valencia, Ireland.

Belfast sent word at 12:30 o'clock in the afternoon (and these and all other time figures given here are New York daylight-saving time), that "Slim" was over the otherwise somnolescent community of Dingle. Then the Government wireless station at Valencia flashed out the news at 2:06 o'clock that the collier *Nogi* had also sighted the plane at Dingle. It was evidently a great day for Dingle.

Cork's Civic Guard next had its turn at the news and announced that Lindbergh was passing over Smerwick Harbor at 2:18. And that was the last message from Ireland, for at 3:24 the French Cable Company electrified millions by the announcement, according to official advices, that the plane was then over Bayeux, France. The French time was then 8:24 o'clock at night.

Six minutes later, the "Spirit of St. Louis" was sighted over Cherbourg, and Paris was at hand.

Paris knew of his coming and a crowd of more than 100,-000 had gathered at Le Bourget, the famous flying field just outside the capital. There rockets and flares were set off.

"Slim" wheeled and brought the "Spirit of St. Louis" to earth.

It was 10:21 o'clock at night, according to Paris time, or 5:21 o'clock in the afternoon in New York.

And in that instant was terminated the greatest air voyage yet made by any one man. A youth of twenty-five had flown for the first time, without a stop, from New York to Paris, a distance of 3,640 miles. He had done it in thirty-three and one-half hours.

THE COAST OF IRELAND

CHARLES A. LINDBERGH · 1953

Is that a cloud on the northeastern horizon, or a strip of low fog—or . . . *can it possibly be land?* It looks like land, but I don't intend to be tricked by another mirage. Framed between two gray curtains of rain, not more than ten or fifteen miles away, a purplish blue band has hardened from the haze . . . flat below, like a waterline . . . curving on top, as though composed of hills or aged mountains.

I'm only sixteen hours out from Newfoundland. I allowed eighteen and a half hours to strike the Irish coast. If that's

Ireland, I'm two and a half hours ahead of schedule. Can this be another, clearer image, like the islands of the morning? Is there something strange about it too, like the fishing fleet and that haunting head? Is each new illusion to become more real until reality itself is meaningless? But my mind is clear. I'm no longer half asleep. I'm awake—alert—aware. The temptation is too great. I can't hold my course any longer. The *Spirit of St. Louis* banks over toward the nearest point of land.

I stare at it intently, not daring to believe my eyes, keeping hope in check to avoid another disappointment, watching the shades and contours unfold into a coast line . . . a coast line coming down from the north . . . a coast line bending toward the east . . . a coast line with rugged shores and rolling mountains. It's much too early to strike England, France, or Scotland. It's early to be striking Ireland; but that's the nearest land.

A fjorded coast stands out as I approach. Barren islands guard it. Inland, green fields slope up the sides of warted mountains. This *must* be Ireland. It can be no other place than Ireland. The fields are too green for Scotland; the mountains too high for Brittany or Cornwall.

Now, I'm flying above the foam-lined coast, searching for prominent features to fit the chart on my knees. I've climbed to two thousand feet so I can see the contours of the country better. The mountains are old and rounded; the farms small and stony. Rain-glistened dirt roads wind narrowly through hills and fields. Below me lies a great tapering bay; a long, bouldered island; a village. Yes, there's a place on the chart where it all fits—line of ink on line of shore—Valentia and Dingle Bay, *on the southwestern coast of Ireland!*

WIND OVER THE ATLANTIC

RICHARD EVELYN BYRD · 1928

Little did we think, as we went into the fog, how many hours would pass before we could see the land or the sea. After we had left the land some hours behind, I again asked Noville for his gasoline consumption. I told him to be conservative. His figures indicated that it was much greater than we had expected. One reason for this, I thought, was our struggle in attempting to get above the clouds and fog. This had caused us to run the motors much faster than we had intended.

I made some careful calculations and showed Noville (in writing, of course, because the roar of the three engines prevented conversation) that, at that rate, with the slightest winds against us, we would drop into the sea from lack of fuel before reaching Europe.

I told him that I was responsible for the lives of all on board and that, regardless of my feelings, I wanted to know how they felt about turning back. He promptly answered that he knew of no landing place between Newfoundland and the States, except St. John's, that was now covered with fog, so that it was just as safe to go ahead as to go back. I was glad he felt that way, because I did not wish to retreat. We didn't mention our predicament to Acosta and Balchen—they had enough troubles of their own.

Here it was that we staked our lives on our theory that if we flew at the proper altitude we should have favoring winds. If I were wrong then we should fall into the sea and be lost before making a landfall on the other side.

I had studied thoroughly the velocity and directions of winds over the Atlantic. So far as I could learn, no reliable data

From *Skyward*, by Richard E. Byrd, copyright, 1928, by Richard E. Byrd, courtesy of G. P. Putnam's Sons.

had been procured upon the winds' strength at high altitudes, but several meteorologists of the Weather Bureau as well as I believed that a plane could fly high enough to get strong winds from the west, even though there might at the same time be easterly winds on the surface.

So that whenever any of us took the wheel we flew as high as possible. If we could have the winds with us, we should easily make Europe; if not, we should fall far short of it, if Noville's estimate of the gasoline on hand was correct. I also knew, from Dr. Kimball's weather map, which I had spread before me on the chart board, that I now was flying at first on the southern side of the storm area and later would be flying on the northern side of a high-pressure area.

We were now flying nearly two miles high. Above the ocean at night, bitterly cold, lost in storm clouds, so dark that we couldn't see our hands before our faces. It was not the pleasantest situation in the world.

I find notations made hour after hour in my log, as follows: "It is impossible to navigate."

Our safety depended upon winds behind us. It was a strain I must admit. Only an aviator knows what it means to fly 2,000 miles without seeing the ground or water beneath. I doubt whether any other plane had ever flown blindly for half that time.

One notation in the log stated: "Ice is forming on the plane." We were at a dangerous temperature. That was to be expected, flying two miles high in fog, because the temperature decreases considerably with altitude. I passed a note to Acosta warning him to make every effort to get out of the clouds, which he very soon did.

From time to time during the night we fought our way above the clouds. It was a weird sight to look down from the pinnacle of black masses we were skimming. Around us were ominous, towering peaks, some of which reached far above us.

As we could not afford to go around those that lay in our path, we would dash through them in a darkness so intense that we could not see the wing tips. The fire from the exhaust pipes of our faithful engines, invisible in the daytime, shone vividly in the dark night. The 30,000 flashes of fire per minute through the exhaust pipes made a cheering sight against the black.

On one occasion in a thick cloud the plane got temporarily out of control. We must have been going downward at a terrific rate, judging from the roaring of the engines. Balchen, with great skill, finally steadied the ship again on her course.

Throughout the long night each man went about his duty efficiently and calmly, taking it as if it were all in a day's work.

I note in our record that I sent the following radio at 6:50 A.M. on June 30: "We have seen neither land or sea since 3 o'clock yesterday. Everything completely covered with fog. Whatever happens I take my hat off to these great fellows."

In those minutes between twilight and dusk we reached sufficient altitude to skim the tops of the clouds, and the spectacle was extraordinary. On the side of the sun, which, of course, was far below the cloud horizon, the clouds took on weird shapes and colors, but on the other side they were ominous and gloomy. During the day we had some terrifying views; there were fog valleys, dark and sinister, hundreds of feet beneath us. At times distant cloud peaks took on shapes and colors of rugged Arctic land and mountains.

About the time we expected to hit Paris we got temporarily out of the thick weather. I saw bright lights ahead and a revolving light which I took to be Le Bourget. Our dead reckoning showed us to be just about at Paris.

Our troubles seemed at an end. It was a relief. I wrote out the following radio for Mr. Wanamaker: "Paris is in sight. It has been a great trip. I wish to tell you with enthusiasm that Noville, Acosta and Balchen have faced grave dangers with the greatest possible courage and calmness. They have been wonderful and we all send our best wishes to you."

That radio was never to be sent. I looked down and saw the revolving light flash for an instant on water. It was a lighthouse. I knew there was no ocean lighthouse near Paris. We were somewhere on the coast of France! I was astonished very greatly indeed.

The compass had gone wrong—had taken us in a great circle. By the flares of our flash lights, I conferred on paper with the pilots and concluded that we had made a circle to the left. There had either been some local affection of the compass in the plane, or the pilot's dial had stuck badly. The only way to get on again would be to lay some course and check up the compasses.

We tapped the dials, checked them with the extra standard compass we carried, and got them O.K. Again we set out for Paris and again were tossed about in the storm and darkness. It was raining very hard on the coast and visibility was bad. It was much stormier inland. We afterwards found that the centre of the storm was over Paris. I watched the course carefully after that and checked compasses every few minutes. I knew we were heading towards Paris. The inky darkness was broken occasionally by the flashes of our lights as we needed them temporarily, and the fire from the engine exhaust pipes. The rough air made it a little difficult to steer, especially in the darkness, but we kept a pretty good general course.

Then arose the necessity of watching the gasoline very carefully, for a forced landing in the darkness would not only have meant certain disaster for us, but also for some of those perchance beneath us.

A decision had to be made. My big job now was to try not to kill anyone beneath us and to save my shipmates. The only thing to do was to turn back to water.

It would probably be difficult for the layman to visualize

our predicament, tossed around in the inky darkness of the storm, drenched by rain.

I doubt if any one could realize the strain of this part of the flight. We had no assurance that the plane could be landed safely on the water, but there was no chance of a safe landing on the land where we could see nothing.

We set a course for the lighthouse we had seen. The wind might blow us off a bit in the darkness, but if the fog were not too thick there, we were confident of hitting it provided we were where we thought we were while over Paris. Much of the way we could see nothing beneath us, and we were flying so low that Noville had to pull in the antenna of his wireless to prevent it from hitting objects on the ground. Finally, when I thought we were near the lighthouse, I asked Balchen to get down lower. He was afraid of running into something but we had to take the risk. We emerged from the mists and there was the lighthouse ahead of us. That shows, again, I think, that we had not been lost—that we had been at Paris.

We cruised over it slowly, but in spite of the light the area around it was black, and we could only guess its topography. We could find no landing place. We had hoped there would be a beach and had written out a message on a weighted streamer asking the people to clear the beach and make some kind of light for our landing.

We then flew over the lighthouse and, by the quick flash of the revolving beacon, we could tell that we were over water and dimly distinguish the shoreline. We could not discern the character of the beach. It was still raining and dismally thick.

We decided to land near enough to the beach line to swim ashore, if necessary, and to salvage the plane, if it were not too badly wrecked. At the same time we had to be far enough away to miss any rocks, should the beach be rocky. That, of course, we could not tell.

We now dropped a number of flares as nearly in a line as we could, about 100 yards from the beach line. They all ignited, and although they made a light in a pool of blackness, we hoped we would be able to judge the distance of the plane above the water as we descended. Of course, if we could not judge it, we should go into the water at flying speed, which would smash everything badly, since water does not give much when hit hard.

Those hours in the black storm had not been pleasant. I felt myself entirely responsible for the lives of my shipmates. I don't believe they thought there was much chance of getting down safely, but still they faced gallantly, with steady courage, whatever fate lay ahead. In a few moments the story would be ended, but to the last they calmly obeyed orders.

The gasoline was running low, we must not wait for it to give out and be forced to land.

Balchen happened to be at the wheel. I gave the orders to land.

We were landing with the plane in control and the engines functioning perfectly. At that moment, in spite of our danger, I marveled at the three engines that for 42 hours had made some 1,500 revolutions a minute without missing a beat. I thought of the Wright Aeronautical Corporation, that made the engines, and of my friend, Charles Lawrance, who had designed them.

Bennett and I had often wondered what would happen to a great three-engine plane landing in the water. Everyone thought the plane would turn over. Some thought the flyers would get hurt. Others thought not. Anyhow we were about to find out. Only we had the added difficulty of landing at night.

As we neared the water we could not see it; only the flares ahead of us and beneath us.

The wheels touched, and though the landing gear is secured to the plane with a tremendous factor of safety, it was sheared off, along with the wheels, with hardly a jar of the plane, as though a great knife had cut it, thus demonstrating the tremendous resistance of water when hit by a rapidly moving object. No one had predicted that.

It seemed just a second after that the crash came. I suppose I was dazed a little. I know I got a stiff blow over the heart that made it beat irregularly for many months afterward. I found myself in the water outside swimming around in pitchy dark and rain. I could hear Noville calling for me, but not another sound in the extraordinary stillness which contrasted so vividly with the roar of the great motors which had been pounding on our eardrums for 42 hours like tom-toms of Hades.

The plane instantly filled with water. Noville was getting out of the window. I yelled at him that I was unharmed and asked him how he was but he did not answer—just kept on yelling for me. I was a little worried about him, but I knew that he could not have been badly hurt. Hearing nothing from Balchen and Acosta and worried beyond measure about them, I swam to where they had been; the cockpit, of course, was under water. I yelled as loud as I could but got no answer.

I found Balchen slightly caught under water and trying to extricate himself. When he got clear I asked him how he felt. He didn't answer but asked me how I felt. He talked a blue streak but didn't talk to me. I couldn't make it out exactly but concluded that he, too, was somewhat dazed.

Thinking that Acosta must have been caught under the water in the cockpit, we dived down, but he was not there. I yelled for him, but there was no answer. A moment later he appeared, apparently from nowhere, swimming toward the wing, the leading edge of which was now down to the water. He must have been swimming around out there somewhere in the darkness all the time.

I asked Acosta the same question I had asked the others, but he too didn't answer—asked me how I felt. Bert also talked a blue streak but not to either one of us. In the course of his talking I found he had broken his collar-bone.

It was a weird sensation to have three shipmates there in the dark who would not talk to me or each other, but it was the most thankful moment of my life to find them still "kicking." The very worst thing we had anticipated had happened, and we had come through.

With grunts and groans we dragged ourselves upon the wing. The wing was down in the water by that time.

So it must have happened with all the land planes that landed in the ocean that summer.

Noville, still functioning perfectly, was carrying out his orders given before leaving the States, which were to rip open the emergency cabin in case of landing in the water and pump up the rubber boat. He was at his job, although he could hardly stand up and was falling every minute or two.

It had been with considerable difficulty that all hands got on top of the wing. I then found that the reason I could not get any answer from them was that the three engines roaring for 42 hours over their heads had temporarily deafened them. As I had used ear protectors my hearing was normal. No plane had ever flown that long for a distant objective though endurance tests where the engine would not have to be run so fast of course had been longer.

The great question was solved at last. We could land without seriously injuring the personnel. The plane did not turn over, as many thought it would, and we had placed the emergency compartment in about the only situation in the ship where we could get our rubber boat and other emergency supplies when landing in the water.

We were stiff and bruised, tired and watersoaked, and it was with some difficulty that we pumped up the rubber boat. As the wing was almost flush with the water there was no difficulty in launching it.

We placed our most precious cargo, which included a piece of the original American Flag, in a compartment we had made in the great wing; this we thought was the safest place. After finding the things in there were only slightly wet, we shipped the oars in the rubber boat, and wearily made for the shore in the dark.

FREEDOM

ANNE MORROW LINDBERGH · 1935

Flying implies freedom to most people. The average person who hears the drone of a motor and looks up from the walls of a city street to see an airplane boring its way through the clear trackless blue above—the average person, if he stops to use his imagination, may say to himself casually, "Free as a bird! What a way to travel! No roads—no traffic—no dust—no heat—just pick up and go!"

In that careless phrase he is apt to overlook what lies behind the word "free." He is apt to forget, or perhaps he never knew, the centuries of effort which have finally enabled man to be a bird, centuries of patient desiring, which reach back

Condensed from *North to the Orient*, by Anne Morrow Lindbergh. Copyright, 1935, by Anne Morrow Lindbergh. Reprinted by permission of Harcourt, Brace and Company, Inc.

at least as far as the Greek world of Icarus. For Icarus, trying to scale the skies with his waxen wings, was merely an early *expression* of man's desire to fly. How long before him the unexpressed wish wrestled in the minds of men, no one can tell.

And since flight is not a natural function of man; since it has been won by centuries of effort; since it has been climbed to arduously, not simply stumbled upon; since it has been slowly built, not suddenly discovered, it cannot be suspended as the word "freedom" is suspended in the mind. It rests, firmly supported, on a structure of laws, rules, principles —laws to which plane and man alike must conform. Rules of construction, of performance, of equipment, for one; rules of training, health, experience, skill, and judgment, for the other.

Not only must a man know how his plane is made, what it will do, how it must be cared for; but also—to mention only a few of the rules that govern him—what the ceiling of his plane is, whether it will go high enough to clear any elevation on the route; what the gas capacity is, how far it will carry him; what points he can reach for refueling; how to navigate through a signless sky; where he will land for the night; where he can get emergency repairs; what weather conditions he may meet on his way; and, keeping in mind the back stairs, what equipment he should carry in case of a forced landing. All this he must know before he can win that freedom of a bird, before he can follow that straight line he has drawn on the map, directly, without deviation, proverbially "as the crow flies."

The firm black lines which we ruled straight across Canada and Alaska, preparatory to our flight, implied a route which, in its directness of purpose and its apparent obliviousness of outside forces, looked as unerring and resistless as the path of a comet. Those firm black lines implied freedom, actual enough, but dearly won. Months, and indeed years, of preparation made such freedom possible.

It is true that as air travelers we were free of many of the difficulties that had beset the early surface travelers in search of a Northwest passage. Our fast monoplane could carry us far above most of the dangers mentioned by Master George Best: "mountaines of yce in the frozen Sea . . . fiercenesse of wilde beastes and fishes, hugenesse of woods, dangerousnesse of Seas, dread of tempestes, feare of hidden rockes." But in any comparison between us and the early navigators, there were disadvantages to offset advantages.

The early travelers, although confined to navigable waters, and restricted by slow speed, nevertheless were favored with a limitless fuel supply. Wherever they went and no matter how long they were gone, they could count on the wind for power. They might have difficulties in using it, now coaxing it, now fighting it; but they would never completely drain their supply. It was inexhaustible. Whereas we must plan and budget our fuel, arrange for its location along the route, sometimes sending it ahead of us by boat or train, sometimes using fuel already cached through the North.

And although they had to be prepared for longer time, we must be prepared for greater space—north and south, sea and land—and therefore more varied conditions. Our equipment had to be as complete as theirs, and our carrying capacity was far more limited in weight as well as space.

Our craft, the *Sirius*, with its six-hundred-horsepower cyclone engine, was equipped with gasoline tanks which would carry us for two thousand miles, and with pontoons that would enable us to land in Hudson Bay, on the many inland lakes throughout Canada, along the coast of Alaska and Siberia, and among the Japanese islands. The general equipment had to include, among other things, instruments for blind flying and night flying; radio and direction-finding apparatus; facilities for fueling and for anchoring. (We had a twenty-five-pound anchor and rope tucked into a small compartment in the pontoons.) Aside from the general equipment indispensable for our everyday flying, we must carry a large amount of emergency supplies: an adequate repair kit and repair materials; a rubber boat, a sail and oars; an extra crash-proof, waterproof radio set; parachutes; general camping equipment and food supplies; firearms and ammunition; a full medicine kit; warm flying suits and boots; and many other articles.

The contingencies to be provided for were many and varied. We must consider the possibility of a parachute jump, and carry in our flying-suit pockets the most concentrated food and the most compact first-aid kit. We must be prepared for a forced landing in the North, where we would need warm bedding and clothes; and in the South, where we ought to have an insect-proof tent; and on the ocean, where we would need, in addition to food, plenty of fresh water.

The twenty-seventh of July, 1931, was clear and hot. The heat of a whole summer was condensed dripping into that afternoon. A small crowd of people pressed tightly against the gates to the long ramp at College Point, Long Island. As we drove in I saw many familiar faces between movie-tone trucks and cameras. We had all spent sweltering days together on that wooden ramp, watching trial flights and the installation of equipment. Now the preparation was over, we were ready to go. I suppose they were as relieved as we.

I turned to look at the plane. Perched on top of the big pontoons, it seemed small and dainty. They were rolling it down the pier. I thought of all the emergency equipment for North and South, land and water, all parts of the world, packed into that little space. I thought of the two of us, ready to go in it anywhere, and I had a sense of our self-contained insularity. Islands feel like this, I am sure, and walled cities, and sometimes men.

FOG

ANNE MORROW LINDBERGH · 1935

My husband pushed back the cockpit cover, put on his helmet and goggles, heightened the seat for better visibility, and leaned forward to look out. Here we are again, I thought, recognizing by this familiar buckling-on-of-armor that the fight had begun.

Here we are again. We seem to be always here, I thought, fear opening for me a long corridor of similar times and making them all one long fight with fog. There was the time over the Alleghenies in the *Falcon:* slicing over the tops of those pine trees, now on one wing, now on another. Then we found the river down below the mist cutting a gully through the mountains. We followed it and came out to safety. But then with a *Falcon* it wasn't so dangerous—not so fast. The *Sirius* now—(He was headed for that peak in the clouds. How did he know there was not a lower peak —a shoal, just covered by this high tide of fog—that might trip us up as we skimmed across the surface?) Then, there had been that time over the pass of the San Bernardino Mountains. "Ceiling, very low," read the weather report. "What does 'very low' mean?" my husband had asked. "Two or three hundred feet?"

"It means nothing at all," laughed the weather man. "You'd better stay here."

"Oh, we'll go see what it looks like—may come back—may find a hole." And up we had climbed until we were face to face with those giants, snow-streaked, and the bright fog sitting on their shoulders. But that time, too, finally we struck a stream and followed it—a beautiful stream with fields to land in and green orchards and houses. It carried us along and spilled us out into the broad valley of San Bernardino. I had it like a ribbon in my hand all through the fog. I held on to it and it led us out.

Here there was nothing to hold on to—nothing, unless it were the sky. The sun still shone. My husband motioned me to reel in the antenna. Emergency landing, that meant. I buckled my belt tighter. We were circling that giant's head now, getting impudently nearer and nearer. Down, down, we were gliding down now, the engine throttled, wisps of fog temporarily blinding us as we descended. I was losing the sky. I did not want to let go until I could grasp something below. Down the sides of the mountain one could see a strip of water gleaming, harebell-blue. We were diving toward it. Down, down—the sky was gone. The sea! Hold on to the sea—that little patch of blue. Oh, the sea was gone too. We were blind—and still going down—oh, God!—we'll hit the mountain! A wave of fear like terrific pain swept over me, shriveling to blackened ashes the meaningless words "courage"—"pride"—"control." Then a lurch, the engine roared on again, and a sickening roller-coaster up. Up, up, up. I felt myself gasping to get up, like a drowning man. There—the sky was blue above—the sky and the sun! Courage flowed back in my veins, a warm, pounding stream. Thank God, there is the sky. Hold on to it with both hands. Let it pull you up. Oh, let us stay here, I thought, up in this clear bright world of reality, where we can see the sky and feel the sun. Let's never go down.

He is trying it again, like a knife going down the side of a pie tin, between fog and mountain. Will he say afterward, "It was nothing at all"? (if there is an "afterward"). That time in the Alleghenies he turned around, when we struck the river, and smiled at me. It was so reassuring. If only he would do it now. But his face was set. I could see it out of the side of the cockpit—his lips tight-closed. The force of the wind blowing against them made them look thin and fearful like a man gritting his teeth in his last fight. Were we there, then, at the last fight? I had never seen him look like that. The wind flattened his face, made the flesh flabby, the brows prominent—like a skeleton.

Down again—and the terror. Up again—and the return of courage and shame. Think of the radio operators sticking to their posts through fire and flood. If only I could send messages, it would help. Think of the air-mail pilots, doing this every night. Think of the war pilots to whom weather was the smallest of their worries. At least weather was impersonal; it had no ax to grind. Think of that old lady in the early days of flying who took her first transcontinental trip fearlessly—how calmly she said, "Tonight I will be in Clovis —or Heaven." Why not accept it philosophically, like that, "Buroton Bay or Heaven," and not struggle through all the intervening stages of fear? But Buroton Bay did not sound like safety to me. It sounded like one of those quiet, unmarked places which, because of an accident, suddenly become steeped with tragedy: "Crashed—south side Buroton Bay." "Buroton Bay"—the name rings crimson like the name of an old battlefield.

Why try Buroton Bay anyway? Why not go somewhere else—anywhere else? Oh, I realized suddenly, that was what he was doing. The giant was floating behind us in the mist now, getting dimmer and dimmer as new veils of mist separated us. Ahead, I could see nothing—but above, the blue sky and the sun. "The sun is shining free of charge," jingled in my mind flippantly. I felt quite gay. After all, we weren't killed. We're still here in this blue sky—and "the sun is shining free of charge." Oh, Lord—here was another mountain peak! Was he going to try it again? Hadn't he learned *anything?* Did he think I really enjoyed this game of tobogganing down volcanoes?—I thought in a kind of bravado anger. Really it was too much—I would never fly again. The sun began to melt away as we spiraled down. It became a thin watery disk in the mist. "Never fly again," echoed in my ears maliciously. No—never fly again—I had said it myself and shivered to think how true it might be. Down, down, into the darkness. We had never been down this far before. That long green slope at the foot of the volcano—could we make a forced landing there? Bushes and rocks—but still the pontoons would take up the shock. It would be wonderful to be down—even there. No—we were going too fast, skimming over the bushes and straight down the slope. For there, over a sharp cliff of fifty feet, under a layer of mist, lay the water. There it was, shifting, changing, hiding tantalizingly below us. That was what we wanted. If we could only lay our hands on it before it disappeared—like the stone one dives for in the bottom of a pool. Could we reach it or would we have to fight our way up again? We dropped off the cliff. We were over the water. Spank, spank, spank—the ship is breaking under us! I am falling through. No—the seat has bounced down, that's all. It must be rough water. We're slowing up now. We're all right—we're down!

My husband turned around for the first time and looked at me. "What's the matter?"

"Nothing," I stammered. "I'm so happy to be down."

He laughed. "We weren't in much danger. We could have

gone back; but I was trying to get into Buroton Bay. I don't like to anchor in open water—going to try to find a more sheltered spot."

THE ELEMENTS

ANTOINE DE SAINT-EXUPÉRY · 1939
Translated by Lewis Galantière

Every airline pilot has flown through tornadoes, has returned out of them to the fold—to the little restaurant in Toulouse where we sat in peace under the watchful eye of the waitress —and there, recognizing his powerlessness to convey what he has been through, has given up the idea of describing hell. His descriptions, his gestures, his big words would have made the rest of us smile as if we were listening to a little boy bragging. And necessarily so. The cyclone of which I am about to speak was, physically, much the most brutal and overwhelming experience I ever underwent; and yet beyond a certain point I do not know how to convey its violence except by piling one adjective on another, so that in the end I should convey no impression at all—unless perhaps that of an embarrassing taste for exaggeration.

It took me some time to grasp the fundamental reason for this powerlessness, which is simply that I should be trying to describe a catastrophe that never took place. The reason why writers fail when they attempt to evoke horror is that horror is something invented after the fact, when one is re-creating the experience over again in the memory. Horror does not manifest itself in the world of reality. And so, in beginning my story of a revolt of the elements which I myself lived through I have no feeling that I shall write something which you will find dramatic.

I had taken off from the field at Trelew and was flying down to Comodoro-Rivadavia, in the Patagonian Argentine. Here the crust of the earth is as dented as an old boiler. The high-pressure regions over the Pacific send the winds past a gap in the Andes into a corridor fifty miles wide through which they rush to the Atlantic in a strangled and accelerated buffeting that scrapes the surface of everything in their path. The sole vegetation visible in this barren landscape is a plantation of oil derricks looking like the after-effects of a forest fire. Towering over the round hills on which the winds have left a residue of stony gravel, there rises a chain of prow-shaped, saw-toothed, razor-edged mountains stripped by the elements down to the bare rock.

Very soon came a slight tremor. As every pilot knows, there are secret little quiverings that foretell your real storm. No rolling, no pitching. No swing to speak of. The flight continues horizontal and rectilinear. But you have felt a warning drum on the wings of your plane, little intermittent rappings scarcely audible and infinitely brief, little cracklings from time to time as if there were traces of gunpowder in the air.

And then everything round me blew up.

Concerning the next couple of minutes I have nothing to say. All that I can find in my memory is a few rudimentary notions, fragments of thoughts, direct observations. I cannot compose them into a dramatic recital because there was no drama. The best I can do is to line them up in a kind of chronological order.

In the first place, I was standing still. Having banked right in order to correct a sudden drift, I saw the landscape freeze abruptly where it was and remain jiggling on the same spot.

I was making no headway. My wings had ceased to nibble into the outline of the earth. I could see the earth buckle, pivot—but it stayed put. The plane was skidding as if on a toothless cogwheel.

Meanwhile I had the absurd feeling that I had exposed myself completely to the enemy. All those peaks, those crests, those teeth that were cutting into the wind and unleashing its gusts in my direction, seemed to me so many guns pointed straight at my defenseless person. I was slow to think, but the thought did come to me that I ought to give up altitude and make for one of the neighboring valleys where I might take shelter against a mountainside. As a matter of fact, whether I liked it or not I was being helplessly sucked down towards the earth.

Trapped this way in the first breaking waves of a cyclone about which I learned, twenty minutes later, that at sea level it was blowing at the fantastic rate of one hundred and fifty miles an hour, I certainly had no impression of tragedy. Now, as I write, if I shut my eyes, if I forget the plane and the flight and try to express the plain truth about what was happening to me, I find that I felt weighed down, I felt like a porter carrying a slippery load, grabbing one object in a jerky movement that sent another slithering down, so that, overcome by exasperation, the porter is tempted to let the whole load drop. There is a kind of law of the shortest distance to the image, a psychological law by which the event to which one is subjected is visualized in a symbol that represents its swiftest summing up: I was a man who, carrying a pile of plates, had slipped on a waxed floor and let his scaffolding of porcelain crash.

There had been granted me one second of respite. Two seconds. Something was collecting itself into a knot, coiling itself up, growing taut. I sat amazed. I opened astonished eyes. My whole plane seemed to be shivering, spreading outward, swelling up. Horizontal and stationary it was, yet lifted before I knew it fifteen hundred feet straight into the air in a kind of apotheosis. I who for forty minutes had not been able to climb higher than two hundred feet off the ground was suddenly able to look down on the enemy. The plane quivered as if in boiling water. I could see the wide waters of the ocean. The valley opened out into this ocean, this salvation.—And at that very moment, without any warning whatever, half a mile from Salamanca, I was suddenly struck straight in the midriff by the gale off that peak and sent hurtling out to sea.

There I was, throttle wide open, facing the coast. At right angles to the coast and facing it. A lot had happened in a single minute. In the first place, I had not flown out to sea. I had been spat out to sea by a monstrous cough, vomited out of my valley as from the mouth of a howitzer. When, what seemed to me instantly, I banked in order to put myself where I wanted to be in respect of the coast-line, I saw that the coast-line was a mere blur, a characterless strip of blue; and I was five miles out to sea. The mountain range stood up like a crenelated fortress against the pure sky while the cyclone crushed me down to the surface of the waters. How hard that wind was blowing I found out as soon as I tried to climb, as soon as I became conscious of my disastrous mistake: throttle wide open, engines running at my maximum, which was one hundred and fifty miles an hour, my plane hanging sixty feet over the water, I was unable to budge. When a wind like this one attacks a tropical forest it swirls through the branches like a flame, twists them into corkscrews, and uproots giant trees as if they were radishes. Here, bounding off the mountain range, it was leveling out the sea.

Hanging on with all the power in my engines, face to the coast, face to that wind where each gap in the teeth of the range sent forth a stream of air like a long reptile, I felt as if

I were clinging to the tip of a monstrous whip that was cracking over the sea.

In this latitude the South American continent is narrow and
the Andes are not far from the Atlantic. I was struggling not
merely against the whirling winds that blew off the east-
coast range, but more likely also against a whole sky blown
down upon me off the peaks of the Andean chain. For the
first time in four years of airline flying I began to worry
about the strength of my wings. Also, I was fearful of bumping the sea—not because of the down currents which, at sea
level, would necessarily provide me with a horizontal air
mattress, but because of the helplessly acrobatic positions
in which this wind was buffeting me. Each time that I was
tossed I became afraid that I might be unable to straighten
out. Besides, there was a chance that I should find myself out
of fuel and simply drown. I kept expecting the gasoline pumps
to stop priming, and indeed the plane was so violently shaken
up that in the half-filled tanks as well as in the gas lines the
gasoline was sloshing round, not coming through, and the
engines, instead of their steady roar, were sputtering in a
sort of dot-and-dash series of uncertain growls.

I had no thoughts. I had no feelings except the feeling of being emptied out. My strength was draining out of me and so
was my impulse to go on fighting. The engines continued their
dot-and-dash sputterings, their little crashing noises that were
like the intermittent cracklings of a ripping canvas. Whenever they were silent longer than a second I felt as if a heart
had stopped beating. There! that's the end. No, they've
started up again.

The thermometer on the wing, I happened to see, stood at
twenty below zero, but I was bathed in sweat from head to
foot. My face was running with perspiration. What a dance!
Later I was to discover that my storage batteries had been
jerked out of their steel flanges and hurtled up through the

roof of the plane. I did not know then, either, that the ribs
on my wings had come unglued and that certain of my steel
cables had been sawed down to the last thread. And I continued to feel strength and will oozing out of me. Any minute
now I should be overcome by the indifference born of utter
weariness and by the mortal yearning to take my rest.

What can I say about this? Nothing. My shoulders ached.
Very painfully. As if I had been carrying too many sacks too
heavy for me. I leaned forward. Through a green transparency
I saw sea-bottom so close that I could make out all the details.
Then the wind's hand brushed the picture away.

In an hour and twenty minutes I had succeeded in climbing
to nine hundred feet. A little to the south—that is, on my
left—I could see a long trail on the surface of the sea, a sort
of blue stream. I decided to let myself drift as far down as that
stream. Here where I was, facing west, I was as good as motionless, unable either to advance or retreat. If I could reach that
blue pathway, which must be lying in the shelter of something not the cyclone, I might be able to move in slowly to
the coast. So I let myself drift to the left. I had the feeling,
meanwhile, that the wind's violence had perhaps slackened.

It took me an hour to cover the five miles to shore. There
in the shelter of a long cliff I was able to finish my journey
south. Thereafter I succeeded in keeping enough altitude to
fly inland to the field that was my destination. I was able to
stay up at nine hundred feet. It was very stormy, but nothing
like the cyclone I had come out of. That was over.

On the ground I saw a platoon of soldiers. They had been
sent down to watch for me. I landed near by and we were
a whole hour getting the plane into the hangar. I climbed
out of the cockpit and walked off. There was nothing to say.
I was very sleepy. I kept moving my fingers, but they stayed
numb. I could not collect my thoughts enough to decide
whether or not I had been afraid. Had I been afraid? I

couldn't say. I had witnessed a strange sight. What strange sight? I couldn't say. The sky was blue and the sea was white. I felt I ought to tell someone about it since I was back from so far away! But I had no grip on what I had been through. "Imagine a white sea . . . very white . . . whiter still." You cannot convey things to people by piling up adjectives, by stammering.

You cannot convey anything because there is nothing to convey. My shoulders were aching. My insides felt as if they had been crushed in by a terrible weight. You cannot make drama out of that, or out of the cone-shaped peak of Salamanca. That peak was charged like a powder magazine; but if I said so people would laugh. I would myself. I respected the peak of Salamanca. That is my story. And it is not a story.

IX

The Pullman Strike, 1894

❋ ❋ ❋ ❋ ❋ ❋ ❋ ❋ ❋ ❋ ❋ ❋ ❋ ❋ ❋ ❋

THE PULLMAN STRIKE was one of the first great American labor conflicts. The American people, ill informed about labor conditions and unprepared for open warfare, responded with self-righteous indignation. Feeling ran high and was passionately partisan. It was a class war, in a small way a civil war, which commanded national attention. The first two of these reports, seen in the perspective of time, appear exaggerated and incredibly naïve. The news writer for the *Washington Post*, hoping for the worst, presents a much too obvious example of the confusion between expectation and actual fact. The use of inflammatory words and of superlatives in this report contrasts sharply with the account of the same situation written three days later by the reporter for the *New York World*. The *World*'s innocent bystanders: "women gayly dressed," "small boys," and "countrymen," are, however, no less journalistic in their way than "the battlefields" and "the dead and wounded" of the first article. The use of a dramatic vocabulary and of censure by association reaches a high point in the article by General Miles, whose emotionalism would defeat his purpose with any but a prejudiced audience. Miles was the general in charge of United States troops sent by President Cleveland to restore order. The reader may well wonder whether he was more temperamentally disposed to incite further riot than to restore peace. *Democracy and Social Ethics* was written ten years after the event in the light of considerable progress in labor relations, but Miss Addams,

161

born though she was to Pullman society, understood from the beginning the claims of her neighbors at Hull House.

❋ ❋ ❋ ❋ ❋ ❋ ❋ ❋ ❋ ❋ ❋ ❋ ❋ ❋ ❋ ❋ ❋

A NEWSPAPER REPORT—1894

Chicago, Ill., July 6.—The situation tonight is more alarming than at anytime since the trouble began. War of the bloodiest kind in Chicago is imminent, and before tomorrow goes by the railroad lines and yards may be turned into battle fields strewn with hundreds of dead and wounded. Lawlessness of the most violent kind was the order of things today. . . . Chicago was never before the scene of such wild and desperate acts as were witnessed today and tonight. Furious mobs have for hours at a time been in complete control of certain sections of the city, and acts of lawlessness were committed without molestation. . . . The 100,000 or more idle men in Chicago, in addition to the strikers, are taking advantage of the situation, and tonight it came to the knowledge of the Federal authorities here that the anarchists and socialist element, made up largely of the unemployed, were preparing to blow up the South end of the Federal building and take possession of the millions in money now stored in the treasury vaults.

From *The Washington Post*, July 7, 1894.

A NEWSPAPER REPORT—1894

There is no sign of mob or riot or strike, even, about the main part of the city. Business goes on as usual. The streets and shops are thronged with women gayly dressed, laughing and chatting. . . . There is no indication anywhere of dread or fear. No throngs gather to talk at street corners, and the strike is scarcely mentioned in the casual conversation one hears about hotels and other public places. Small boys yell constantly, "Extra! Full account o' de bloody riot!" but nobody except countrymen and New Yorkers just come to town buy the papers. It is day before yesterday's riot and yesterday's news warmed over.

The mass of people evidently do not bother about the strike. . . . Of mob rule and riot, in the sense in which it is generally understood—that of reckless and wanton destruction of life and property regardless of ownership—there has been none. The violence has been directed solely against railroad property. There has been a deplorable lot of it, but the tales of its extent have been greatly exaggerated.

From *The New York World*, July 10, 1894.

FEDERAL INTERVENTION

GENERAL NELSON MILES · 1894

The papers of the city state that during the strike more than a thousand freight cars were set on fire and burned. Forty-five trains were stoned and fired upon by the mobs along the line of the railways. Buildings, station-houses, and railroad

From *The North American Review*, clix, 1894.

property were set on fire and burned. Innocent people travelling in the cars were injured by rocks and pieces of iron and bullets thrown through the windows of the cars. Locomotives were started on the tracks and sent wild along the roads, endangering lives of hundreds of people. On July 5 a mob of ten thousand people gathered in one part of the city and moved nearly three miles along through a dense part of the city, destroying and burning property, and the universal cry of that mob was "To hell with the government!" How near this comes to the carrying out of the declaration of the anarchists of Pennsylvania, who proclaimed that they were "opposed to all private property, and, as the state is the bulwark of property, they were opposed to all government," I need not stop to inquire.

If the property of a corporation or company in which the laboring men, the capitalists, the widows and orphans, the savings banks, properties in which any or all our people are interested, cannot be respected and protected, then the cottage, the hamlet, and the little personal property of the humblest citizen is in jeopardy, liable at any moment to be confiscated, seized, or destroyed by any travelling band of tramps. Then any combination or any body of men that threaten the peace, the prosperity, the personal liberty, the life and property of our citizens must be regarded as revolutionary and dangerous, and it is a misfortune that the laboring men employed in railroad transportation have been misled by the harangues of professional agitators into an attitude of this character. The insurrection must be met and overcome in one of two ways: first by the strong arm of the municipal, State, and Federal governments enforcing the guarantee to all the people, from the humblest to the most exalted, of perfect security in life and property. Otherwise our government would be a rope of sand. The other method of meeting the crisis is for American manhood to assert its principles. Men must take sides either for anarchy, secret conclaves, unwritten law, mob violence, and universal chaos under the red or white flag of socialism on the one hand; or on the side of established government, the supremacy of law, the maintenance of good order, universal peace, absolute security of life and property, the rights of personal liberty, all under the shadow and folds of "Old Glory," on the other.

IS THE STRIKE JUSTIFIABLE?

SAMUEL GOMPERS · 1894

Thousands of miles of railroads in all directions have been at a stand-still, and nearly a hundred thousand workmen in voluntary idleness to secure what they regard as justice to their fellow workmen. It has been questioned whether the boycott or strike was wise or whether it was justifiable.

The policy or wisdom of entering into so great a movement without consultation with, or against the advice of, the older railroad and *bona-fide* labor organizations of the country is open to serious question. Nor will I attempt from the usual standpoint of trade dispute to justify the strike. Sufficient for me are the facts which provoked it and to which I shall allude later; but that the railroadmen deliberately entered a contest which entailed many sacrifices and dangers in an attempt to redress grievances not of their own, but of other workmen, who, having become thoroughly enervated and impoverished, without organization or previous understanding, in sheer desperation threw down their work, is indeed to their credit.

A little more than twenty years ago George M. Pullman

From *The North American Review*, clix, 1894.

conceived the idea of starting, in connection with his car shops, a town—one that should bear his name and hand down to posterity a monument of his enterprise and philanthropy. He built houses for his employees to live in, stores to make their purchases in, and churches to do their praying in. The workers were told their interests and Mr. Pullman's were one and the same, that what would bring him a greater prosperity would redound to their advantage. They were warned that to belong to a trade-union would be inimical to their *joint* enterprise, hence workmen who would purpose forming a union among them would be discharged, regarded as a common enemy, and driven out of town. They were to depend entirely upon Mr. Pullman's generosity and foresight in all things.

The result was that the workers at Pullman were huddled together in the (outwardly) neat houses, for which they were required to pay higher rents than are paid for similar accommodations in Chicago. They were reduced in wages as often as the seasons would recur and opportunities either arose or were made. This was carried on until last February, when a reduction in wages was offered varying from 25 to 33 1/3 and in a few instances 50 per cent.

The workmen being driven to desperation, a meeting was held. Who called it no one knows; how it came about not a vestige of evidence is at hand. It was held and a committee appointed to wait upon Mr. Pullman or a representative of the company, to show that it was absolutely impossible to live on the wages offered; that a middle ground should be sought; that if wages were to be reduced the rents should also come down. Instead of the request of the men being considered by Mr. Pullman, the committee was summarily dismissed and discharged almost instantly. Is it surprising that these men in their rude awakening, finding themselves in-

jured and insulted and their spokesmen discharged and black-
listed, and themselves without an organization to protect or
defend them, without the means of properly laying their
grievances before organized labor of the country, struck work,
declaring that they might as well remain idle and starve as
work and slowly meet that fate?

COMMISSION REPORT

A SUMMARY THIRTY YEARS LATER · 1924

The United States Strike Commission discovered nothing to
justify the belief that "the officers of the American Railway
Union at any time participated in or advised intimidation,
violence, or destruction of property." While "strikers were
concerned in the outrages against law and order, the number
was undoubtedly small as compared with the whole number
out"; and "the mobs that took possession of railroad yards,
tracks and crossings after July 3, and that stoned, tipped over,
burned, and destroyed cars and stole their contents, were,
by general concurrence in the testimony, composed generally
of hoodlums, women, a low class of foreigners, and recruits
from the criminal classes. Few strikers were recognized or
arrested in these mobs, which were without leadership, and
seemed simply bent upon plunder and destruction." "In the
view that this railroad strike was wrong; that such mobs are
well known to be incidental to strikes, and are thereby given
an excuse and incentive to gather and to commit crime, the
responsibility rests largely with the American Railway Union;

otherwise that association, its leaders, and a very large majority of the railroad men on strike are not shown to have had any connection therewith."

Early in the course of the strike, a prominent citizens' organization of Chicago known as the Civic Federation twice sent a committee to urge upon the Pullman company the conciliation or arbitration of differences with its employees. Upon both occasions the company took the position that there was nothing to arbitrate. Efforts toward the same end made by the common council of Chicago were equally unsuccessful; and the company repeated its stereotyped answer when appealed to by Mayor Pingree of Detroit, who claimed to have telegrams from the mayors of more than fifty large American cities urging recourse to arbitration. Upon this point, the report of the United States Strike Commission makes the following significant comments:

The policy of both the Pullman company and the General Managers' Association in reference to applications to arbitrate closed the door to all attempts at conciliation and settlement of differences. The commission is impressed with the belief, by the evidence and by the attendant circumstances as disclosed, that a different policy would have prevented the loss of life and great loss of property and wages occasioned by the strike.

DEMOCRACY AND SOCIAL ETHICS

JANE ADDAMS · 1902

At times of social disturbance the law-abiding citizen is naturally so anxious for peace and order, his sympathies are so justly and inevitably on the side making for the restoration of law, that it is difficult for him to see the situation fairly. He becomes insensible to the unselfish impulse which may prompt a sympathetic strike in behalf of the workers in a nonunion shop, because he allows his mind to dwell exclusively on the disorder which has become associated with the strike. He is completely side-tracked by the ugly phases of a great moral movement. It is always a temptation to assume that the side which has respectability, authority, and superior intelligence, has therefore righteousness as well, especially when the same side presents concrete results of individual effort as over against the less tangible results of associated effort.

It is as yet most difficult for us to free ourselves from the individualistic point of view sufficiently to group events in their social relations and to judge fairly those who are endeavoring to produce a social result through all the difficulties of associated action. The philanthropist still finds his path much easier than do those who are attempting a social morality. In the first place, the public, anxious to praise what it recognizes as an undoubted moral effort often attended with real personal sacrifice, joyfully seizes upon this manifestation and overpraises it, recognizing the philanthropist as an old friend in the paths of righteousness, whereas the others are strangers and possibly to be distrusted as aliens. It is easy to confuse the response to an abnormal number of individual claims with the response to the social claim. An exaggerated personal morality is often mistaken for a social morality, and until it attempts to minister to a social situation its total inadequacy is not discovered. To attempt to attain a social morality without a basis of democratic experience results in the loss of the only possible corrective and guide, and ends in an exaggerated individual morality but not in social morality at all.

X

Woman Suffrage

❋ ❋ ❋ ❋ ❋ ❋ ❋ ❋ ❋ ❋ ❋ ❋ ❋ ❋ ❋ ❋ ❋

THESE ESSAYS are a record of controversy in England and the United States. They are a lesson not in writing but in reading. The subject of Votes for Women was too inflammatory to inspire good writing, and the disgracefully emotional, diversionary, and superficial character of what became the central points of disagreement scarcely supported or admitted of clear or perceptive essays. Feminism, sex, domestic concord, and childbearing were all deliberately confused with woman suffrage to arouse prejudice and to identify the battle for votes with the battle of the sexes. Important, then, for an understanding of these selections is a separation, relatively easy at this distance in time, of relevant from irrelevant points and of fact from assumption. The same critical reading should be applied, under the difficult circumstances of partisan prejudice, fear, and hate, to questions which are currently lively and upon which we lack the wise perspective of nearly half a century.

Unfortunately the proponents of woman suffrage were not always so logically restrained and so clearly indifferent to extraneous argument as they appear in the sound statement of their position sent to the Presidential Conventions of 1900. An attempt to separate the controversy from traditional prejudices about sex is clear in this Open Letter signed by the most distinguished American suffragettes. Their lack of success in controlling either their advocates or their opponents is unhappily revealed by the fact that fourteen years later

Samuel McChord Crothers made the same effort to get down
to the essential question in his amiable and persuasive essay
on Democracy and Feminism.

❋ ❋ ❋ ❋ ❋ ❋ ❋ ❋ ❋ ❋ ❋ ❋ ❋ ❋ ❋ ❋ ❋

OPEN LETTER
TO THE NATIONAL PRESIDENTIAL
CONVENTIONS OF 1900

GENTLEMEN: You are respectfully requested by the National-
American Woman Suffrage Association to place the following plank in your platform:

Resolved, That we favor the submission by Congress, to
the various State Legislatures, of an Amendment to the Federal
Constitution forbidding disfranchisement of United States
citizens on account of sex.

The chief contribution to human liberty made by the
United States is the establishment of the right of personal
representation in government. In other countries suffrage often
has been called "the vested right of property," and as such
has been extended to women the same as to men. Our country
at length has come to recognize the principle that the elective
franchise is inherent in the individual and not in his property,
and this principle has become the cornerstone of our republic.
Up to the beginning of the twentieth century, however, the
application of this great truth has been made to but one-half
the citizens.

The women of the United States are now the only disfranchised class, and sex is the one remaining disqualification.

As quoted in Susan B. Anthony and Ida Husted Harper, *History of Woman
Suffrage*, 1902.

A man may be idle, corrupt, vicious, utterly without a single quality necessary for purity and stability of government, but through the exercise of the suffrage he is a vital factor. A woman may be educated, industrious, moral and law-abiding, possessed of every quality needed in a pure and stable government, but, deprived of that influence which is exerted through the ballot, she is not a factor in affairs of State. Who will claim that our government is purer, wiser, stronger and more lasting by the rigid exclusion of what men themselves term "the better half" of the people?

Every argument which enfranchises a man, enfranchises a woman. There is no escape from this logic except to declare sex the just basis of suffrage. But this position can not be maintained in view of the fact that women already have full suffrage in Wyoming, Colorado, Utah and Idaho, municipal suffrage in Kansas, school suffrage in twenty-five States, a vote on tax levies in Louisiana, on bond issues in Iowa, and on minor questions in various other States. They have every franchise except the Parliamentary in England, Scotland and Ireland, the full ballot in New Zealand and South and West Australia, and some form of suffrage in every English colony. In a large number of the monarchical countries certain classes of women vote. On this fundamental question of individual sovereignty surely the United States should be a leader and not a follower. The trend of the times is clearly toward equal suffrage. It will add to the credit and future strength of any party to put itself in line with the best modern and progressive thought on this question.

In the division of the world's labor an equal share falls to woman. As property holder and wage-earner her material stake in the government is equal to that of man. As wife, as mother, as individual, her moral stake is certainly as great as his. The perpetuity of the republic depends upon the careful performance of the duties of both. One is just as necessary as the other to the growth and prosperity of the country. All of these propositions are self-evident, but they are wholly foreign to the question at issue. The right of the individual to a vote is not founded upon the value of his stake in government, upon his moral character, his business ability or his physical strength, but simply and solely upon that guarantee of personal representation which is the essence of a true republic, a true democracy.

The literal definition of these two terms is, "a State in which the sovereign power resides in the whole body of the people and is exercised by representatives elected by them." By the Declaration of Independence, by the rules of equity, by the laws of justice, women equally with men are entitled to exercise this sovereign power through the franchise, the only legal means provided. But whatever may be regarded as the correct basis of suffrage—character, education, property, or the inherent right of the person who is subject to law and taxation—women possess all the qualifications required of men.

At this dawn of a new century are not the sons of the Revolutionary Fathers sufficiently progressive to remove the barriers which for more than a hundred years have prevented women from exercising this citizen's right? We appeal to this great national delegate body, representing the men of every State, gathered to outline the policy and select the head of the Government for the next four years, to adopt in your platform a declaration approving the submission by Congress of an amendment enfranchising women. We urge this action in order that the question shall be carried to the various Legislatures, where women may present their arguments before the representative men, instead of being compelled to plead their cause before each individual voter of the forty-one States where they are still disfranchised.

We make this earnest appeal on behalf of the hundreds of thousands of women who, from year to year, have petitioned

Congress to take the action necessary for their enfranchisement; and of those millions who are so engrossed in the struggle for daily bread, or in the manifold duties of the home, that they are compelled to leave this task to others. We make it also on behalf of the generations yet to come, for there will be no cessation of this demand until this highest privilege of citizenship has been accorded to women.

ELIZABETH CADY STANTON, ⎫
SUSAN B. ANTHONY, ⎬ Honorary Presidents.
⎭
CARRIE CHAPMAN CATT, President

ANNA HOWARD SHAW, Vice-President-at-Large.	HARRIET TAYLOR UPTON, Treasurer.
RACHEL FOSTER AVERY, Corresponding Secretary.	LAURA CLAY, First Auditor.
ALICE STONE BLACKWELL, Recording Secretary.	CATHARINE WAUGH McCULLOCH, Second Auditor.

TIME TO STOP IT

EDITORIAL · 1912

If the feminist cause has any real friends in Great Britain, it is time for them to get together and apply decisive measures to the feline band of finger nail and hat pin rioters ridiculously self-named "militant" suffragets. Their disgraceful antics have gone far enough. The political enfranchisement of women is bound to come. These female hoodlums cannot prevent its coming any more than the McNamaras and the Industrial Workers of the World can prevent the onmoving course of social reform.

The enfranchisement of women will come because it is

From *The Independent*, lxxiii, December 19, 1912.

right, because self-respecting men and women believe in it. It will come because it is a part of the inevitable moral evolution of the human race. It will come because the vast majority of women, like the vast majority of men, are endowed with common sense, self-control and a decent regard for civilization. It will come thru the operation of the same causes that have opened to women the opportunities for higher education, and for business and professional life. It will come because humanity is, on the whole, a law making and law abiding association of intelligent and reasonably conscientious beings.

It is time to stop the rioting of the hoodlums for a number of reasons. One is that for more than a generation high minded and self-sacrificing workers in the cause of woman's advancement have been telling the world that woman's influence in politics would work for reasonableness, orderliness, graciousness, considerateness and the things of good report. It will, in the long run, work in just that way, because, in the long run, decently behaved women will assert themselves and relegate their disorderly sisters to the rear ranks or, if necessary, to the penitentiaries. The outbreak of violence retards the cause because it makes the unconverted and the indifferent sceptical upon the validity of the rational and moral arguments in its behalf.

It is time to stop these violent tactics also because civilization is face to face with the necessity of taking resolute action against the propaganda of violence in all of its abhorrent and threatening manifestations. McNamara methods have been carried altogether too far in the economic class war. The most priceless achievements of man's collective struggle for advantage and enlightenment are put in jeopardy. Criminality has become assertive, flagrant and impudent. That these methods should now be carried into the struggle for the enfranchisement of woman is a thing incredible and unspeakable.

To those misguided or addle-pated creatures who attempt

to justify the campaign of violence on historical grounds, we have just one word to say. Their historical argument is preposterous. It is true that men have won liberty and defended it thruout the generations by fighting for it, and if the day ever comes when women have to fight for liberty we shall do whatever may be in our power to arm them with the most up-to-date munitions of war and shall wish them God speed. If we are not too old we will undertake to handle a few guns for them ourselves. But organized fighting, in which enemies meet face to face in open encounter, is one thing. Sneaking, cowardly, secret, underhanded violence and sabotage are a totally different thing. They have never been resorted to by men worthy of the name, and they have never yet promoted liberty in any age or in any place.

And what if they had? Has mankind made any progress, or has it not? If it could be shown that rioting and machinery smashing had helped to emancipate the British workingman and establish his legal rights, would that prove that women now in these days of steady and resistless advancement of their cause thru law and reason must fall back upon the methods of ignorance, brutality and barbarism?

The Independent has fought for years for the emancipation of woman. It will continue to fight for it; and because it will continue to fight for it, it will speak in language that nobody can possibly mistake against the incredible folly and wickedness of the so-called militant suffragets who, at this moment, are the chief obstacle to the triumphant progress of the cause of woman.

MILITANT METHODS

TERESA BILLINGTON-GREIG · 1913

To remove servile conditions, or conditions of imposed disability, rebellion of some kind and degree always has been necessary. Change is born of aspiration and discontent; these are its creative forces. But they do not become fruitful in silence and inaction; only when by protest and organisation they have found voice and form, only when they are expressed in rebellion, can the desired revolution follow. It is true that the statement of a grievance has sufficed in some rare instances to procure redress—but this is pecularily uncommon. As a rule the attitude of governing bodies tends to make rebellion necessary, and to make it necessary in a further degree than that which the malcontents contemplate or desire.

But the necessity for organised movements of protest does not wholly proceed from the conservatism of governments; it is in great part due to the inertia of the mass of humanity, to the multifarious and conflicting interests and detachments of the governing and the governed, to the indifference and ignorance of the victims, and—in these modern days—to the many avenues of interest and amusement, opened by wider knowledge and applied science, which absorb us in pleasure, forgetfulness, and solace.

The repeated postponement of the woman suffrage demand, and its relegation to a wholly academic position in the political world, provided full justification for the extension of the suffrage agitation into more vigorous channels at the beginning of this century. An active protestant movement was essential, if the apathy of the public and the contempt of Parliament were to be replaced by support, understanding, and

From *The Fortnightly Review*, xciv, December 1, 1913. With the kind permission of the Editor.

respect. The older suffrage societies had been losing ground for years. Their methods of work, which had fully satisfied the needs of the day in which they were first applied, had become antiquated and ineffective. While politics crept ever closer to women, intruding into their homes, regulating their working conditions, shutting them out of this avenue and making new restrictions for them in the other, their claim to be consulted about all these matters had receded rather than advanced. The women who wished to share in the determination of their own legal, domestic, social, and industrial conditions were brushed aside by the legislators. They were come to be regarded as negligible. Politicians assumed as an axiom that women should be content to be legislated for, and should show fitting gratitude that a certain number of the laws enacted with regard to them were benevolently intended.

There was here clear need for protest and propaganda, and this need was made the more emphatic and the more urgent by the rapid growth of the labour representation movement among working men. The re-inforced demands of the male workers tended to submerge more completely the needs of women who were politically more helpless than themselves; and their emergence into the political arena at this critical time hastened the outbreak of that campaign of protest which many women had now realised was inevitable. The magnification of political issues and political machinery has reached its height in the present day. It was inevitable when men had persuaded themselves that by the manipulation of legislative machinery they could bring about national reformation, economic peace, and individual well-being, that women should set up the suffrage as the central and primary right of an emancipated womanhood. When all progress had come to be viewed through political spectacles the liberty of woman naturally received a political interpretation.

Every observer of the conditions which prevailed at the opening of the twentieth century must admit a need for revolt. It was beyond question; it could not be gainsaid. The stress of the industrial struggle, the wide changes that education had wrought, not only in culture and books and tools for the earning of livelihood, but in the stuff of life itself, the greater ambition and resentment with which trained women struggled against artificial restrictions, the contrast between intellectual equality and the petty social and political bonds imposed on women—these supplied at every turn the raw material for the making of rebels. The conditions which in a political age barred the avenues of political reform determined the direction of the rebellion. Women set out to play the part of the political importunate widow.

And rightly and naturally so. Rebellion against subjection is not only a justifiable but a desirable thing. A spiritless race cannot achieve emancipation, however wide the doors of liberty and opportunity be held open. Without rebellion there would be no progress. All the later work of thought, of constructive organisation, of concrete establishment, spring from the seeds of discontent and aspiration which compose rebellion. And just as naturally this rebellion took a political channel. It would have been odd if at the beginning any other arena, unless perhaps the economic, had been selected for the first rebel protest.

Therefore condemnation of the forms and character now assumed by the revolt which originated in 1905 must not be misunderstood. Such criticism has become an imperative duty, but it does not imply, it is not meant to imply, any negation of the pressing need for rebellion. The destructive criticism which has been formulated, chiefly from within the suffrage movement, has been a criticism of methods, an exposure of the blindness of leaders, of the errors of judgment by which the great opportunity of the women of this generation has been restricted in effect and degraded in character and expression. Not because rebellion itself is opposed, but because the need for rebellion is recognised as great, must the misdirection of the movement's energies be so gravely condemned.

Those who undertake any campaign of reform must be prepared to serve a novitiate to propaganda. For a reform which depends upon individual conviction and acceptance progress may be early, measurable and steady; there may be laurels for wearing every day. But a very much greater length of service and strength of appeal is demanded before success can be obtained when the reform sought requires a legislative enactment; and the demands are multiplied when the enactment is claimed by a body of non-electors. This is especially so at present when the parliamentary machine is permanently overburdened and an accumulating overplus of ungranted demands marks the end of every session, and when the system of Cabinet control in conjunction with the extension of political action into new areas deprives the House of Commons of all real power of successfully initiating legislation. It is easier nowadays for politically powerless persons to establish a new creed than to carry a new law. The one requires only the conversion of individuals; the other requires propaganda carried to the point of satiety, and sufficient influence to secure for a body of outsiders a temporary predominance over the insiders who generally control the political machine.

In order to obtain effective support for any demand it is necessary to enlist in its behalf emotion and numbers. This can only be done by awakening public interest and sympathy. Protest, propaganda, persistent appeals and demands, energetic organisation and advertisement, must all play their part. The evils to be redressed and the advantages to be gained must be set forth in every possible way, so that sympathisers may be moved to adherence and adherents to activity. But paramount among the forces which must be employed to produce momentum for a reform movement is that of feeling. The average British person is not moved by appeals to abstract justice, nor by aspirations after better things, as he or she is moved by suffering. As a nation we have no desire for change unless there is a hurt to be remedied. But produce a victim, a victim from whom we are not allowed to escape, and we will act. A victim will stir us to the deeps and give momentum to the deadest of old Causes. We are a nation of sentimentalists. We love to believe in our own good name. We love to feel satisfied with ourselves. And when this is not possible without action we will act. When an evil is so thrust upon our notice that we cannot escape it we will organise against it, or boycott it, or legislate it away.

This fact has to be recognised and reckoned with in every reform movement. It had to be recognised and reckoned with by the first militant suffragists; no doubt assailed us upon this point. We knew that the mere act of voting would never appeal to the imagination of women as in itself so desirable a thing as to call for strenuous effort and bitter sacrifice. It was also clear to us that the vote as a symbol would appeal only to those who were already self-emancipated, and not therefore in need of awakening. Our task was to stir the imaginations and enlist the feelings of great numbers of indifferent and unthinking people, the great mass of the community. To do this we recognised clearly that we must appeal to the emotions; that we must produce evidence of injustice in practice; that we must show victims to the eyes of the nation.

This policy has been put into practice; victims have been provided to move the hearts of the people. But from the beginning the task has been carried out on false lines and founded on a wrong basis. Those who from the early days have kept in their own hands the control of the militant suffrage organisation decided upon a policy of making victims—of creating them specially to meet the need. They did not seek for true cases of victimisation caused by the conditions of which we complained, but set out to create an arbitrary supply of artificial victims. They made it a policy of the society to train women to seek martyrdom in order that they might pose later upon platforms to waken the enthusiasm of other women, and to stir the sympathy and admiration and conscience of the multitude. They abandoned the natural way of revolution which would centre round real victims a demand for change. They invented an artificial way. And to this fundamental mistake may be traced almost all, if not all, of that amazing harvest of heroic foolishness and futile greatness, of doubly-dealt blows which struck both for and against the cause, of shallowness and emptiness and blindness and wastefulness, by which the later years have been made into a very path to Calvary.

Why was the artificial method of revolt preferred before the natural? Once the distinction has been made there can be no argument as to their comparative merits. The seeking out of real victims of our present sex-subjection is not an impossible task; such victims are to be found on every side. There can be no excuse that they cannot be found; suffragists themselves are every day proclaiming their existence from Press and platform. There may be too many such victims for effective use; certainly there are not too few.

The final propaganda value of a fact depends upon its being true. Similarly, it must be clear at once that the propaganda value of a victim depends upon her being real, not self-made, but a product of the conditions complained of. Such a real victim produced before the public has a great potentiality for the conversion of previously indifferent individuals, where a specially manufactured victim can by her very nature appeal only to the already converted.

It is further to be noted in comparing the martyr-creation

method with the victim-seeking policy that the one brings the movement into close touch with real life, while at the best the other creates only a special simulation of life of its own, apart from the great currents of human interest. All the big reasons of principle, all the arguments of sound and earnest thought, are ranged on the side of selecting real victims for a real revolution in the minds of the people rather than creating artificial ones and leaving the minds of the people either estranged or unmoved.

It has been argued that the method employed was the only one which left the control of individuals and events in the hands of the militant directors, and that it provided that the women best fitted to act as propagandists should wear the martyr crown and interpret the new gospel to the multitude; and these claims must be granted for what they are worth. The method chosen has retained in the hands of the leaders greater power than the one rejected. This scarcely needs emphasis. A true victim has to be taken as she is found. She is not a follower to be directed and controlled, and she may never become a follower.

Other reasons of expediency have weighed in the determination of the leaders. They have known that the predominant position of suffrage in the rebel woman's outlook depended upon precarious supports. To by far the greater number of their supporters the suffrage is only a means to an end; it is what the vote has come to represent, not what it is, that stirs them to enthusiasm. Hence the vote can only remain the most important of all things so long as it is accepted as the only highway to all things. If the things beyond can be achieved without it the vote loses in value.

Yet the production of artificial victims as a method of appeal to the multitude, taken apart entirely from the considerations already examined, could never be regarded as sound. It is not even politically advisable. It fails at the first test. It proves nothing. The world is used to mistaken martyrs; its records of the past are full of them, of fanatics who have been willing to suffer any measure of pain and despoilment for a super- stition, for a tyrant, for a pretender, or for the dream of an overwrought brain. The world has learned to admire the martyr while seeing the mistake. If its mental processes are not always careful and accurate, it is still not mentally blind enough to accept self-sacrifice as a proof of logical reasoning and super-human certainty.

Undoubtedly there has been excuse for much bitter anger in the parliamentary record of the last seven years. And this is not unknown to the general public. Had the rebel suffrage campaign proceeded on truly revolutionary lines there might by this time have been sufficient sympathy and understanding in the body of the people to have made the latest evasion of the issue impossible. But that sympathy has not been created. The man in the street and the woman in the home appear to believe that between the Government and the suffragette it is a case of six of one and half a dozen of the other. And they do not see why they should be made scapegoats by the angry militant martyrs whose sacrifices, being ill-directed, have been crowned with failure.

The militant movement has been killed, as all movements that lack reality are killed, by the blindness of its adherents. It has lost the public ear; it has become politically futile. And only a recourse to some alternative method of revolt which will link the suffrage demand with the real lives of women, with the real evils from which they suffer, with the crying needs by the neglect of which they die, will save the wider suffrage movement itself from sharing in the decay and death of militancy.

WOMAN THE HELPMATE

MRS. EDMUND PENNINGTON · 1916

Nature teaches us that permanent growth is slow, almost imperceptible. Our Anti-suffrage Association has grown in the same gradual but deliberate way and many are doubtless astonished to see it already so strong and far-reaching.

It is said "An empty vessel makes the most sound." If our great anti-suffrage ship has ploughed quietly the turbulent ocean of present-day conditions it is a sign the cargo is heavy. The enthusiastic manner in which the supporters of the *Woman's Protest* have organized and quietly carried on a remarkable work shows the direction and current of the wind in our beautiful State of Minnesota. However, in times when each day has its isms and each week its 'ology—when dictionaries a few years old ignore the familiar word "feminist"—it may be a real novelty to fix our attention upon elementary conditions of nature, and face a few stubborn facts. The truth, eternally old, must sometimes be the fashion —as the hat worn twenty years by a woman of the old school found itself at the top of the style three times.

We recognize in the suffrage ranks many magnificent women—self-sacrificing, earnest, philanthropic—who are spending themselves in that work because they sincerely believe franchise is the remedy for all the trouble, and evils besetting the path of women to-day. But we also see that the emotional nature of woman has carried many suffragists to the disgraceful conduct of the militant, and the repelling doctrine of the feminist. Where would emotionalism carry these women in the political arena? Would the militant accept the will of the majority? Would the feminist not destroy

From *The Woman's Protest*, October, 1916.

the ideals that have grown with the triumphs of civilization and Christianity?

We also are seeking a remedy for the injustices and wrongs that beset the path of women. Our object is the same as theirs. We are not protesting against franchise directly. If their principles can be fairly proven to lead to woman's best emancipation, or to her most rational influence—to the city of true peace—we shall all fall in line. We are protesting against the sacrilegious license and Babylonian confusion to which suffrage seems to be leading. To us the ballot-box idea seems held so near—it hides the great scope and glorious mission of woman's world outside and beyond it. Is there any actual relation between woman's personal world and franchise? Could woman's sphere be enlarged or strengthened by the ballot-box?

This brings us to the consideration of that time-worn expression "woman's sphere." The word "sphere" in this connection is not a happy selection, for it suggests ceaseless revolution in a determined orbit—unchanging routine. The application of the word to woman's activity—because of its erroneous interpretation and superficiality—arouses a determination not to submit—a sense of suffocation. Woman is perfectly conscious that no limit can be placed upon the radii of her mind and heart—they reach to infinite truth and infinite goodness. To bring peace and happiness to women we must have a deeper, fuller understanding of woman's nature and give her an opportunity for the expansion and growth of her faculties. Then we must recognize the element in which such growth is possible—take into it all "modern improvements," and finally win women back to live and rule in it.

We anti-suffragists do not protest against suffrage or anything else that may help the condition of women and restore peace and unity to the women of our land—but we do protest against suffrage and *everything* that may tend to foster difficulties, protract restlessness and bring endless contention. *We* see the peculiar positions in which women find themselves to-day, *we* feel the feminine unrest with which all woman-hood seems to tremble, *we* hear the heartrending cries from overtired, struggling, bread-winning sisters and *we* feel the overpowering circumstances which call aloud for readjust-ment. We recognize the crisis is at hand—we are willing, indeed eager to launch out and courageously, enthusiastically give a helping hand. With all our energy we wish to strive to bring peace to every woman's heart and to save the dignity of true womanhood. But we must be sane in our endeavor and wise in our enthusiasms. What we wish is to find some path-way that will lead women to pure air in which their womanly natures can breathe freely and their womanly minds see clearly.

Woman's suffrage stands for "equal rights," which means competition in man's kingdom. This is against nature and might not the inevitable result of such an attempt be social, moral and religious anarchy? As women, we must keep our eyes well fixed on our real destiny—on Nature's eternal truths—and not strand ourselves on the sand-bars of a passing hour.

Women have a larger choice than they had formerly—and we are grateful; but in the broadening of their field of labor women seem to rebel against any limitation. With all choice placed before them, many refuse to acknowledge that Nature has a primal law, or any true demand. But woman must remain woman, with a woman's nature. She can be happy in any occupation to which her capacity entitles her if she be true to that nature. By seeking equality in the realm of man, she cannot change her nature. By ignoring or repudiating her femininity, she may create for herself a veritable Hades on earth.

On the contrary, if she recognizes the undeniable fact that

her physical obligation to the human race creates the limitation of her activities and is more than offset by the spiritual acquisition it should bring, she makes herself the center of a physical and spiritual orbit of which earth is the smaller part.

It is not my purpose to make any exhaustive argument against woman's suffrage; but to speak of it only as it bears upon my deep, heartfelt conviction that woman's sphere is in the moral world, and that her freedom and happiness, whatever may be her circumstances in life, depend upon her recognition of this fact. While suffrage may not be identical with the repelling beliefs advanced by some of our women to-day, it is hand in hand with them. Therefore, we must protest with all the earnestness of our minds and hearts and souls against anything that seems, directly or indirectly, to lead to the moral degradation of women.

Let us unite to save the true nature of womanhood—the dignity of motherhood—the unity of the family and the influence of the home. How? Let us declare ourselves, not only by words, but by our actions—let us demand morality in the theaters where we and our daughters seek entertainment; let us wage war against immoral posters and extravagant shop windows—let us make the woman wage earner less necessary by making marriage more possible, and marriage more possible by making economy respectable and extravagance vulgar. You may smile and say—"beautiful sentiments, but theory." Can it not be made practical? Individually we are helpless against these forces, but if each one will pledge herself to join a crusade—not alone against suffrage, but against beliefs and abuses that threaten the true nature of womanhood and the influence of the family and the home, we may rescue the Holy Land of woman's moral Kingdom.

COMPETITION OR CO-OPERATION

JULIA D. HENRY · 1913

Those funny little sisters of ours, who are so busy demonstrating their fitness to rule, claim that the only women opposed to suffrage are those who cling to some sturdy oak and peer with timid eyes from his sheltering branches into the big, wide world.

Now, I am no clinging vine. I am managing a successful business, which employs twenty men, and have actively assisted in the election or defeat of various political candidates. And from my experience I am *opposed* to woman suffrage.

The reasons for the faith that is in me are: First, the biological necessity of conserving woman's strength for her great function of motherhood; second, the fundamental difference between woman the individualist and man the gregarious creature; third, the economic need of removing woman from industry and restoring her to the natural duty of home-making, so that she may co-operate rather than compete with man; lastly, the progressive movement of our time, which is bringing in the day when man, the bread-winner, will again be able to wed his woman, and to provide for her and her children.

Woman is inferior to man in bodily strength. To do a man's work woman must consume her vital reserve. Such a woman approaches motherhood a bankrupt. Too often her marriage is barren, or her offspring defective in mind or body. Our debt to nature for the gift of life is the continuance of the race. Beside that duty the privilege of voting is child's play.

When nature gave concentration to the setting hen it was to ensure the hatching of eggs. Likewise has she endowed

From *The Woman's Protest*, June, 1913.

woman with a narrow and intense interest in life, and for much the same reason. Man is a mixer. From the first tribal war-dance down to the Stock Exchange man has worked with man for common ends, and that is the essence of government. Woman is passionately loyal to her own. She is unmoved by abstract justice and the common good when they conflict with her personal interests. He who governs must seek the common advantage or he will fail. Man has proven capable for the task, while woman's very nature unfits her for it.

Woman is competing with man for his job. They who should be helpmeets are rivals. Because woman is doing his work man is less able to provide a home, and therefore woman must continue to do man's work. And this is the endless chain of our industrial folly. Votes for women would prove only another chain to bind woman to her present false place.

The industrial slavery of women will not last. The spirit of our time spells progress. Already living conditions are improving and capital and labor are coming together to work out the problem of poverty. Within our generation the young man will be able to marry and the young woman will be transferred from the shop to the home. And with her will go the only plausible argument for woman suffrage.

DEMOCRACY AND FEMINISM

SAMUEL MC CHORD CROTHERS · 1914

There are doubtless some women who seek the vote because they think it would give a distinctly feminine cast to the government, and lead to the triumph of ideals held by

From *Meditations on Votes for Women,* by Samuel McChord Crothers. Reprinted by kind permission of and arrangement with Houghton Mifflin Company, the authorized publishers.

women and not by men. But the vast majority seek it because they are interested in those public questions in which men and women are equally concerned. They believe in a democratic order of society, and this is one of its expressions.

Democracy does not promise much to any special class. It allows no one to have all he asks. Because you are rich, or have had a classical education, or an excellent set of grandfathers, is no reason why you should have more than one vote. You shall cast one ballot and the garbage-man shall do the same. If you do not acquiesce cheerfully in this arrangement, you may be a gentleman and a scholar, but you are not a good democrat.

Or because you are a woman and have a charming personality, your opinion shall have no more than its proper arithmetical value. You shall not, on election day, count for more than one.

To those who desire special consideration, democracy is not pleasing. It takes away more than it seems to give. It is an equalizing tendency by which every valley shall be exalted and every mountain and hill shall be made low. The democratization of society has gone on by slow degrees. The democratic mind cannot accept the disfranchisement of any class as permanent. It represents a vacuum that must be filled. When once the idea of popular government has been accepted, there must be a definition of the term "the people." What is meant by "We the people of the United States"? In what sense do American women use the phrase? Or do they prefer not to use it, but rather to say, "they the people"?

These are democratic queries which cannot be escaped. They continue to recur so long as the political status of women is uncertain. The programmes of feminism and democracy may coincide up to a certain point but they are not identical. The enthusiastic Feminist is thinking of the maximum of woman's influence. Democracy is chiefly concerned about the irreducible minimum.

XI

Merry England

❋ ❋ ❋ ❋ ❋ ❋ ❋ ❋ ❋ ❋ ❋ ❋ ❋ ❋ ❋ ❋

FORSTER'S TITLE, "Peeping at Elizabeth," cautions the reader to expect a "backstairs" attitude toward the most highly idealized period in English history. It further suggests that Forster is aware that he is approaching his subject from an unusual angle. The essay was written, actually, out of respect for the age; it is designed to be a vigorous corrective to the quaint, sentimentalized, "merrie England" conception of what was in reality a tough and hazardous time. These selections present extremes in attitude and a variety of intentions, and have been chosen to illustrate the problems and methods of interpreting a great wealth of conflicting evidence on a large subject. They represent the difficulties presented by the synthesis of what men do with what their actions mean. Contradictions in historical statement are a recognized and constructive element in the interpretation of the past. These passages, which present several seemingly incompatible opinions about the spacious days of great Elizabeth, reflect also the constantly growing understanding of the age.

It is important to note that the writings included here are few of them primarily historical in intention. Forster's essay and Virginia Woolf's were both written as book reviews; Symonds's as an introduction to the glory of the age, its theater. Christopher Hollis presents the Roman Catholic attitude, though indeed his title is quoted from the great Protestant, John Knox. Ideally this collection should represent more pure historical writing, but it is a significant commentary upon the complexity of the historian's task that sound historical statement on so large a topic can scarcely be condensed into this length. The excerpt from Trevelyan describing a single characteristic of the time is, for instance, only a fragment of his discussion.

❀ ❀ ❀ ❀ ❀ ❀ ❀ ❀ ❀ ❀ ❀ ❀ ❀ ❀ ❀ ❀ ❀ ❀ ❀

PEEPING AT ELIZABETH

E. M. FORSTER · 1925

[*The Elizabethan Home.* Discovered in Two Dialogues by Claudius Hollyband and Peter Erondell. Edited by M. St. Clare Byrne. (The Haslewood Books. 12s. 6d.)]

Do you wish you had lived in the days of Queen Elizabeth? I am thankful to have escaped them. The noise, the hopefulness, the vitality, the cant about chastity—I should have found them hard to bear, nor would a Reformed Religion have consoled. Gone was the dear Pope, overseas, underground; gone the traditions that echoed out of the past and whispered of future unity, and in their place, closing every vista, stood a portentous figure shaped like a dinner-bell. The hard reverberations of this creature filled the air, her feet twinkled in a septuagenarian dance, she made progresses and rude metallic jokes, she exploited a temper naturally violent, she was a public virgin—and all she did she did for the honour of England. Could one have psycho-analyzed her, one would have obtained relief, but that was not yet to be. Spenser, Sidney, Raleigh—no, psycho-analysis did not occur to them; they

From *The Nation and The Athenaeum*, August 8, 1925. Reprinted with the kind permission of the author.

accepted the dinner-bell as solid woman; they did not venture
to think. There was very little thought in those spacious times,
just as there was little unashamed or uncontorted passion.
Socrates, Cleopatra—no, they do not occur. Continents were
discovered, beards singed, bowls bowled, but for all its bravery
life had retreated to the muscles and the will, and even Shakespeare, who could have contained so much, suffered from the
surrounding impoverishment as he pegged away at his thirty-
seven plays.

Nevertheless, viewed from a sufficient distance, the Elizabethan age has two great attractions—lyric beauty and quaintness. Much good they would have done us on the spot, for
beauty is rare always, and requires perspective to thicken
it into an atmosphere, and as for quaintness, it disappears entirely when we form part of it. Open this quaint little book. It
is so naive and disarming that we are tempted to hail it as a
masterpiece. It is nothing of the sort, as its able editor realizes,
and is of genuine importance only to the antiquarian. But
open its pages! Schoolboys and servants elbow with old-world
angularity, we dine with square merchants or my domical
Lady Ri Mellaine; we have the illusion of sharing the daily
life of a sixteenth-century woodcut. Even the writing imposes
itself and asks to be considered fine prose.

"You mayd, goe fetch the childes cradle, make his bed, where
is his pillowe? seeke a cleane pillow-bere, Set on the coverlet, now
put him in his cradle and rocke him till he sleepe, but bring him
to me first that I may kisse him: God send thee good rest my little
boykin. I pray you good Nurse have a care of him."
"Dout not of it Madame with the grace of God."
"Well then, God be with you till anon."

It seems profoundly charming and tender, and because the
arrangements of the words and the punctuation are unfamiliar,
they assume the inevitability of art. But who wrote the words,

and why? The author was a Huguenot schoolmaster, and his aim was not to touch our hearts or even to depict his times, but to assist his pupils and attract new ones. On the opposite page of the book was a French translation. So the effect produced on us is not simply quaint, it is doubly quaint. Two influences have to be discounted before we can peep at that far-off age.

"From whence come you good scholar? is it time to rise, and come to schole at nine? where have you beene?"

"Maister, I met him by the way which did leape, did slide uppon the ice: which did cast snow: which fowght with his fist, and balles of snow: which did scorge his top: which played for pointes, pinnes, cherie stones, counters, dice, cardes."

"Enter in galland, I will teach you a game which you know not."

The delightful catalogue, "pointes, pinnes," etc., is really an exercise in vocabulary, and the same need explains the enormous menu at the Lady Ri Mellaine's dinner. Beginning with oysters and grace, her guests tackle every variety of boiled and roast meat, game, salad, and fish, she urging them on with such hospitable cries as:—

"Come on, let me give you some of this Quince pye, of this Tarte of Almonds, of that of Cherrie, of Gooseberries, of Prunes."

"Certainly Madame, I know not how we should eat any more, unlesse we should borrowe other bellyes."

"Take away then all this, And bring us the Fruite. Doe you loue Cheese? There is holland Cheese, Some Angelot, Auvergne cheese, Parmesan. Will you have some grated cheese with sage and Sugar? If you find the same too strong, take some of that Banbury cheese, For it is mileder in taste (to the mouth)."

Nine kinds of fruit follow, and the meal ends with an aggrieved "Why have we no Chest-nuts?" A superb performance . . . but it has been no more real than a banquet in Ollendorff.

The origins of the volume are explained by the editor in his introduction. He has taken four of these curious French lesson-books—three by Hollyband, who taught in the late sixteenth century, and one by Erondell which was published in 1605—he has made extracts from them, added notes, and served up with woodcuts taken from the Roxburghe Ballads. The result is a most entertaining little volume, solidly quaint, and sometimes charming. Is it good literature? No. Can it be read with profit? Probably not. But it has, in its minute, in-offensive fashion, the commanding quality we attribute to that age; it compels; we are obliged to read it with pleasure.

For the Elizabethans excelled at putting things across. There was a vigour and swagger about them which all must admire and which some would adore. England begins to splash and send ripples all over the world, and English literature makes its big splash too. Epics, treatises, hundreds of plays, thou-sands of sonnets bounce about and would overwhelm the critic by their copiousness, but most of them have proved less permanent than the British Empire. Oblivion engulfed them because they had not spiritual sincerity. Freshness and vitality were not enough. It is in their treatment of love that their falsity becomes most obvious, but the roots of the trouble lie far deeper. Quite what was amiss we can see when we come to a less confident age, and read the poems of Donne. Donne tried to be straight about love and about other things also: he attempted the process known as thought. And though thought may betray a man individually and bring Empires to ruin, it is nevertheless the only known preservative, the only earnest of immortality. The Elizabethans, even the greatest of them, plumped for the native hue of resolution, and are receiving their reward; they increased our political power and glorified our race, and are rightly commended on public occasions. But they were at once too violent and too hazy to contribute much towards the development of the human mind.

THE SPACIOUS DAYS

JOHN ADDINGTON SYMONDS · 1924

England was in a state of transition when the Drama came to perfection. That was one of those rare periods when the past and the future are both coloured by imagination, and both shed a glory on the present. The medieval order was in dissolution; the modern order was in process of formation. Yet the old state of things had not faded from memory and usage; the new had not assumed despotic sway. Men stood then, as it were, between two dreams—a dream of the past, thronged with sinister and splendid reminiscences; a dream of the future, bright with unlimited aspirations and indefinite hopes. Neither the retreating forces of the Middle Ages nor the advancing forces of the modern era pressed upon them with the iron weight of actuality. The brutalities of feudalism had been softened; but the chivalrous sentiment remained to inspire the Surreys and the Sidneys of a milder epoch—its high enthusiasm and religious zeal, its devotion to women, its ideal of the knightly character, its cheerful endurance of hardship, its brave reliance on a righteous cause. The Papacy, after successive revolutions of opinion, had become odious to the large majority of the nation; but Protestantism had not yet condensed into a compact body of sectarian doctrines. The best work of our dramatists, so far from reticent, so comprehensive as it is, reveals no theological orthodoxy, no polemical antagonism to dogmatic creeds. The poet, whether he sounds the depths of sceptical despair or soars aloft on wings of aspiration, appeals less to religious principle than to human emotion, to doubts and hopes instinctive in the breast of man. It is as though in this transition state of thought, humanity

From *Shakespere's Predecessors in the English Drama*, by John Addington Symonds. London: John Murray, Ltd., 1924. Used with the kind permission of the publishers.

were left alone, surveying with clear eyes the universe, sustained by its own adolescent fearlessness and strength. The fields, again, of wealth, discovery, and science, over which we plod with measured and methodic footsteps, spread before those men like a fairyland of palaces and groves, teeming with strange adventures, offering rich harvests of heroic deeds. To the New World Raleigh sailed with the courage of a Paladin, the boyishness of Astolf mounted on his hippogriff.

The genius of youthfulness, renascent, not new-born, was dominant in that age. Adam stepped forth again in Eden, gazed with bold eyes upon the earth and stars, felt himself master there, plucked fruit from the forbidden tree. But though still young, though 'bright as at creation's day,' this now rejuvenescent Adam had six thousand centuries of conscious life, how many countless centuries of dim unconscious life, behind him! Not the material world alone, not the world of his unquenchable self alone, not the world of unscrutable futurity alone, but, in addition to all this, a ruinous world of his own works awaiting reconstruction lay around him. The nations moved 'immersed in rich foreshadowings' of the future, amid the dust of creeds and empires, which crumbled like 'the wrecks of a dissolving dream.' Refreshed with sleep, the giant of the modern age rose up strong to shatter and create. Thought and action were no longer to be fettered. Instead of tradition and prescription, passion and instinct ruled the hour. Every nerve was sensitive to pleasure bordering on pain, and pain that lost itself in ecstasy. Men saw and coveted and grasped at their desire. If they hated, they slew. If they loved and could not win, again they slew. If they climbed to the height of their ambition and fell toppling down, they died with smiles upon their lips like Marlowe's Mortimer:

> Weep not for Mortimer,
> That scorns the world, and, as a traveller
> Goes to discover countries yet unknown.

Turbulence, not the turbulence of a medieval barony, but the turbulence of artists, lovers, pleasure-seekers, aspirants after pomp and spiritual empire, ruffled the ocean of existence.

THE MONSTROUS REGIMENT

CHRISTOPHER HOLLIS · 1929

Some Catholics, speaking of the Elizabethan Government, begin by condemning its religious policy but then turn and echo a conventional panegyric upon the age and the England of that time; they say to us "after all, Queen Elizabeth was the maker of modern England" or some words of the sort. Again, other Catholics speak as if, had Mary, Queen of Scots, succeeded to the throne, all modern England would have been exactly as it is to-day except only that everybody would have gone to Mass. It is important, therefore, that we try to form an estimate of the probable effect upon our lives, had the great Elizabethan experiment failed.

Before entering upon an examination such as that which I have proposed, it is first necessary to get the mind clear upon one large preliminary obstacle. What is the meaning of the language of rhetoric in which it is to-day so common to talk about the Elizabethan age? "England then truly great" —"a race of immortals"—"made us a nation"—"the spacious times of great Elizabeth"—"Drake and Hawkins, Raleigh and Frobisher"—what does it all amount to? What do we owe to the Elizabethans?

Elizabethan literature? It is true. The nationalism of the

From *The Monstrous Regiment*, by Christopher Hollis. London and New York, 1929. Used by kind permission of the author and of the publishers in the United States, G. P. Putnam's Sons.

Renaissance was the cause of two effects, the one good and rational, a national literature, the other bad and irrational, a national religion (if the phrase "national religion" be not a contradiction in terms).

The first foundations of our empire? Strictly the claim is false. Such men as Drake were not empire-builders. They made no attempt to rob Spain of her territory nor to annex it to England. Their spirit, for good or bad, had very little in common with the spirit which has built and maintained our great commercial empire. Raleigh's colony of Virginia was a fiasco and had to be abandoned. The surviving American settlements are all of Stuart foundation. Yet it is certainly true that interest in America dates from the Elizabethan era. It was natural for such a country as England to exploit the new discovery of America. The only wonder was that she was so slow in doing so and allowed other nations to get so large a start on her. In any case there would doubtless have been plenty of good English pirates to prey upon the Spanish galleons, but the happy accident of religious difference certainly gave a zest to that piracy which it would otherwise have lacked. To flout the papal decision which divided the New World between Spain and Portugal became a patriotic and religious duty.

The world has seen many viler deeds than those of the Elizabethan pirates. Yet at the same time, if they were not abominably vicious, it is hard to understand how anyone can pretend to find them excessively virtuous nor why such men should be held up to us, as no others in English history are held up, as models. We are told that the Elizabethans beat the Spanish Armada? It is true. But Englishmen have fought and won and lost wars in every generation since Rome fell. Why is this one war so especially singled out and those who took part in it spoken of in a peculiar and uncritical language that we are not expected to employ about the men and women of any other generation in our history? It is the fashion to discuss religious questions in non-religious, and therefore false, language and there is no better example of this fashion than that of popular rhetoric about the Elizabethans. Is it not clear that the cause of all that rhetoric is one thing alone? This was the first English generation that had thrown over Catholicism. All other reasons are but pretence. The Spanish war is singled out for praise, when twenty other wars just as important are relegated to the mustiest corner of the text-book, simply because in that war the English cause was more clearly and certainly an anti-Catholic cause than any which she has championed before or since. Of the peculiar institutions of England there is but one that we owe to the reign of Elizabeth—the Church of England. The rhetoric which says that Elizabeth made England means only that she first established the separation of England from the Catholic unity.

THE ENGLISH RENAISSANCE

GEORGE MACAULAY TREVELYAN · 1926

Outside the politico-religious sphere, intellectual and poetic freedom had already reached their fullest expansion by the end of Elizabeth's reign. The Renaissance, with its spirit of enquiry and its vision of the ancient freedom of Greek and Roman thought, had been transplanted from Italy, where it was fast withering away under the hands of Spaniards and Jesuits. It bloomed afresh in England, tended by poets who grafted it on English trees in the Forest of Arden. There the imagination was free indeed,—freer than in our own day,

From *A History of England*, by G. M. Trevelyan. London and New York: Longmans, Green & Co., 1926. Reprinted by permission.

when it is burdened by too great a weight of knowledge, and hemmed in by the harsh realism of an age of machinery. Shakespeare and his friends, standing as they did outside the dangerous world of religious and political controversy, enjoyed in their own spacious domains a freedom of spirit perhaps irrecoverable.

But though Shakespeare may be in retrospect the greatest glory of his age, he was not in his own day its greatest influence. By the end of Elizabeth's reign, the book of books for Englishmen was already the Bible, although the Authorized Version that is still in use was only drawn up by James I's Bishops in the years immediately following her death. For every Englishman who had read Sidney or Spenser, or had seen Shakespeare acted at the Globe, there were hundreds who had read or heard the Bible with close attention as the word of God. The effect of the continual domestic study of the book upon the national character, imagination and intelligence for nearly three centuries to come, was greater than that of any literary movement in our annals, or any religious movement since the coming of St. Augustine. New worlds of history and poetry were opened in its pages to a people that had little else to read. Indeed it created the habit of reading and reflection in whole classes of the community, and turned a tinker into one of the great masters of the English tongue. Through the Bible, the deeds and thoughts of men who had lived thousands of years before in the eastern Mediterranean, translated into English during the period when our language reached its brief perfection, coloured the daily thought and speech of Britons, to the same degree as they are coloured in our own day by the commonplaces of the newspaper press. The Bible in English history may be regarded as a 'Renaissance' of Hebrew literature far more widespread and more potent than even the Classical Renaissance which, thanks to the reformed Grammar Schools, provided the mental background of the better educated. The Bible and the Classics together stimulated and enlarged the culture of the British, as their ocean voyages stimulated and enlarged their practical outlook on life.

Another source of popular inspiration and refinement in the great age that lies between the Armada and the Civil War, was music and lyrical poetry. They flourished together: many of the best poems, like the songs in Shakespeare's plays, were written to be sung. Europe recognized Elizabethan England as the country of music *par excellence*. German travellers noted with admiration how they 'heard beautiful music of violas and pandoras, for in all England it is the custom that even in small villages the musicians wait on you for a small fee.' Throughout Tudor times, fine Church music was written in England, indifferently for the Roman Mass or the Anglican service, while the Renaissance inspired non-ecclesiastical music with a fresh spirit, so that it reached its zenith under Elizabeth. The genius of Byrd adorned impartially the religious and the profane sphere, and whole troops of able composers flourished in that great age of the madrigal. The arena of Tudor and Stuart music was not the concert-hall but the domestic hearth. In days when there were no newspapers, and when books were few and ponderous, the rising middle class, not excluding Puritan families, practised vocal and instrumental music assiduously at home. The publication of music by the printing-press helped to diffuse the habit, and Elizabeth set the example to her subjects by her skill upon the virginals.

Music and song were the creation and inheritance of the whole people. The craftsman sang over his task, the pedlar sang on the footpath way, and the milkmaid could be heard 'singing blithe' behind the hedgerow, or in the north country crooning the tragic ballads that told of Border fight and foray. The common drama was a poetical drama, and in that age was popular because it appealed to the imaginative faculties. Poetry was not an affair solely of intellectual circles, nor was music yet associated mainly with foreign composers. It was no mere accident that Shakespeare and Milton came when they did. Among a whole people living in the constant presence of nature, with eyes and ears trained to rejoice in the best pleasures of the mind, the perfect expansion of Shakespeare's poetic gifts was as much a part of the general order of society as the development of a great novelist out of a journalist would be to-day. And in the life of John Milton, born five years after Elizabeth died, we read clearly how the three chief elements in the English culture of that day—music, the Classics and the Bible—combined to inspire the 'God-gifted organ-voice of England.'

THE ELIZABETHAN UNDERWORLD

A. V. JUDGE · 1930

It is not always the social historian's good fortune to discover among the principal sources for his subject a body of material in which are combined the qualities of romantic fiction and close observation. And when this occurs he hardly knows whether to congratulate himself after all. For while it is satisfactory to be able to gather together the sweeping generalizations of those contemporary writers who were conscious of the existence of a social problem, and to savour the atmosphere of their discussions, the topics may have become too exciting both to themselves and their public for them to be able to restrain their imaginative impulses.

From the book *The Elizabethan Underworld*, by A. V. Judge. Published by E. P. Dutton & Co., Inc., and by Routledge & Kegan Paul Ltd.

In their studies of rogue life and behaviour, the pamphleteers of the Elizabethan period broke several of the rules which ought to govern scientific observation. And such has been the literary success of their achievement that we love them for it. Who, after all, will presume to quarrel with a man who turns a reforming tract into a novel, even when he so far forgets himself as to exalt the character of the intended villain?

Whatever exaggeration we may discover in panicky appeals for rigorous deeds, or read into official acts and regulations, it is clear that a problem of the first magnitude did exist, not only in the minds of justices and legislators, but also in actual fact. All accounts affirm that the number of beggars was prodigious; thieves abounded everywhere; and in the unruly north their bands were still a menace to the villages after the borderland ceased to be a frontier. Figures giving the numbers of beggars and masterless men, and estimating the gallows' harvest of thieves are not lacking; but few can be accepted without criticism, so that quantitative judgment must be reserved until further work has been done upon the sessions rolls. The remarks of an Italian visiting England at the end of the fifteenth century are often quoted. In spite, he says, of the severe laws and the extensive powers of the magistracy, "there is no country in the world where there are so many thieves and robbers as in England; insomuch that few venture to go alone in the country, excepting in the middle of the day, and fewer still in the towns at night, and least of all in London." Twenty years earlier Chief Justice Fortescue had a similar comparison to make. "There be . . . more men hanged in England in a year for robbery and manslaughter than be hanged in France for such manner of crime in seven years."

Discharged retainers and serving-men, flung off by their employers when convention, if not necessity, called for the partial disbandment of the military personnel of the great house-

holds, made effective additions to the ranks of roguery. Servants of all descriptions seem to have found the vagrant's life
an attractive one.

The poorer servants of the state were also subject to vicissitudes of fortune. Inadequate provision for discharged soldiers
left these turbulent and demoralized men to fend for themselves,
and they frequently took the easy course. Such penniless vagrants were doubly dangerous; for unused, as many
of them were, to the arts of peace, it was difficult to find
means of assimilating them; and with their military training
in mass discipline they responded readily to the invitation
of any robber leader who could offer pillage.

It seems probable that most of the beggars of the more re-
doubtable kind began their lives as soldiers, sailors or retainers.
These, together with the "wild rogues," or men born in the
profession, and a sprinkling of "young shifting gentlemen,
which oftentimes do bear more port than they are able to
maintain," formed the backbone of the ragged army, and
insofar as it possessed any organization at all, they provided
the nerves and sinews. They were feared by gentry and
common people alike, because they had courage, resource and
versatile talents, had often too a good address and plausible
appearance, and knew how to stir up trouble in a district when
it served their purpose. Joseph Hext, one of the Somerset
justices, wrote a long account to a member of the Privy
Council in 1596, describing the terrorism exercised by these
people in his own county, where local juries, out of sympathy or fear, refused to bring indictments against them.

I do not see how it is possible for the poor countryman to bear
the burdens duly laid upon him, and the rapines of the infinite
numbers of the wicked wandering idle people of the land; so as
men are driven to watch their sheep folds, their pastures, their
woods, their cornfields, all things growing too too common. Others
there be (and I fear me emboldened by the wandering people)

that stick not to say boldly they must not starve, they will not starve. And this year there assembled eighty in a company, and took a cartload of cheese from one driving it to a fair, and dispersed it amongst them, for which some of them have endured long imprisonment and fine by the judgment of the good Lord Chief Justice at our last Christmas sessions; which may grow dangerous by the aid of such numbers as are abroad, especially in this time of dearth; who no doubt animate them to all contempt both of noblemen and gentlemen, continually buzzing into their ears that the rich men have gotten all into their hands and will starve the poor. And I may justly say that the infinite numbers of the idle wandering poor and robbers of the land are the chiefest cause of the dearth, for, though they labour not, and yet they spend doubly as much as the labourer doth, for they lie idly in the ale-houses day and night, eating and drinking excessively. And within these three months I took a thief, that was executed this last assizes, that confessed unto me that he and two more lay in an ale-house three weeks in which time they ate twenty fat sheep, whereof they stole every night one, besides they break many a poor man's plough by stealing an ox or two from him. . . . I may justly say that the able men that are abroad seeking the spoil and confusion of the land are able, if they were reduced to good subjection, to give the greatest enemy her Majesty hath a strong battle; and as they are now they are so much strength unto the enemy; besides, the generation that daily springeth from them is like to be most wicked.

THE STRANGE ELIZABETHANS

VIRGINIA WOOLF · 1932

There are few greater delights than to go back three or four hundred years and become in fancy at least an Elizabethan. That such fancies are only fancies, that this "becoming an Elizabethan," this reading sixteenth-century writing as cur-

From *The Second Common Reader*, by Virginia Woolf, copyright, 1932, by Harcourt, Brace and Company, Inc.

rently and certainly as we read our own is an illusion, is no doubt true. Very likely the Elizabethans would find our pronunciation of their language unintelligible; our fancy picture of what it pleases us to call Elizabethan life would rouse their ribald merriment. Still, the instinct that drives us to them is so strong and the freshness and vigour that blow through their pages are so sweet that we willingly run the risk of being laughed at, of being ridiculous.

And if we ask why we go further astray in this particular region of English literature than in any other, the answer is no doubt that Elizabethan prose, for all its beauty and bounty, was a very imperfect medium. It was almost incapable of fulfilling one of the offices of prose which is to make people talk, simply and naturally, about ordinary things. In an age of utilitarian prose like our own, we know exactly how people spend the hours between breakfast and bed, how they behave when they are neither one thing nor the other, neither angry nor loving, neither happy nor miserable. Poetry ignores these slighter shades; the social student can pick up hardly any facts about daily life from Shakespeare's plays; and if prose refuses to enlighten us, then one avenue of approach to the men and women of another age is blocked. Elizabethan prose, still scarcely separated off from the body of its poetry, could speak magnificently, of course, about the great themes —how life is short, and death certain; how spring is lovely, and winter horrid—perhaps, indeed, the lavish and towering periods that it raises above these simple platitudes are due to the fact that it has not cheapened itself upon trifles. But the price it pays for this soaring splendour is to be found in its awkwardness when it comes to earth—when Lady Sidney, for example, finding herself cold at nights, has to solicit the Lord Chamberlain for a better bedroom at Court. Then any housemaid of her own age could put her case more simply and with greater force. Thus, if we go to the Elizabethan prose-writers to solidify the splendid world of Elizabethan poetry as we should go now to our biographers, novelists, and journalists to solidify the world of Pope, of Tennyson, of Conrad, we are perpetually baffled and driven from our quest. What, we ask, was the life of an ordinary man or woman in the time of Shakespeare? Even the familiar letters of the time give us little help. Sir Henry Wotton is pompous and ornate and keeps us stiffly at arm's-length. Their histories resound with drums and trumpets. Their broadsheets reverberate with meditations upon death and reflections upon the immortality of the soul. Our best chance of finding them off their guard and so becoming at ease with them is to seek one of those unambitious men who haunt the outskirts of famous gatherings, listening, observing, sometimes taking a note in a book. But they are difficult to find. Gabriel Harvey perhaps, the friend of Spenser and of Sidney, might have fulfilled that function. Unfortunately the values of the time persuaded him that to write about rhetoric, to write about Thomas Smith, to write about Queen Elizabeth in Latin, was better worth doing than to record the table talk of Spenser and Sir Philip Sidney. But he possessed to some extent the modern instinct for preserving trifles, for keeping copies of letters, and for making notes of ideas that struck him in the margins of books. If we rummage among these fragments we shall, at any rate, leave the highroad and perhaps hear some roar of laughter from a tavern door, where poets are drinking; or meet humble people going about their milking and their lovemaking without a thought that this is the great Elizabethan age, or that Shakespeare is at this moment strolling down the Strand and might tell one, if one plucked him by the sleeve, to whom he wrote the sonnets, and what he meant by Hamlet.

The first person whom we meet is indeed a milkmaid—Gabriel Harvey's sister Mercy. In the winter of 1574 she was milking in the fields near Saffron Walden accompanied by an old woman, when a man approached her and offered her cakes and malmsey wine. When they had eaten and drunk in a wood and the old woman had wandered off to pick up sticks, the man proceeded to explain his business. He came from Lord Surrey, a youth of about Mercy's own age—seventeen or eighteen that is—and a married man. He had been bowling one day and had seen the milkmaid; her hat had blown off and "she had somewhat changed her colour." In short, Lord Surrey had fallen passionately in love with her; and sent her by the same man gloves, a silk girdle, and an enamel posy ring which he had torn from his own hat though his Aunt, Lady W——, had given it him for a very different purpose. Mercy at first stood her ground. She was a poor milkmaid, and he was a noble gentleman. But at last she agreed to meet him at her house in the village. Thus, one very misty, foggy night just before Christmas, Lord Surrey and his servant came to Saffron Walden. They peered in at the malthouse, but saw only her mother and sisters; they peeped in at the parlour, but only her brothers were there. Mercy herself was not to be seen; and "well mired and wearied for their labour," there was nothing for it but to ride back home again. Finally, after further parleys, Mercy agreed to meet Lord Surrey in a neighbour's house alone at midnight. She found him in the little parlour "in his doublet and hose, his points untrust, and his shirt lying round about him." He tried to force her on to the bed; but she cried out, and the good wife, as had been agreed between them, rapped on the door and said she was sent for. Thwarted, enraged, Lord Surrey cursed and swore, "God confound me, God confound me," and by way of lure emptied his pockets of all the money in them—thirteen shillings in shillings and testers it came to—and made her finger it. Still, however, Mercy made off, untouched, on condition that she would come again on Christmas Eve. But when Christmas Eve dawned she was up betimes and had put seven miles be-

tween her and Saffron Walden by six in the morning, though
it snowed and rained so that the floods were out, and P., the
servant, coming later to the place of assignation, had to pick
his way through the water in pattens. So Christmas passed.
And a week later, in the very nick of time to save her honour,
the whole story very strangely was discovered and brought
to an end. On New Year's Eve her brother Gabriel, the
young fellow of Pembroke Hall, was riding back to Cambridge when he came up with a simple countryman whom he
had met at his father's house. They rode on together, and
after some country gossip, the man said that he had a letter
for Gabriel in his pocket. Indeed, it was addressed "To my
loving brother Mr. G. H.," but when Gabriel opened it there
on the road, he found that the address was a lie. It was not
from his sister Mercy, but to his sister Mercy. "Mine Own
Sweet Mercy," it began; and it was signed "Thine more than
ever his own Phil." Gabriel could hardly control himself—
"could scarcely dissemble my sudden fancies and comprimitt
my inward passions"—as he read. For it was not merely a love-
letter; it was more; it talked about possessing Mercy according
to promise. There was also a fair English noble wrapped up
in the paper. So Gabriel, doing his best to control himself
before the countryman, gave him back the letter and the coin
and told him to deliver them both to his sister at Saffron
Walden with this message: "To look ere she leap. She may
pick out the English of it herself." He rode on to Cambridge;
he wrote a long letter to the young lord, informing him with
ambiguous courtesy that the game was up. The sister of
Gabriel Harvey was not to be the mistress of a married nobleman. Rather she was to be a maid, "diligent, and trusty and
tractable," in the house of Lady Smith at Audley End. Thus
Mercy's romance breaks off; the clouds descend again; and
we no longer see the milkmaid, the old woman, the treacherous serving man who came with malmsey and cakes and rings

and ribbons to tempt a poor girl's honour while she milked her cows.

This is probably no uncommon story; there must have been many milkmaids whose hats blew off as they milked their cows, and many lords whose hearts leapt at the sight so that they plucked the jewels from their hats and sent their servants to make treaty for them. But it is rare for the girl's own letters to be preserved or to read her own account of the story as she was made to deliver it at her brother's inquisition. Yet when we try to use her words to light up the Elizabethan field, the Elizabethan house and living-room, we are met by the usual perplexities. It is easy enough, in spite of the rain and the fog and the floods, to make a fancy piece out of the milkmaid and the meadows and the old woman wandering off to pick up sticks. Elizabethan song-writers have taught us too well the habit of that particular trick. But if we resist the impulse to make museum pieces out of our reading, Mercy herself gives us little help. She was a milkmaid, scribbling love-letters by the light of a farthing dip in an attic. Nevertheless, the sway of the Elizabethan convention was so strong, the accent of their speech was so masterful, that she bears herself with a grace and expresses herself with a resonance that would have done credit to a woman of birth and literary training. When Lord Surrey pressed her to yield she replied:

The thing you wot of, Milord, were a great trespass towards God, a great offence to the world, a great grief to my friends, a great shame to myself, and, as I think, a great dishonour to your lordship. I have heard my father say, Virginity is ye fairest flower in a maid's garden, and chastity ye richest dowry a poor wench can have. . . . Chastity, they say, is like unto time, which, being once lost, can no more be recovered.

Words chime and ring in her ears, as if she positively enjoyed the act of writing. When she wishes him to know that she is only a poor country girl and no fine lady like his wife, she exclaims, "Good Lord, that you should seek after so bare and country stuff abroad, that have so costly and courtly wares at home!" She even breaks into a jog-trot of jingling rhyme, far less sonorous than her prose, but proof that to write was an art, not merely a means of conveying facts. And if she wants to be direct and forcible, the proverbs she has heard in her father's house come to her pen, the biblical imagery runs in her ears: "And then were I, poor wench, cast up for hawk's meat, to mine utter undoing, and my friends' exceeding grief." In short, Mercy the milkmaid writes a natural and noble style, which is incapable of vulgarity, and equally incapable of intimacy. Nothing, one feels, would have been easier for Mercy than to read her lover a fine discourse upon the vanity of grandeur, the loveliness of chastity, the vicissitudes of fortune. But of emotion as between one particular Mercy, and one particular Phillip, there is no trace. And when it comes to dealing exactly in a few words with some mean object—when, for example, the wife of Sir Henry Sidney, the daughter of the Duke of Northumberland, has to state her claim to a better room to sleep in, she writes for all the world like an illiterate servant girl who can neither form her letters nor spell her words nor make one sentence follow smoothly after another. She haggles, she niggles, she wears our patience down with her repetitions and her prolixities. Hence it comes about that we know very little about Mercy Harvey, the milkmaid, who wrote so well, or Mary Sidney, daughter to the Duke of Northumberland, who wrote so badly. The background of Elizabethan life eludes us.

ELIZABETHAN ENGLAND

ROY LAMSON AND HALLETT SMITH · 1942

England, when Elizabeth Tudor came to the throne in 1558, was a country small in population, backward in industrial techniques and in exploration and discovery, and poor in the production of wealth and the consumption of goods. She was relatively isolated and provincial. During the previous century and a half her social fabric had been torn by the civil wars of the Roses in the fifteenth century and by the dispossession of the monastic orders under Henry VIII. The two short reigns of Edward VI and Mary had sharply focused the struggle, which was both religious and political, between Catholics and Protestants. There was little reason to suppose that the next half century would be one of the most glorious periods in English history.

How it came about is one of the complexes of history, and no narrative does real justice to the facts. Probably the most important development is the growth of the population, from the two and a half to three millions for England and Wales at the beginning of the reign, to a point at which the need for new markets, new sources of raw materials, new country for settlers caused the expansion and energy we think of as typical of the age. Since the feudal aristocracy and the vested interests of Rome had been destroyed, the men who felt the new spirit and who profited from it were new people, the middle class.

Chief among these was the Queen herself. Her royal line went back only two generations before her, and she was still able to feel and see like the new men who were her most gifted statesmen and her most enterprising adventurers. To be sure,

From *The Golden Hind*, copyright 1942 by W. W. Norton & Company, Inc.

she had more political talent than any of them, and this ability, coupled with a set of fortunate circumstances, brought about the unification of England and the growth of a real feeling of nationality. It was painfully evident to Englishmen that any alternative to Elizabeth, such as Mary Queen of Scots, would mean civil war. And the Papal bull excommunicating Elizabeth, issued in 1570, made it a pious act for any Catholic to assassinate her. The response of Englishmen was fervent and typical: they did not like civil war and they did not like political interference by a foreign power. So national spirit and loyalty to the crown rose to a great pitch, climaxed by the glorious defeat of the Spanish Armada in 1588. After that there was a certain disillusionment. The Queen had not married and the succession to the crown was in some doubt; the two extremist parties were not fundamentally reconciled; and even though England had successfully challenged the might of Spain and established herself as a sea power, one felt that domestic peace and security were only temporary. Elizabeth's middle ground in religion was to insist upon outward conformity, order, and discipline, without prying too much into men's private opinions. Naturally, the religious compromise, or Settlement as it was called, was attacked by the Catholics on one side and the Puritans on the other. Although no compromise would work permanently, Elizabeth's position was probably closer than either of its alternatives to the hearts of the majority of Englishmen.

In spite of the prominence of the religio-political controversy, English civilization became markedly more secular during the second half of the sixteenth century. England was not ready for the influences of the Italian Renaissance when they were first offered in the fourteenth and fifteenth centuries. Chaucer was an early but false spring. And when these influences, for the glorification of life on this earth, for the realization of the tremendous possibilities inherent in man, began to be really felt in England, they coincided with a great economic and social change. The enclosure of fields for pasture altered the whole agricultural character of the country and carried with it profound social disruption. The decrease in the supply of wood for fuel led to the exploitation of coal and laid a foundation for the industrial revolution. The one great English export trade, wool and woolen cloth, was supplemented by others, and these new businesses offered to any enterprising English yeoman the opportunity to become a capitalist, as many of them did. The difficulties of trade with Europe and the East forced Englishmen to turn to the Western Hemisphere. Strange as it may seem, the Atlantic was a safer highway for English ships than the Mediterranean. Enterprise in America meant, of course, rivalry with the Spaniard; but conveniently enough, Spain was also the enemy on political and religious grounds. So Francis Drake, in harassing the ships of King Philip, was a kind of pirate-patriot. (Besides, his ventures sometimes returned a profit on the investment of as high as 5,000 per cent!)

The influx of American mineral wealth, the argosies that yearly stuffed old Philip's treasury and sometimes the coffers of English stockholders, naturally produced in Europe in the latter half of the century an ever-increasing rise in prices. This phenomenon meant great hardship for the poor, and the literature of the time is full of pictures of beggars, rogues, and vagabonds. At the other extreme, those who had money spent it lavishly. The English were conscious of their lack of splendor in comparison with continental countries, and they indiscriminately aped the fashions of the continent. Dress was expensive, luxurious, and sometimes fantastic. Houses were no longer built of timber and clay, but of oak (formerly reserved for churches, noblemen's houses, and ships) or even of stone, lath, and plaster. And as usual in such periods, there were many complaints that the accumulation of wealth meant the decay of men.

In the court the greatest opportunities existed, but there also were the greatest disappointments to be found. "It was overrun with place-seekers," says Miss Byrne's account of it, "but it was also undeniably the focus of the national life. It drew to it the clever mountebanks, but also the real vigour and talent. It captured and stimulated men's imaginations, even if, eventually, it disheartened them." Men like Sir Christopher Hatton and Sir Walter Ralegh leaped from obscurity to great power and prominence as a result of their success as courtiers, but it must not be forgotten that they had abilities other than those of the gallantry and dancing which have made them famous in anecdote.

Though most of the literature which is still considered worth reading shows the predominant influence of the court, it would be a mistake to underestimate the influence of the city of London on the literary taste and production of the period. London had grown tremendously since the time of Chaucer. Instead of a population of about 50,000 it had 93,-276 in 1563; 123,034 in 1580; 152,478 in 1593–1595; and 224,-275 in 1605. It was by far the most important city in the realm, and the political history of the seventeenth century is understandable only if one recognizes the great power the city had, even as against the crown. The printing press was located in London, the publishers were located in London, and the mass of the middle-class population which set the style for the literature written for the ordinary man lived in London.

The Tudor sovereigns of England were themselves highly literate, and Henry VIII and Elizabeth, at least, had definite ambitions as authors. What more natural, therefore, than that the writers should see in the glorification of their ruler a service which was both humanistic and political? Much of the praise of the Queen which is so prominent in Elizabethan literature seems to modern taste fulsome and fawning, and no doubt the possibility of personal reward was present in the mind of most authors. But there was also a social service performed by this propaganda; it was the concentration of the feeling of many inarticulate Englishmen, and it was a great builder of what we would now call public morale.

The Elizabethans, having a very different view of history from the one we now hold, were extremely conscious of posterity. They did not consider that future ages would look down on them with contempt, because they thought the world was not getting better, but worse. Rather they felt that it was the duty of their generation to give posterity something worthy of the veneration the future would feel for them. Hamlet, in many ways a representative of the English Renaissance, makes his last concern in this life a concern for the fame that will outlive him. Every sixteenth-century gentleman would have understood and sympathized. From the time of Homer's celebration of Achilles it had been notorious that the poet had more to do with the fame of a great man than anyone else. The social utility of poetry was that it preserved and recorded for the admiration and guidance of the future the heroism of the past. Poetry could do this more effectively than history, and it could preserve the memory of greatness far longer than material monuments or inscriptions. "Not marble nor the gilded monuments of princes shall outlive this powerful rhyme," promised Shakespeare, and other poets with less justification felt equal assurance.

XII

The Gilded Age

❋ ❋ ❋ ❋ ❋ ❋ ❋ ❋ ❋ ❋ ❋ ❋ ❋ ❋ ❋ ❋ ❋

THIS SECTION presents, in four portraits of an age, the lavish entertainments given by American millionaires during the eighties and nineties. The extravagance of that era is epitomized in the grand ball, originally an object of wonder and admiration, but almost immediately a symbol of selfish materialism and bad taste. The dilemma of the *Tribune* reporters, whose exuberant descriptions of the late Roman splendor of the Bradley Martin entertainment contributed to popular riots, is revealed within twenty-four hours. There are few more amusing examples of mending a fence and at the same time straddling it than that in the paragraphs written for the *Tribune* "after the ball."

The tone of these descriptions is complex: at once scornful and nostalgic, satiric, self-righteous, and frankly hostile. The honest confusion of the *Tribune* reports contrasts sharply with the dedicated attack made by the Beards; and Crouse's sly ridicule is mingled with a secret excitement very different from Edith Wharton's affectionate but sharp rejection of the ruthlessness in this society which she really understood. These subtleties of tone are achieved by combining the extravagant and colorful details of wealth and display with unblushingly loaded editorial comment. Gold, sables, velvets, and dollar bills become glaring and gaudy in the white light of commentary characterized by words such as "parvenu," "stampede," "shabby," and the figures of speech which stud the Beards' account. None of these portraits of an era can be

219

called purely factual or unbiased. Each should be measured in the spectrum from naïveté to malice, from photograph to caricature.

❊ ❊ ❊ ❊ ❊ ❊ ❊ ❊ ❊ ❊ ❊ ❊ ❊ ❊ ❊ ❊ ❊ ❊

THE BRADLEY MARTIN BALL

A NEWSPAPER ACCOUNT · FEBRUARY 10, 1897

After weeks of anticipation on the part of the public and of preparation on the part of the hostess and her guests, the Bradley Martin fancy dress ball took place last night at the Hotel Waldorf. The affair had been censured by some, highly commended by more and awaited with interest by all. It is safe to say that no affair of the sort in this city has aroused more widespread attention than the ball that took place in the famous Fifth-avenue hostelry between the hours of 11 o'clock last evening and 5 o'clock this morning. A variety of circumstances combined to induce this condition of affairs. The ball in itself was bound to arouse a great deal of interest both in society and among the millions who do not form a part of that body, but whose interest in its doings is both great and continuous.

A new turn was given to the anticipation of the public, however, by the utterance of one of the city's clergymen, who was not only among the best known of the metropolitan wearers of the cloth, but whose congregation included many

An abridgement of five full columns of report upon the ball published in the *New York Daily Tribune*, Thursday, February, 11, 1897, and from an account of preparations for the ball which appeared in the *Tribune* on the Sunday preceding. In a few cases it has been necessary to modify the tense of verb forms in order to combine the events described by different reporters.

of the most fashionable and wealthy citizens of New York. This clergyman, the Rev. Dr. Rainsford, rector of St. George's Protestant Episcopal Church, while disclaiming any desire to attack the propriety of the Bradley Martin ball in particular, declared that all exhibitions of wealth and its lavish use were much out of place in hard times such as the present. Dr. Rainsford furthermore said that he had advised some of his parishioners against countenancing the Bradley Martin ball by attending it. This utterance naturally provoked a storm of comment, for and against, which did not die away up to the day of the ball.

But in spite of all criticisms the preparations for the ball went steadily on and interest in the affair rather increased than diminished. To no social function, not even to the visit of the Prince of Wales to this country, or the fancy dress ball given by Mrs. W. K. Vanderbilt, have the newspapers of the country given anything like the amount of attention.

The expense attending Mrs. Martin's ball, which was the cause of much adverse criticism, was doubtless great, but that it was greater than that attending any similar function given in this country is not certain. Mrs. Martin limited the period to be covered by the costumes to the sixteenth, seventeenth and eighteenth centuries, while the costumes at Mrs. Vanderbilt's ball in 1883 were not limited to any period. Mrs. Martin too waited before making her final announcements until it was too late for her guests to have their costumes made abroad. This delay Mrs. Martin made purposely, in order that American tailors and costumers might reap the benefits of the money spent on the preparation of clothes for the ball. Preparations were made at the Waldorf for something more than 1,050 guests, probably at least 400 more than were present at the famous ball in 1883.

Mrs. Martin arranged for the 200 attendants at the ball to wear the usual evening livery of the Waldorf, with the addition that the lapels and fronts of their dress coats were embellished with gold embroidery and brass buttons. Mrs. Martin's servants appeared in costumes of the sixteenth, seventeenth and eighteenth centuries.

The florist who had charge of the decorations spent weeks in laying his plans. His men, eighty in number, took charge of the entire western end of the two lower floors of the Waldorf on Tuesday night and did not stop work until an hour before the guests began to arrive last night. The entire force of the hotel servants was on duty; the number mounted up to something more than 750. A force of French hairdressers took possession of one of the smaller rooms on the second floor and devoted themselves to the care of the coiffures of the guests.

Outside the hotel the people who wanted to see what they could not see continued to increase in number, and by 9 o'clock the policemen in the block were obliged to argue with them to prevent them from forming a blockade in front of the Waldorf. In the next hour fifty more policemen were summoned and formed lines across Thirty-third-street at Fifth-avenue. The crowds became so dense that at 10 o'clock the police, who were present in large numbers, were obliged to clear Thirty-third-street in order to allow the carriages of the guests to deposit their owners. In Fifth-avenue the crowd was even greater, and a great mass of people stood packed together to look at the carriages although their curiosity could not have been gratified to any great extent.

Mrs. Martin, in a costume of the Marie Stuart period, the entire dress richly and elaborately embroidered with pearls and jewels, received the guests in the small ballroom. Guests and their costumes: Mrs. Astor, in a gown of dark plum-colored velvet with Van Dyke collar and white lace, the corsage covered with a stomacher of jewels which Mrs. Astor did not wear when painted for her portrait in the same gown by Carolus Duran. Miss Edith Blight in an Empire gown embroidered all over with gold spangles and a court train from the shoulders of coral colored velvet trimmed with sable. Elisha Dyer, jr. a Francis I costume cloak of purple velvet lined with a violet satin and heavily embroidered with gold. Walter Poultney of Baltimore a Kohler costume made full of white satin, 200 slashes of blue silk profusely trimmed with pearls. . . .

The principal feature of the ball after it had really been opened was the quadrille d'honneur, which was organized and rehearsed in the ballroom of Mrs. Astor's house. The dancers entered the room to Beethoven's music in pairs, and the three intricate figures of which the dance is made up were gone through precisely as they were when danced 100 years ago by kings and queens and their court attendants.

Supper was served continuously from midnight until the last guest had entered his carriage. The café and the winter garden, with their 125 flower-laden tables, were utilized for supper rooms, while the small reception-room to the left of the main entrance was given over for the service to guests of all sorts of liquid refreshments from champagne to bouillon.

The arrangements for the departure of the guests were somewhat unique. Instead of being called for by their own carriages, Mrs. Martin arranged for 400 other carriages to be on hand when the ball was over, and for the guests to take whatever carriage was at the door when they left the hotel.

A NEWSPAPER COMMENT: AFTER THE BALL · FEBRUARY 12, 1897

Now that the Bradley Martin ball is a matter of social history, many of the opinions that were formed of it in advance will have to undergo considerable revision. It is certain that most

Condensed from the *New York Daily Tribune*, Friday, February 12, 1897.

of the estimates of its cost, which were the bases of much of
the hostile criticism, were greatly in excess of the real figures.
This does not mean that Mrs. Martin's ball was not a lavish,
even a sumptuous, affair. It was undoubtedly complete in all
its appointments . . . The estimates of the cost of the ball
which appeared in several newspapers were sufficiently large
to reach the point of absurdity. One of these estimates was
$500,000, another $350,000, still another $250,000—a quarter
of a million dollars. All of these estimates are plainly so far
beyond the truth as to make this contradiction scarcely worth
while.

Various wild guesses have been made at the cost of the use
of the Waldorf for the ball. As a matter of fact, that cost
is known to have been less than $5,000. It had been predicted
that the supper would be more profuse and more varied than
any before provided for any social function in this city. A
glance at the menu card will suffice to show that while it was
of an elaborate and expensive nature, its like is not unprece-
dented. The wines used at the ball were brought by Mr.
Martin from Europe.

The bill for carriage hire, too, could not have been nearly
so large as it is said to be in the extravagant estimates mentioned.
The floral decorations aside from the extent of the space upon
which they were bestowed, were not of a character to involve
enormous expense. They were faithfully described in yesterday's *Tribune* and were seen to be tasteful throughout, but
neither profuse nor heavy nor especially rare.

THE FOUR HUNDRED

RUSSEL CROUSE · 1931

It was in the late '80's that society at last threatened to get out of hand. Parvenus were storming the doors. Gentlefolk were resentful but helpless. They might have given way to the stampede had it not been for a shrewd, somewhat shabby Southerner with a gift for organization and an ability to capitalize snobbishness. Ward McAllister was a Georgian, who came to New York to live with a wealthy aunt, in the self-confessed hope that she would enrich him in her will.

Society recognized that prospect, too, and admitted him to its fringes. But the dear old lady, when at last she released the ghost, left a million to the Presbyterian Church and the Georgia Historical Society. Mr. McAllister's legacy was a meagre $1,000, which he promptly spent for a fancy-dress costume in which to plunge deeper into the social whirl he had chosen for a career.

Within a few years he had formed an alliance with Mrs. Astor which was to establish that austere lady as an empress with strange and far-reaching power. In her day it would have been unnecessary to explain that she was Mrs. William Astor. She was simply Mrs. Astor. There were other wives of Astors, but there was only one Mrs. Astor.

Society had wanted to be snobbish but had not known how. It was Mr. McAllister who capitalized the desire. Unwittingly, he coined the expression "The Four Hundred," which is still in use, although in its last edition the Social Register contained more than forty thousand names. It came about because Mrs. Astor's ballroom would hold no more than that number. And

From *It Seems Like Yesterday*, by Russel Crouse. Copyright 1931 by Russel Crouse; reprinted by permission of Doubleday & Company, Inc.

so he pared the list of the elect to a figure embraceable by its four walls.

Mrs. Astor gave her receptions, sitting in a high-backed chair beneath Carolus Duran's portrait of her. She gave three dinners a year and one ball. She went to Europe in February and returned in July to open her home in Newport. Mr. McAllister did his best to make the Rhode Island resort gay, but his imagination pictured nothing more thrilling than picnics—lawn picnics, beach picnics, picnics in the woods, yacht picnics.

Throughout the years of the Astor dynasty the nouveau riche sought in vain to find a foothold on the social ladder. There was none for them. It was a revolt within the ranks of the elect themselves that brought the downfall of the imperious strategist Mr. McAllister. With increasing frequency he overstepped the bounds of graciousness in his manipulations.

Finally, when he assumed complete charge of the Centennial Ball in 1889, ignoring the members of a committee that had been named to arrange it, he found rebels on his hands. He sought to override them with intimidating hauteur, but his secret was so easily discovered—the secret of organization —that it was not at all difficult to depose him. He died, discredited and almost forgotten, in 1895.

The revolt, however, was not aimed at Mrs. Astor, and she continued to reign, now with a new prime minister. This one was far more colorful, impudent rather than insolent.

He was to teach Mrs. Astor a thing or two in loftiness that had not occurred to Mr. McAllister. It was Mr. Lehr's idea that the queen of society should show a royal contempt for practically everything. It was his idea that she should attend the opera only for an hour. And so Mrs. Astor would time her stay in Box No. 7, and when she left, all who would be fashionable left with her.

It was this contempt that almost toppled the aristocracy in

1897. It was a year of widespread depression in which not a few of those born free and equal were actually starving. And yet Mr. and Mrs. Bradley-Martin chose the moment for the most lavish display of wealth the city has ever known.

The occasion was a costume ball at the new Waldorf Hotel. The Four Hundred—now Eight Hundred—threw every jewel into an ill-timed display of wealth. Mrs. Bradley-Martin herself was a gold-embroidered, pearl-bedecked Mary Stewart. Other royalty was impersonated as extravagantly. Five florists were necessary for the decorations and three orchestras for the music.

It was as though society had decided to flaunt its wealth in the face of bread lines. Preachers inveighed against the display, and yellow journals stormed. The rabble began to murmur threats of anarchy, and in the end the gilded guests had to have police escort to and from the proceedings.

Mrs. Astor's throne survived the incident. She was too firmly intrenched for disorganized discontent. However, age at last began to dim the glory of the empress. Crushed under the weight of the conventions she herself had established, her shoulders began to sag. She gave her last ball in 1904 and began slowly to recede into the shadows.

THE GILDED AGE

CHARLES A. AND MARY R. BEARD · 1927

Housed in a grand style, like the great of old, the American captains of business enterprise poured out their riches in the purchase of goods. As the new men of Rome in Cicero's day,

From *The Rise of American Civilization*, by Charles and Mary Beard. Used by permission of The Macmillan Company.

more acquisitive than creative, despoiled Egypt and Greece
of their treasures, so the plutocracy of the United States ran-
sacked the palaces, churches, abbeys, castles, and ateliers of
Europe for statuary, paintings, pottery, rugs, and every other
form of art. Even the Orient was forced to yield up graven
goddesses of mercy and complacent Buddhas to decorate the
buildings of men absorbed in making soap, steel rails, whisky,
and cotton bagging and to please the women who spent the
profits of business enterprise. The armor of mediaeval knights
soon stood in the halls of captains of industry whose boldest
strokes were courageous guesses on the stock market or the
employment of Pinkerton detectives against striking working-
men; while Mandarin coats from Peking sprawled on the
pianos of magnates who knew not Ming or Manchu and perhaps could not tell whether their hired musicians were grinding out Wagner or Chopin. Grand ladies, who remembered
with a blush the days when they laundered the family clothes,
shone idly resplendent in jewels garnered by a search of two
hemispheres. European tutors were imported to teach the "new
people" and their offspring "parlor and table etiquette," music
and "appreciation," as Greek preceptors had served Roman
families in the time of Cicero. European artists were brought
over to design and decorate for them as the artists of Athens
were summoned to beautify the homes of Trimalchio's con-
temporaries. Private libraries of the "sets," rare editions, and
rich bindings were quickly assembled in job lots to give tone to
establishments—a diversion that afforded gratifying appearances of culture with none of its laborious penalties. Almost
buried in a deluge of alien goods, the vestiges of colonial taste,
which though derivative had become acclimatized, survived
only in rural districts, North and South, out of the range of
the grand plutocracy.

Having discovered that they could buy palaces and import

them to America, sticks, stones, carvings, and tiles, the *novi homines* assumed, by no means without respectable sanction, that they could buy their way into "the best families" of two hemispheres. On the eve of the Civil War there had been many "seasoned clans" on the eastern seaboard, some of them dating their origins back a hundred years or more, and boasting of ancestors who had served as preachers, judges, warriors, and statesmen in colonial times, in the heroic epoch of the Revolution, and in the momentous age of the new republic. Able to hold their own socially, if not politically, these select families had absorbed with facility the seepage of rising fortunes that gradually oozed into their ranks—until the flood of the new plutocracy descended upon them. In that crisis all who were not fortunate enough to multiply their estates had to be content with genteel poverty or surrender to the owners of riches reeking of the market.

Since there was no legalized aristocracy into which Dives could be compelled to win his way by purchase, politics, cajolery, or philanthropy, it was necessary to resort to a kind of dictatorship. It was by this process that a portion of the plutocracy of New York was brought for a time under the sway of a social sovereign, Mrs. William Astor, capable of setting a fashionable standard for the city and thus for the nation. The founder of the house had come over as a penniless immigrant at the close of the eighteenth century but had quickly laid the basis of a family fortune by operations in furs, hides, and real estate, making it possible for his children to work wonders in the cultural line.

At last when the queenly heiress by wifely right assumed the reins in New York society, she had all the material substance required for her rôle. She wore regal jewelry and wore it regally; she erected a court and selected its courtiers— limited to four hundred because that was the number which her ballroom would comfortably hold; she had heralds to announce her activities, a public dazzled by her splendor, and newspapers, as eager as any court gazette, to make known her magnificence to those that sat in outer gloom. Moreover, she was ably assisted by a southern gentleman, Ward McAllister, the last Beau Brummel of his school. Thus conditioned, her experiment was successful beyond all hopes for many years—indeed until the invasion of "steel barons, coal lords, dukes of wheat and beef," decribed by Mrs. John King Van Rensselaer, broke the floodgates at the close of the century. But by that time the dictatorship had won recognition abroad; it had paved the way for the leaders to ascend into English society; and it had won titles for many of the high participants.

With extraordinary swiftness a wedge was driven into the English line in 1874 by the marriage of Miss Jennie Jerome, daughter of a Wall Street broker, and Lord Randolph Churchill. There had of course been earlier conquests; Miss Bingham, daughter of a rich Philadelphia merchant in Washington's time, had married Alexander Baring, later Lord Ashburton, but that leap into the nobility had been by accident rather than carefully nourished design. It was the marriage of Miss Jerome that broke the ice, for her exploit was quickly followed by other international matches. The daughter of a railway king married a descendant of the hero of Blenheim; a granddaughter of a daring speculator in stocks and gold wedded a French count; the Leiter millions of Chicago were merged with the estate of Lord Curzon, that "very superior person." Finally the conquering power of the almighty dollar was completely demonstrated when William Waldorf Astor shook the dust of the United States from his feet, invaded the British Isles, acquired an English peerage by the usual method, and landed in the House of Lords among a host of English cotton spinners, soap magnates, tobacconists, journalists, and successful brokers.

THE AGE OF INNOCENCE

EDITH WHARTON · 1920

It invariably happened in the same way. Mrs. Julius Beaufort, on the night of her annual ball, never failed to appear at the Opera; indeed, she always gave her ball on an Opera night in order to emphasise her complete superiority to household cares, and her possession of a staff of servants competent to organise every detail of the entertainment in her absence.

The Beauforts' house was one of the few in New York that possessed a ball-room (it antedated even Mrs. Manson Mingott's and the Headly Chiverses); and at a time when it was beginning to be thought "provincial" to put a "crash" over the drawing-room floor and move the furniture up-stairs, the possession of a ballroom that was used for no other purpose, and left for three-hundred-and-sixty-four days of the year to shuttered darkness, with its gilt chairs stacked in a corner and its chandelier in a bag; this undoubted superiority was felt to compensate for whatever was regrettable in the Beaufort past.

Mrs. Archer, who was fond of coining her social philosophy into axioms, had once said: "We all have our pet common people—" and though the phrase was a daring one, its truth was secretly admitted in many an exclusive bosom. But the Beauforts were not exactly common; some people said they were even worse. Mrs. Beaufort belonged indeed to one of America's most honoured families; she had been the lovely Regina Dallas (of the South Carolina branch), a penniless beauty introduced to New York society by her cousin, the imprudent Medora Manson, who was always doing the wrong

thing from the right motive. When one was related to the
Mansons and the Rushworths one had a *"droit de cité"* (as
Mr. Sillerton Jackson, who had frequented the Tuileries,
called it) in New York society; but did one not forfeit it in
marrying Julius Beaufort?

The question was: who *was* Beaufort? He passed for an
Englishman, was agreeable, handsome, ill-tempered, hospitable
and witty. He had come to America with letters of recom-
mendation from old Mrs. Manson Mingott's English son-in-
law, the banker, and had speedily made himself an important
position in the world of affairs; but his habits were dissipated,
his tongue was bitter, his antecedents were mysterious; and
when Medora Manson announced her cousin's engagement to
him it was felt to be one more act of folly in poor Medora's
long record of imprudences.

Mr. Beaufort's secret, people were agreed, was the way
he carried things off. It was all very well to whisper that he
had been "helped" to leave England by the international
banking-house in which he had been employed; he carried
off that rumour as easily as the rest—though New York's business conscience was no less sensitive than its moral standard
—he carried everything before him, and all New York into
his drawing-rooms, and for over twenty years now people
had said they were "going to the Beauforts' " with the same
tone of security as if they had said they were going to Mrs.
Manson Mingott's, and with the added satisfaction of knowing
they would get hot canvas-back ducks and vintage wines, instead of tepid Veuve Clicquot without a year and warmed-up
croquettes from Philadelphia.

Mrs. Beaufort, then, had as usual appeared in her box just
before the Jewel Song; and when, again as usual, she rose at
the end of the third act, drew her opera cloak about her lovely
shoulders, and disappeared, New York knew that meant that
half an hour later the ball would begin.

The Beaufort house was one that New Yorkers were proud to show to foreigners, especially on the night of the annual ball. The Beauforts had been among the first people in New York to own their own red velvet carpet and have it rolled down the steps by their own footmen, under their own awning, instead of hiring it with the supper and the ball-room chairs. They had also inaugurated the custom of letting the ladies take their cloaks off in the hall, instead of shuffling up to the hostess's bedroom and recurling their hair with the aid of the gas-burner; Beaufort was understood to have said that he supposed all his wife's friends had maids who saw to it that they were properly *coiffées* when they left home.

Then the house had been boldly planned with a ball-room, so that, instead of squeezing through a narrow passage to get to it (as at the Chiverses') one marched solemnly down a vista of enfiladed drawing-rooms (the sea-green, the crimson and the *bouton d'or*), seeing from afar the many-candled lustres reflected in the polished parquetry, and beyond that the depths of a conservatory where camellias and tree-ferns arched their costly foliage over seats of black and gold bamboo.

Newland Archer, as became a young man of his position, strolled in somewhat late. He had left his overcoat with the silk-stockinged footmen (the stockings were one of Beaufort's few fatuities), had dawdled a while in the library hung with Spanish leather and furnished with Buhl and malachite, where a few men were chatting and putting on their dancing-gloves, and had finally joined the line of guests whom Mrs. Beaufort was receiving on the threshold of the crimson drawing-room.

XIII
The Sea

❋ ❋ ❋ ❋ ❋ ❋ ❋ ❋ ❋ ❋ ❋ ❋ ❋ ❋ ❋ ❋ ❋ ❋

THE EMOTIONAL IMPACTS of the sea are at once so varied and so universally effective that it presents a challenging and difficult subject, though an endlessly attractive one. The most clear-headed scientist is moved to poetry, even when his sights are set upon the sea currents or the sea's creatures. These selections were chosen to emphasize the nonsubjective treatments of the sea and to illustrate scientific prose. In each of them, however, the author is moved by the very nature of the subject from the literal to what might be called a literary description. Miss Carson, for instance, constructs her essay upon a balance of great elemental forces: eternity and time, cycles and tides, land and sea, winter and spring. Conrad finds the sea aged and gray, with furrowed face and white locks. Melville, like Miss Carson, translates the sea into the vocabulary of the prairie: "sea-pastured," "flowery earth," "grasslands," "grazing." Beston enlarges the subject, as Miss Carson does, by association with the fundamental life cycle through such words as "fulfilment," "fecundity," "death." Because he is concerned particularly with the sound of the sea, Beston uses many onomatopoetic words: "hiss," "seethe," "grinding." The rhythms of the sea waves are echoed by the parallel clauses and repeated phrases of one after another of these descriptions.

Beston and Conrad, though they are impressed with the giant power of the sea, consider it intimately and immediately on Cape Cod and on a small steamer, but Miss Carson and

Melville extend the sea's edge to far, unknown places of the mind and the imagination. Miss Carson not only invokes the rolling proper names associated with places, but also makes the most romantic use of the strange scientific names of the minute sea creatures. Melville extends his short passage with biblical and mythological suggestions which associate the sea with the half-light of ancient gods and inspired wisdom.

The passage from Stephen Crane is introduced for contrast to the other selections. This bare recital, tense with uncertainty and physical strain, cruel with the ironic contrast between the safe indifferent shore and the fatal indifferent sea, depends for its effect upon understatement and the monotony of tired repetition, reflecting not only the endless power of the waves, but the fruitless exhaustion of shipwrecked men afloat for days in a lifeboat.

❋ ❋ ❋ ❋ ❋ ❋ ❋ ❋ ❋ ❋ ❋ ❋ ❋ ❋ ❋ ❋

THE OCEAN YEAR

RACHEL CARSON · 1950

For the sea as a whole, the alternation of day and night, the passage of the seasons, the procession of the years, are lost in its vastness, obliterated in its own changeless eternity. But the surface waters are different. The face of the sea is always changing. Crossed by colors, lights, and moving shadows, sparkling in the sun, mysterious in the twilight, its aspects and its moods vary hour by hour. The surface waters move with the tides, stir to the breath of the winds, and rise and fall to the endless, hurrying forms of the waves. Most of all, they

From *The Sea Around Us*, by Rachel Carson. Copyright, 1950, 1951, by Rachel L. Carson. Reprinted by permission of Oxford University Press, Inc.

change with the advance of the seasons. Spring moves over the temperate lands of our Northern Hemisphere in a tide of new life, of pushing green shoots and unfolding buds, all its mysteries and meanings symbolized in the northward migration of the birds, the awakening of sluggish amphibian life as the chorus of frogs rises again from the wet lands, the different sound of the wind which stirs the young leaves where a month ago it rattled the bare branches. These things we associate with the land, and it is easy to suppose that at sea there could be no such feeling of advancing spring. But the signs are there, and seen with understanding eye, they bring the same magical sense of awakening.

In the sea, as on land, spring is a time for the renewal of life. During the long months of winter in the temperate zones the surface waters have been absorbing the cold. Now the heavy water begins to sink, slipping down and displacing the warmer layers below. Rich stores of minerals have been accumulating on the floor of the continental shelf—some freighted down the rivers from the lands; some derived from sea creatures that have died and whose remains have drifted down to the bottom; some from the shells that once encased a diatom, the streaming protoplasm of a radiolarian, or the transparent tissues of a pteropod. Nothing is wasted in the sea; every particle of material is used over and over again, first by one creature, then by another. And when in spring the waters are deeply stirred, the warm bottom water brings to the surface a rich supply of minerals, ready for use by new forms of life.

Just as land plants depend on minerals in the soil for their growth, every marine plant, even the smallest, is dependent upon the nutrient salts or minerals in the sea water. Diatoms must have silica, the element of which their fragile shells are fashioned. For these and all other microplants, phosphorus is an indispensable mineral. Some of these elements are in short supply and in winter may be reduced below the minimum necessary for growth. The diatom population must tide itself over this season as best it can. It faces a stark problem of survival, with no opportunity to increase, a problem of keeping alive the spark of life by forming tough protective spores against the stringency of winter, a matter of existing in a dormant state in which no demands shall be made on an environment that already withholds all but the most meager necessities of life. So the diatoms hold their place in the winter sea, like seeds of wheat in a field under snow and ice, the seeds from which the spring growth will come.

These, then, are the elements of the vernal blooming of the sea: the 'seeds' of the dormant plants, the fertilizing chemicals, the warmth of the spring sun.

In a sudden awakening, incredible in its swiftness, the simplest plants of the sea begin to multiply. Their increase is of astronomical proportions. The spring sea belongs at first to the diatoms and to all the other microscopic plant life of the plankton. In the fierce intensity of their growth they cover vast areas of ocean with a living blanket of their cells. Mile after mile of water may appear red or brown or green, the whole surface taking on the color of the infinitesimal grains of pigment contained in each of the plant cells.

The plants have undisputed sway in the sea for only a short time. Almost at once their own burst of multiplication is matched by a similar increase in the small animals of the plankton. It is the spawning time of the copepod and the glass-worm, the pelagic shrimp and the winged snail. Hungry swarms of these little beasts of the plankton roam through the waters, feeding on the abundant plants and themselves falling prey to larger creatures. Now in the spring the surface waters become a vast nursery. From the hills and valleys of the continent's edge lying far below, and from the scattered shoals and banks, the eggs or young of many of the bottom animals rise to the surface of the sea. Even those which, in their maturity, will sink down to a sedentary life on the bottom, spend the first weeks of life as freely swimming hunters of the plankton. So as spring progresses new batches of larvae rise into the surface each day, the young of fishes and crabs and mussels and tube worms, mingling for a time with the regular members of the plankton.

Under the steady and voracious grazing, the grasslands of the surface are soon depleted. The diatoms become more and more scarce, and with them the other simple plants. Still there are brief explosions of one or another form, when in a sudden orgy of cell division it comes to claim whole areas of the sea for its own. So, for a time each spring, the waters may become blotched with brown, jellylike masses, and the fishermen's nets come up dripping a brown slime and containing no fish, for the herring have turned away from these waters as though in loathing of the viscid, foul-smelling algae. But in less time than passes between the full moon and the new, the spring flowering of Phaeocystis is past and the waters have cleared again.

In the spring the sea is filled with migrating fishes, some of them bound for the mouths of great rivers, which they will ascend to deposit their spawn. Such are the spring-run chinooks coming in from the deep Pacific feeding grounds to breast the rolling flood of the Columbia, the shad moving in to the Chesapeake and the Hudson and the Connecticut, the alewives seeking a hundred coastal streams of New England, the salmon feeling their way to the Androscoggin and the Kennebec. For months or years these fish have known only the vast spaces of the ocean. Now the spring sea and the maturing of their own bodies lead them back to the rivers of their birth.

Other mysterious comings and goings are linked with the

advance of the year. Capelin gather in the deep, cold water of the Barents Sea, their shoals followed and preyed upon by flocks of auks, fulmars, and kittiwakes. Cod approach the banks of Lofoten, and gather off the shores of Iceland. Birds whose winter feeding territory may have encompassed the whole Atlantic or the whole Pacific converge upon some small island, the entire breeding population arriving within the space of a few days. Whales suddenly appear off the slopes of the coastal banks where the swarms of shrimplike krill are spawning, the whales having come from no one knows where, by no one knows what route.

With the subsiding of the diatoms and the completed spawning of many of the plankton animals and most of the fish, life in the surface waters slackens to the slower pace of midsummer. Along the meeting places of the currents the pale moon jelly Aurelia gathers in thousands, forming sinuous lines or windrows across miles of sea, and the birds see their pale forms shimmering deep down in the green water. By midsummer the large red jellyfish Cyanea may have grown from the size of a thimble to that of an umbrella. The great jellyfish moves through the sea with rhythmic pulsations, trailing long tentacles and as likely as not sheperding a little group of young cod or haddock, which find shelter under its bell and travel with it.

A hard, brilliant, coruscating phosphorescence often illuminates the summer sea. In waters where the protozoan Noctiluca is abundant it is the chief source of this summer luminescence, causing fishes, squids, or dolphins to fill the water with racing flames and to clothe themselves in a ghostly radiance. Or again the summer sea may glitter with a thousand thousand moving pinpricks of light, like an immense swarm of fireflies moving through a dark wood. Such an effect is produced by a shoal of the brilliantly phosphorescent shrimp Meganyctiphanes, a creature of cold and darkness and of the places where icy water rolls upward from the depths and bubbles with white ripplings at the surface.

Out over the plankton meadows of the North Atlantic the dry twitter of the phalaropes, small brown birds, wheeling and turning, dipping and rising, is heard for the first time since early spring. The phalaropes have nested on the arctic tundras, reared their young, and now the first of them are returning to the sea. Most of them will continue south over the open water far from land, crossing the equator into the South Atlantic. Here they will follow where the great whales lead, for where the whales are, there also are the swarms of plankton on which these strange little birds grow fat.

As the fall advances, there are other movements, some in the surface, some hidden in the green depths, that betoken the end of summer. In the foggy waters of Bering Sea, down through the treacherous passes between the islands of the Aleutian chain and southward into the open Pacific, the herds of fur seals are moving. Left behind are two small islands, treeless bits of volcanic soil thrust up into the waters of Bering Sea. The islands are silent now, but for the several months of summer they resounded with the roar of millions of seals come ashore to bear and rear their young—all the fur seals of the eastern Pacific crowded into a few square miles of bare rock and crumbling soil. Now once more the seals turn south, to roam down along the sheer underwater cliffs of the continent's edge, where the rocky foundations fall away steeply into the deep sea. Here, in a blackness more absolute than that of arctic winter, the seals will find rich feeding as they swim down to prey on the fishes of this region of darkness.

Autumn comes to the sea with a fresh blaze of phosphorescence, when every wave crest is aflame. Here and there the whole surface may glow with sheets of cold fire, while below schools of fish pour through the water like molten metal. Often the autumnal phosphorescence is caused by a fall flowering of the dinoflagellates, multiplying furiously in a short-lived repetition of their vernal blooming.

Sometimes the meaning of the glowing water is ominous. Off the Pacific coast of North America, it may mean that the sea is filled with dinoflagellate Gonyaulax, a minute plant that contains a poison of strange and terrible virulence. About four days after Gonyaulax comes to dominate the coastal plankton, some of the fishes and shellfish in the vicinity become toxic. This is because, in their normal feeding, they have strained the poisonous plankton out of the water. Mussels accumulate the Gonyaulax toxins in their livers, and the toxins react on the human nervous system with an effect similar to that of strychnine. Because of these facts, it is generally understood along the Pacific coast that it is unwise to eat shellfish taken from coasts exposed to the open sea where Gonyaulax may be abundant, in summer or early fall. For generations before the white men came, the Indians knew this. As soon as the red streaks appeared in the sea and the waves began to flicker at night with the mysterious blue-green fires, the tribal leaders forbade the taking of mussels until these warning signals should have passed. They even set guards at intervals along the beaches to warn inlanders who might come down for shellfish and be unable to read the language of the sea.

But usually the blaze and glitter of the sea, whatever its meaning for those who produce it, implies no menace to man. Seen from the deck of a vessel in open ocean, a tiny, man-made observation point in the vast world of sea and sky, it has an eerie and unearthly quality. Man, in his vanity, subconsciously attributes a human origin to any light not of moon or stars or sun. Lights on the shore, lights moving over the water, mean lights kindled and controlled by other men, serving purposes understandable to the human mind. Yet here are lights that flash and fade away, lights that come and go for reasons meaningless to man, lights that have been doing this very thing over the eons of time in which there were no men to stir in vague disquiet.

Like the blazing colors of the autumn leaves before they wither and fall, the autumnal phosphorescence betokens the approach of winter. After their brief renewal of life the flagellates and the other minute algae dwindle away to a scattered few; so do the shrimps and the copepods, the glassworms and the comb jellies. The larvae of the bottom fauna have long since completed their development and drifted away to take up whatever existence is their lot. Even the roving fish schools have deserted the surface waters and have migrated into warmer latitudes or have found equivalent warmth in the deep, quiet waters along the edge of the continental shelf. There the torpor of semi-hibernation descends upon them and will possess them during the months of winter.

The surface waters now become the plaything of the winter gales. As the winds build up the giant storm waves and roar along their crests, lashing the water into foam and flying spray, it seems that life must forever have deserted this place.

But the symbols of hope are not lacking even in the grayness and bleakness of the winter sea. On land we know that the apparent lifelessness of winter is an illusion. Look closely at the bare branches of a tree, on which not the palest gleam of green can be discerned. Yet, spaced along each branch are the leaf buds, all the spring's magic of swelling green concealed and safely preserved under the insulating, overlapping layers. Pick off a piece of the rough bark of the trunk; there you will find hibernating insects. Dig down through the snow into the earth. There are the eggs of next summer's grasshoppers; there are the dormant seeds from which will come the grass, the herb, the oak tree.

So, too, the lifelessness, the hopelessness, the despair of the winter sea are an illusion. Everywhere are the assurances that the cycle has come to the full, containing the means of its own renewal. There is the promise of a new spring in the very iciness of the winter sea, in the chilling of the water, which must, before many weeks, become so heavy that it will plunge downward, precipitating the overturn that is the first act in the drama of spring. There is the promise of new life in the small plantlike things that cling to the rocks of the underlying bottom, the almost formless polyps from which, in spring, a new generation of jellyfish will bud off and rise into the surface waters. There is unconscious purpose in the sluggish forms of the copepods hibernating on the bottom, safe from the surface storms, life sustained in their tiny bodies by the extra store of fat with which they went into this winter sleep.

Already, from the gray shapes of cod that have moved, unseen by man, through the cold sea to their spawning places, the glassy globules of eggs are rising into the surface waters. Even in the harsh world of the winter sea, these eggs will begin the swift divisions by which a granule of protoplasm becomes a living fishlet.

Most of all, perhaps, there is assurance in the fine dust of life that remains in the surface waters, the invisible spores of the diatoms, needing only the touch of warming sun and fertilizing chemicals to repeat the magic of spring.

THE HEADLONG WAVE

HENRY BESTON · 1928

This morning I am going to try my hand at something that I do not recall ever having encountered either in a periodical or

From *The Outermost House*, by Henry Beston. Copyright, 1928, 1949, by Henry Beston. Reprinted by permission of Rinehart & Company, Inc.

in a book, namely, a chapter on the ways, the forms, and the sounds of ocean near a beach. Friends are forever asking me about the surf on the great beach and if I am not sometimes troubled or haunted by its sound. To this I reply that I have grown unconscious of the roar, and though it sounds all day long in my waking ears, and all night long in my sleeping ones, my ears seldom send on the long tumult to the mind. I hear the roar the instant I wake in the morning and return to consciousness, I listen to it a while consciously, and then accept and forget it; I hear it during the day only when I stop again to listen, or when some change in the nature of the sound breaks through my acceptance of it to my curiosity.

They say here that great waves reach this coast in threes. Three great waves, then an indeterminate run of lesser rhythms, then three great waves again. On Celtic coasts it is the seventh wave that is seen coming like a king out of the grey, cold sea. The Cape tradition, however, is no half-real, half-mystical fancy, but the truth itself. Great waves do indeed approach this beach by threes. Again and again have I watched three giants roll in one after the other out of the Atlantic, cross the outer bar, break, form again, and follow each other in to fulfilment and destruction on this solitary beach. Coast guard crews are all well aware of this triple rhythm and take advantage of the lull that follows the last wave to launch their boats.

It is true that there are single giants as well. I have been roused by them in the night. Waked by their tremendous and unexpected crash, I have sometimes heard the last of the heavy overspill, sometimes only the loud, withdrawing roar. After the roar came a briefest pause, and after the pause the return of ocean to the night's long cadences. Such solitary titans, flinging their green tons down upon a quiet world, shake beach and dune. Late one September night, as I sat reading, the very father of all waves must have flung himself down before the house, for the quiet of the night was suddenly overturned by a gigantic, tumbling crash and an earthquake rumbling; the beach trembled beneath the avalanche, the dune shook, and my house so shook in its dune that the flame of a lamp quivered and pictures jarred on the wall.

The three great elemental sounds in nature are the sound of rain, the sound of wind in a primeval wood, and the sound of outer ocean on a beach. I have heard them all, and of the three elemental voices, that of ocean is the most awesome, beautiful, and varied. For it is a mistake to talk of the monotone of ocean or of the monotonous nature of its sound. The sea has many voices. Listen to the surf, really lend it your ears, and you will hear in it a world of sounds: hollow boomings and heavy roarings, great watery tumblings and tramplings, long hissing seethes, sharp, rifle-shot reports, splashes, whispers, the grinding undertone of stones, and sometimes vocal sounds that might be the half-heard talk of people in the sea. And not only is the great sound varied in the manner of its making, it is also constantly changing its tempo, its pitch, its accent, and its rhythm, being now loud and thundering, now almost placid, now furious, now grave and solemn-slow, now a simple measure, now a rhythm monstrous with a sense of purpose and elemental will.

Every mood of the wind, every change in the day's weather, every phase of the tide—all these have subtle sea musics all their own. Surf of the ebb, for instance, is one music, surf of the flood another, the change in the two musics being most clearly marked during the first hour of a rising tide. With the renewal of the tidal energy, the sound of the surf grows louder, and fury of battle returns to it as it turns again on the land, and beat and sound change with the renewal of the war.

Sound of surf in these autumnal dunes—the continuousness of it, sound of endless charging, endless incoming and gathering, endless fulfilment and dissolution, endless fecundity, and end-less death. I have been trying to study out the mechanics of that mighty resonance. The dominant note is the great spilling crash made by each arriving wave. It may be hollow and booming, it may be heavy and churning, it may be a tumbling roar. The second fundamental sound is the wild seething cataract roar of the wave's dissolution and the rush of its foaming waters up the beach—this second sound *diminuendo*. The third fundamental sound is the endless dissolving hiss of the inmost slides of foam. The first two sounds reach the ear as a unisonance —the booming impact of the tons of water and the wild roar of the uprush blending—and this mingled sound dissolves into the foam-bubble hissing of the third. Above the tumult, like birds, fly wisps of watery noise, splashes and counter splashes, whispers, seethings, slaps, and chucklings. An overtone sound of other breakers, mingled with a general rumbling, fells earth and sea and air.

Here do I pause to warn my reader that although I have recounted the history of a breaker—an ideal breaker—the surf process must be understood as mingled and continuous, waves hurrying after waves, interrupting waves, washing back on waves, overwhelming waves. Moreover, I have described the sound of a high surf in fair weather. A storm surf is mechanically the same thing, but it *grinds*, and this same long, sepulchral grinding—sound of utter terror to all mariners—is a development of the second fundamental sound; it is the cry of the breaker water roaring its way ashore and dragging at the sand. A strange underbody of sound when heard through the high, wild screaming of a gale.

Breaking waves that have to run up a steep tilt of the beach are often followed by a dragging, grinding sound—the note of the baffled water running downhill again to the sea. It is loudest when the tide is low and breakers are rolling beach stones up and down a slope of the lower beach.

I am, perhaps, most conscious of the sound of surf just after I have gone to bed. Even here I read myself to drowsiness, and, reading, I hear the cadenced trampling roar filling all the dark. So close is the Fo'castle to the ocean's edge that the rhythm of sound I hear oftenest in fair weather is not so much a general tumult as an endless arrival, overspill, and dissolution of separate great seas. Through the dark, mathematic square of the screened half window, I listen to the rushes and the bursts, the tramplings, and the long, intermingled thunderings, never wearying of the sonorous and universal sound.

Away from the beach, the various sounds of the surf melt into one great thundering symphonic roar. Autumnal nights in Eastham village are full of this ocean sound. The "summer people" have gone, the village rests and prepares for winter, lamps shine from kitchen windows, and from across the moors, the great levels of the marsh, and the bulwark of the dunes resounds the long wintry roaring of the sea. Listen to it a while, and it will seem but one remote and formidable sound; listen still longer and you will discern in it a symphony of breaker thunderings, an endless, distant, elemental cannonade. There is beauty in it, and ancient terror. I heard it last as I walked through the village on a starry October night; there was no wind, the leafless trees were still, all the village was abed, and the whole sombre world was awesome with the sound.

ACROSS THE PACIFIC

THOR HEYERDAHL · 1950

Two days later we had our first storm. It started by the trade wind dying away completely, and the feathery, white trade-wind clouds, which were drifting over our heads up in the top-

most blue, being suddenly invaded by a thick black cloud bank
which rolled up over the horizon from southward. Then there
came gusts of wind from the most unexpected directions, so
that it was impossible for the steering watch to keep control.
As quickly as we got our stern turned to the new direction
of the wind, so that the sail bellied out stiff and safe, just as
quickly the gusts came at us from another quarter, squeezed
the proud bulge out of the sail, and made it swing round and
thrash about to the peril of both crew and cargo. But then
the wind suddenly set in to blow straight from the quarter
whence the bad weather came, and, as the black clouds rolled
over us, the breeze increased to a fresh wind which worked itself up into a real storm.

In the course of an incredibly short time the seas round about
us were flung up to a height of fifteen feet, while single crests
were hissing twenty and twenty-five feet above the trough of
the sea, so that we had them on a level with our masthead when
we ourselves were down in the trough. All hands had to
scramble about on deck bent double, while the wind shook
the bamboo wall and whistled and howled in all the rigging.

To protect the radio corner we stretched canvas over the
rear wall and port side of the cabin. All loose cargo was lashed
securely, and the sail was hauled down and made fast around
the bamboo yard. When the sky clouded over, the sea grew
dark and threatening, and in every direction it was white-
crested with breaking waves. Long tracks of dead foam lay
like stripes to windward down the backs of the long seas; and
everywhere, where the wave ridges had broken and plunged
down, green patches like wounds lay frothing for a long time
in the blue-black sea. The crests blew away as they broke,
and the spray stood like salt rain over the sea. When the
tropical rain poured over us in horizontal squalls and whipped
the surface of the sea, invisible all round us, the water that ran
from our hair and beards tasted brackish, while we crawled

about the deck naked and frozen, seeing that all the gear was in order to weather the storm.

When the storm rushed up over the horizon and gathered about us for the first time, strained anticipation and anxiety were discernible in our looks. But when it was upon us in earnest, and the *Kon-Tiki* took everything that came her way with ease and buoyancy, the storm became an exciting form of sport, and we all delighted in the fury round about us which the balsa raft mastered so adroitly, always seeing that she herself lay on the wave tops like a cork, while all the main weight of the raging water was always a few inches beneath. The sea had much in common with the mountains in such weather. It was like being out in the wilds in a storm, up on the highest mountain plateaus, naked and gray. Even though we were right in the heart of the tropics, when the raft glided up and down over the smoking waste of sea we always thought of racing downhill among snowdrifts and rock faces.

The steering watch had to keep its eyes open in such weather. When the steepest seas passed under the forward half of the raft, the logs aft rose right out of the water, but the next second they plunged down again to climb up over the next crest. Each time the seas came so close upon one another that the hindmost reached us while the first was still holding the bow in the air. Then the solid sheets of water thundered in over the steering watch in a terrifying welter, but next second the stern went up and the flood disappeared as through the prongs of a fork.

We calculated that in an ordinary calm sea, where there were usually seven seconds between the highest waves, we took in about two hundred tons of water astern in twenty-four hours. But we hardly noticed it because it just flowed in quietly round the bare legs of the steering watch and as quietly disappeared again between the logs. But in a heavy storm more than ten thousand tons of water poured on board astern in the course of twenty-four hours, seeing that loads varying from a few gallons to two or three cubic yards, and occasionally much more, flowed on board every five seconds. It sometimes broke on board with a deafening thunderclap, so that the helmsman stood in water up to his waist and felt as if he were forcing his way against the current in a swift river. The raft seemed to stand trembling for a moment, but then the cruel load that weighed her down astern disappeared overboard again in great cascades.

When the weather moderated, it was as though the big fish around us had become completely infuriated. The water round the raft was full of sharks, tunnies, dolphins, and a few dazed bonitos, all wriggling about close under the timber of the raft and in the waves nearest to it. It was a ceaseless life-and-death struggle; the backs of big fishes arched themselves over the water and shot off like rockets, one chasing another in pairs, while the water round the raft was repeatedly tinged with thick blood. The combatants were mainly tunnies and dolphins, and the dolphins came in big shoals which moved much more quickly and alertly than usual. The tunnies were the assailants; often a fish of 150 to 200 pounds would leap high into the air holding a dolphin's bloody head in its mouth. But, even if individual dolphins dashed off with tunnies hard on their heels, the actual shoal of dolphins did not give ground, although there were often several wriggling round with big gaping wounds in their necks. Now and again the sharks, too, seemed to become blind with rage, and we saw them catch and fight with big tunnies, which met in the shark a superior enemy.

Not one single peaceful little pilot fish was to be seen. They had been devoured by the furious tunnies, or they had hidden in the chinks under the raft or fled far away from the battle-field. We dared not put our heads down into the water to see.

THE MIRROR OF THE SEA

JOSEPH CONRAD · 1906

It seems to me that no man born and truthful to himself could declare that he ever saw the sea looking young as the earth looks young in spring. But some of us, regarding the ocean with understanding and affection, have seen it looking old, as if the immemorial ages had been stirred up from the undisturbed bottom of ooze. For it is a gale of wind that makes the sea look old.

From a distance of years, looking at the remembered aspects of the storms lived through, it is that impression which disengages itself clearly from the great body of impressions left by many years of intimate contact.

If you would know the age of the earth, look upon the sea in a storm. The greyness of the whole immense surface, the wind furrows upon the faces of the waves, the great masses of foam, tossed about and waving, like matted white locks, give to the sea in a gale an appearance of hoary age, lustreless, dull, without gleams, as though it had been created before light itself.

Looking back after much love and much trouble, the instinct of primitive man, who seeks to personify the forces of Nature for his affection and for his fear, is awakened again in the breast of one civilized beyond that stage even in his infancy. One seems to have known gales as enemies, and even as enemies one embraces them in that affectionate regret which clings to the past.

Gales have their personalities, and, after all, perhaps it is not strange; for, when all is said and done, they are adversaries whose wiles you must defeat, whose violence you must resist,

From *The Mirror of the Sea*, by Joseph Conrad. Reprinted by permission of J. M. Dent & Sons, Ltd.

and yet with whom you must live in the intimacies of nights and days.

Here speaks the man of the masts and sails, to whom the sea is not a navigable element, but an intimate companion. The length of passages, the growing sense of solitude, the close dependence upon the very forces that, friendly to-day, without changing their nature, by the mere putting forth of their might, become dangerous to-morrow, make for that sense of fellow-ship which modern seamen, good men as they are, cannot hope to know.

I remember a few nights in my lifetime, and in a big ship, too (as big as they made them then), when one did not get flung out of one's bed simply because one never even at-tempted to get in; one had been made too weary, too hopeless, to try. The expedient of turning your bedding out on a damp floor and lying on it there was no earthly good, since you could not keep your place or get a second's rest in that or any other position. But of the delight of seeing a small craft run bravely amongst the great seas there can be no question to him whose soul does not dwell ashore. Thus I well remember a three days' run got out of a little barque of 400 tons somewhere between the islands of St. Paul and Amsterdam and Cape Ot-way on the Australian coast. It was a hard, long gale, grey clouds and green sea, heavy weather undoubtedly, but still what a sailor would call manageable. Under two lower topsails and a reefed foresail the barque seemed to race with a long, steady sea that did not becalm her in the troughs. The solemn thundering combers caught her up from astern, passed her with a fierce boiling up of foam level with the bulwarks, swept on ahead with a swish and a roar: and the little vessel, dipping her jib-boom into the tumbling froth, would go on running in a smooth, glassy hollow, a deep valley between two ridges of the sea, hiding the horizon ahead and astern. There was such fascination in her pluck, nimbleness, the continual exhibition of unfailing seaworthiness, in the semblance of courage and endurance, that I could not give up the delight of watching her run through the three unforgettable days of that gale which my mate also delighted to extol as "a famous shove."

And this is one of those gales whose memory in after-years returns, welcome in dignified austerity, as you would remember with pleasure the noble features of a stranger with whom you crossed swords once in knightly encounter and are never to see again. In this way gales have their physiognomy. You remember them by your own feelings, and no two gales stamp themselves in the same way upon your emotions. Some cling to you in woebegone misery; others come back fiercely and weirdly, like ghouls bent upon sucking your strength away; others, again, have a catastrophic splendour; some are unvenerated recollections, as of spiteful wildcats clawing at your agonized vitals; others are severe like a visitation; and one or two rise up draped and mysterious with an aspect of ominous menace. In each of them there is a characteristic point at which the whole feeling seems contained in one single moment. Thus there is a certain four o'clock in the morning in the confused roar of a black and white world when coming on deck to take charge of my watch I received the instantaneous impression that the ship could not live for another hour in such a raging sea.

I wonder what became of the men who silently (you couldn't hear yourself speak) must have shared that conviction with me. To be left to write about it is not, perhaps, the most enviable fate; but the point is that this impression resumes in its intensity the whole recollection of days and days of desperately dangerous weather. We were then, for reasons which it is not worth while to specify, in the close neighbourhood of Kerguelen Land; and now, when I open an atlas and look at the tiny dots on the map of the Southern Ocean, I see as if engraved upon the paper the enraged physiognomy of that gale.

THE PACIFIC

HERMAN MELVILLE · 1851

I

When gliding by the Bashee isles we emerged at last upon the great South Sea; were it not for other things, I could have greeted my dear Pacific with uncounted thanks, for now the long supplication of my youth was answered; that serene ocean rolled eastwards from me a thousand leagues of blue.

There is, one knows not what sweet mystery about this sea, whose gently awful stirrings seem to speak of some hidden soul beneath; like those fabled undulations of the Ephesian sod over the buried Evangelist St. John. And meet it is, that over these sea-pastured, wide-rolling watery prairies and Potters' Fields of all four continents, the waves should rise and fall, and ebb and flow unceasingly; for here, millions of mixed shades and shadows, drowned dreams, somnambulisms, reveries; all that we call lives and souls, lie dreaming, dreaming, still; tossing like slumberers in their beds; the ever-rolling waves but made so by their restlessness.

To any meditative Magian rover, this serene Pacific, once beheld, must ever after be the sea of his adoption. It rolls the mid-most waters of the world, the Indian Ocean and Atlantic being but its arms. The same waves wash the moles of the new-built Californian towns, but yesterday planted by the recent-est race of men, and lave the faded but still gorgeous skirts of Asiatic lands, older than Abraham; while all between float milky-ways of coral isles, and low-lying, endless, unknown

From *Moby Dick*, 1851.

Archipelagoes, and impenetrable Japans. Thus this mysterious, divine Pacific zones the world's whole bulk about; makes all coasts one bay to it; seems the tide-beating heart of earth. Lifted by those eternal swells, you needs must own the seductive god, bowing your head to Pan.

II

Penetrating further and further into the heart of the Japanese cruising ground, the *Pequod* was soon all astir in the fishery. Often, in mild, pleasant weather, for twelve, fifteen, eighteen, and twenty hours on the stretch, they were engaged in the boats, steadily pulling, or sailing, or paddling after the whales, or for an interlude of sixty or seventy minutes calmly awaiting their uprising; though with but small success for their pains.

At such times, under an abated sun; afloat all day upon smooth, slow heaving swells; seated in his boat, light as a birch canoe; and so sociably mixing with the soft waves themselves, that like hearth-stone cats they purr against the gunwale; these are the times of dreamy quietude, when beholding the tranquil beauty and brilliancy of the ocean's skin, one forgets the tiger heart that pants beneath it; and would not willingly remember, that this velvet paw but conceals a remorseless fang.

These are the times, when in his whale-boat the rover softly feels a certain filial, confident, land-like feeling towards the sea; that he regards it as so much flowery earth; and the distant ship revealing only the tops of her masts, seems struggling forward, not through high rolling waves, but through the tall grass of a rolling prairie: as when the western emigrants' horses only show their erected ears, while their hidden bodies widely wade through the amazing verdure. The long-drawn virgin vales; the mild blue hill-sides; as over these there steals the hush, the hum; you almost swear that play-wearied children lie sleeping in these solitudes, in some glad May-time, when the flowers of the woods are plucked. And all this mixes with your most mystic mood; so that fact and fancy, half-way meeting, interpenetrate, and form one seamless whole.

Oh, grassy glades! oh, ever vernal endless landscapes in the soul; in ye,—though long parched by the dead drought of the earthy life,—in ye, men yet may roll, like young horses in new morning clover; and for some few fleeting moments, feel the cool dew of the life immortal on them. Would to God these blessed calms would last. But the mingled, mingling threads of life are woven by warp and woof: calms crossed by storms, a storm for every calm. There is no steady unretracing progress in this life; we do not advance through fixed gradations, and at the last one pause:—through infancy's unconscious spell, boyhood's thoughtless faith, adolescence's doubt (the common doom), then scepticism, then disbelief, resting at last in manhood's pondering repose of If. But once gone through, we trace the round again; and are infants, boys, and men, and Ifs eternally. Where lies the final harbor, whence we unmoor no more? In what rapt ether sails the world, of which the weariest will never weary? Where is the foundling's father hidden? Our souls are like those orphans whose unwedded mothers die in bearing them: the secret of our paternity lies in their grave, and we must there to learn it.

THE OPEN BOAT

STEPHEN CRANE · 1898

When the correspondent again opened his eyes, the sea and the sky were each of the grey hue of the dawning. Later,

Reprinted from *Stephen Crane: An Omnibus*, edited by Robert Wooster Stallman, by permission of Albert A. Knopf, Inc. Copyright, 1952, by Alfred A. Knopf, Inc.

carmine and gold was painted upon the waters. The morning appeared finally, in its splendor, with a sky of pure blue, and the sunlight flamed on the tips of the waves.

On the distant dunes were set many little black cottages, and a tall white windmill reared above them. No man, nor dog, nor bicycle appeared on the beach. The cottages might have formed a deserted village.

The voyagers scanned the shore. A conference was held in the boat. "Well," said the captain, "if no help is coming we might better try a run through the surf right away. If we stay out here much longer we will be too weak to do anything for ourselves at all." The others silently acquiesced in this reasoning. The boat was headed for the beach. The correspondent wondered if none ever ascended the tall wind-tower, and if then they never looked seaward. This tower was a giant, standing with its back to the plight of the ants. It represented in a degree, to the correspondent, the serenity of nature amid the struggles of the individual—nature in the wind, and nature in the vision of men. She did not seem cruel to him then, nor beneficent, nor treacherous, nor wise. But she was indifferent, flatly indifferent. It is, perhaps, plausible that a man in this situation, impressed with the unconcern of the universe, should see the innumerable flaws of his life, and have them taste wickedly in his mind and wish for another chance. A distinction between right and wrong seems absurdly clear to him, then, in this new ignorance of the grave-edge, and he understands that if he were given another opportunity he would mend his conduct and his words, and be better and brighter during an introduction or at a tea.

"Now, boys," said the captain, "she is going to swamp, sure. All we can do is to work her in as far as possible, and then when she swamps, pile out and scramble for the beach. Keep cool now, and don't jump until she swamps sure."

The oiler took the oars. Over his shoulders he scanned the

surf. "Captain," he said, "I think I'd better bring her about, and keep her head-on to the seas and back her in."

"All right, Billie," said the captain. "Back her in." The oiler swung the boat then and, seated in the stern, the cook and the correspondent were obliged to look over their shoulders to contemplate the lonely and indifferent shore.

The monstrous in-shore rollers heaved the boat high until the men were again enabled to see the white sheets of water scudding up the slanted beach. "We won't get in very close," said the captain. Each time a man could wrest his attention from the rollers, he turned his glance toward the shore, and in the expression of the eyes during this contemplation there was a singular quality. The correspondent, observing the others, knew that they were not afraid, but the full meaning of their glances was shrouded.

As for himself, he was too tired to grapple fundamentally with the fact. He tried to coerce his mind into thinking of it, but the mind was dominated at this time by the muscles, and the muscles said they did not care. It merely occurred to him that if he should drown it would be a shame.

There were no hurried words, no pallor, no plain agitation. The men simply looked at the shore. "Now, remember to get well clear of the boat when you jump," said the captain.

Seaward the crest of a roller suddenly fell with a thunderous crash, and the long white comber came roaring down upon the boat.

"Steady now," said the captain. The men were silent. They turned their eyes from the shore to the comber and waited. The boat slid up the incline, leaped at the furious top, bounced over it, and swung down the long back of the wave. Some water had been shipped and the cook bailed it out.

But the next crest crashed also. The tumbling, boiling flood of the white water caught the boat and whirled it almost perpendicular. Water swarmed in from all sides. The correspondent had his hands on the gunwale at this time, and when the water entered at that place he swiftly withdrew his fingers, as if he objected to wetting them.

The little boat, drunken with this weight of water, reeled and snuggled deeper into the sea.

"Bail her out, cook! Bail her out," said the captain.

"All right, captain," said the cook.

"Now, boys, the next one will do for us, sure," said the oiler. "Mind to jump clear of the boat."

The third wave moved forward, huge, furious, implacable. It fairly swallowed the dingey, and almost simultaneously the men tumbled into the sea. A piece of lifebelt had lain in the bottom of the boat, and as the correspondent went overboard he held this to his chest with his left hand.

The January water was icy, and he reflected immediately that it was colder than he had expected to find it on the coast of Florida. This appeared to his dazed mind as a fact important enough to be noted at the time. The coldness of the water was sad; it was tragic. This fact was somehow so mixed and confused with his opinion of his own situation that it seemed almost a proper reason for tears. The water was cold.

When he came to the surface he was conscious of little but the noisy water. Afterward he saw his companions in the sea. The oiler was ahead in the race. He was swimming strongly and rapidly. Off to the correspondent's left, the cook's great white and corked back bulged out of the water, and in the rear the captain was hanging with his one good hand to the keel of the overturned dingey.

There is a certain immovable quality to a shore, and the correspondent wondered at it amid the confusion of the sea.

It seemed also very attractive, but the correspondent knew that it was a long journey, and he paddled leisurely. The piece of life-preserver lay under him, and sometimes he whirled down the incline of a wave as if he were on a hand-sled.

But finally he arrived at a place in the sea where travel was beset with difficulty. He did not pause swimming to inquire what manner of current had caught him, but there his progress ceased. The shore was set before him like a bit of scenery on a stage, and he looked at it and understood with his eyes each detail of it.

As the cook passed, much farther to the left, the captain was calling to him, "Turn over on your back, cook! Turn over on your back and use the oar."

"All right, sir." The cook turned on his back, and, paddling with an oar, went ahead as if he were a canoe.

Presently the boat also passed to the left of the correspondent with the captain clinging with one hand to the keel. He would have appeared like a man raising himself to look over a board fence, if it were not for the extraordinary gymnastics of the boat. The correspondent marvelled that the captain could still hold to it.

They passed on, nearer to shore—the oiler, the cook, the captain—and following them went the water-jar, bouncing gaily over the seas.

The correspondent remained in the grip of this strange new enemy—a current. The shore, with its white slope of sand and its green bluff, topped with little silent cottages, was spread like a picture before him. It was very near to him then, but he was impressed as one who in a gallery looks at a scene from Brittany or Holland.

He thought: "I am going to drown? Can it be possible? Can it be possible? Can it be possible?" Perhaps an individual must consider his own death to be the final phenomenon of nature.

But later a wave perhaps whirled him out of this small, deadly current, for he found suddenly that he could again make progress toward the shore. Later still, he was aware that the captain, clinging with one hand to the keel of the dingey, had his face turned away from the shore and toward him, and was calling his name. "Come to the boat! Come to the boat!"

In his struggle to reach the captain and the boat, he reflected that when one gets properly wearied, drowning must really be a comfortable arrangement, a cessation of hostilities accompanied by a large degree of relief, and he was glad of it, for the main thing in his mind for some months had been horror of the temporary agony. He did not wish to be hurt.

Presently he saw a man running along the shore. He was undressing with most remarkable speed. Coat, trousers, shirt, everything flew magically off him.

"Come to the boat," called the captain.

"All right, captain." As the correspondent paddled, he saw the captain let himself down to bottom and leave the boat. Then the correspondent performed his one little marvel of the voyage. A large wave caught him and flung him with ease and supreme speed completely over the boat and far beyond it. It struck him even then as an event in gymnastics, and a true miracle of the sea. An over-turned boat in the surf is not a plaything to a swimming man.

The correspondent arrived in water that reached only to his waist, but his condition did not enable him to stand for more than a moment. Each wave knocked him into a heap, and the under-tow pulled at him.

Then he saw the man who had been running and undressing, and undressing and running, come bounding into the water. He dragged ashore the cook, and then waded towards the captain, but the captain waved him away, and sent him to the correspondent. He was naked, naked as a tree in winter, but a halo was about his head, and he shone like a saint. He gave a strong pull, and a long drag, and a bully heave at the correspondent's hand. The correspondent, schooled in the minor formulae, said: "Thanks, old man." But suddenly the man cried: "What's that?" He pointed a swift finger. The correspondent said: "Go."

In the shallows, face downward, lay the oiler. His forehead touched sand that was periodically, between each wave, clear of the sea.

The correspondent did not know all that transpired afterward. When he achieved safe ground he fell, striking the sand with each particular part of his body. It was as if he had dropped from a roof, but the thud was grateful to him.

It seems that instantly the beach was populated with men with blankets, clothes, and flasks, and women with coffeepots and all the remedies sacred to their minds. The welcome of the land to the men from the sea was warm and generous, but a still and dripping shape was carried slowly up the beach, and the land's welcome for it could only be the different and sinister hospitality of the grave.

When it came night, the white waves paced to and fro in the moonlight, and the wind brought the sound of the great sea's voice to the men on shore, and they felt that they could then be interpreters.

XIV

The Great Plains

❋ ❋ ❋ ❋ ❋ ❋ ❋ ❋ ❋ ❋ ❋ ❋ ❋ ❋ ❋ ❋ ❋ ❋

THE ROMANCE of the Great Plains, like many another dream, depends for its survival upon the enchantment of distance either in time or in space. Seen from the overcivilized East or in the perspective of advancing years, the prairie lies on the horizon in western glow. Clark remarked, on looking out over "one Continued Plain as fur as can be seen," "the most beautiful prospect of the river up and down and the country opposite . . . which ever I beheld." But the men who crossed these prairies, arriving gratefully at the fording of the Platte, record in their diaries the searing heat, the sudden violent storms, the dust, the agonizing distances.

The contradictions of beauty and hardship, nature benevolent and nature untamed, the elements and man, are the continuing themes of all the interpreters of the Prairie—scientists, authors, or artists. Parkman's first sentences present the contradictions between the paradise of the imagination and the great American desert. His attitude toward the Platte River valley contrasts sharply with the nostalgic recollections of Willa Cather, who sees the prairie in the light of a childhood memory of glorious autumn. Sears and Steinbeck were inspired by the ravages of drought in the "dust bowl." Sears's is the point of view of the agricultural economist; Steinbeck's that of the socially conscious artist; yet, in a similar way, they focus attention upon the particles of dust, the grass blades, the corn stalks, the weeds. All these descriptions demonstrate

263

in some degree the contrast between the vastness of prairie and the significance of the minutiae which compose it.

❀ ❀ ❀ ❀ ❀ ❀ ❀ ❀ ❀ ❀ ❀ ❀ ❀ ❀ ❀ ❀ ❀ ❀

THE ROUTE OF THE PLATTE

FRANCIS PARKMAN · 1849

I

Should any one of my readers ever be impelled to visit the prairies, and should he choose the route of the Platte (the best, perhaps, that can be adopted), I can assure him that he need not think to enter at once upon the paradise of his imagination. A dreary preliminary, a protracted crossing of the threshold, awaits him before he finds himself fairly upon the verge of the "great American desert,"—those barren wastes, the haunts of the buffalo and the Indian, where the very shadow of civilization lies a hundred leagues behind him. The intervening country, the wide and fertile belt that extends for several hundred miles beyond the extreme frontier, will probably answer tolerably well to his preconceived ideas of the prairie; for this it is from which picturesque tourists, painters, poets, and novelists, who have seldom penetrated farther, have derived their conceptions of the whole region. If he has a painter's eye, he may find his period of probation not wholly void of interest. The scenery, though tame, is graceful and pleasing. Here are level plains, too wide for the eye to measure; green undulations, like motionless swells of the ocean; abundance of streams, followed through all their windings by lines of woods and scattered groves. But let him be

From *The Oregon Trail*, 1849.

as enthusiastic as he may, he will find enough to damp his ardor. His wagons will stick in the mud; his horses will break loose; harness will give way; and axle-trees prove unsound. His bed will be a soft one, consisting often of black mud of the richest consistency. As for food, he must content himself with biscuit and salt provisions; for, strange as it may seem, this tract of country produces very little game. As he advances, indeed, he will see, mouldering in the grass by his path, the vast antlers of the elk, and farther on the whitened skulls of the buffalo, once swarming over this now deserted region. Perhaps, like us, he may journey for a fortnight, and see not so much as the hoof-print of a deer; in the spring, not even a prairie-hen is to be had.

II

A low, undulating line of sand-hills bounded the horizon before us. That day we rode ten hours, and it was dusk before we entered the hollows and gorges of these gloomy little hills. At length we gained the summit, and the long-expected valley of the Platte lay before us. We all drew rein, and sat joyfully looking down upon the prospect. It was right welcome; strange, too, and striking to the imagination, and yet it had not one picturesque or beautiful feature; nor had it any of the features of grandeur, other than its vast extent, its solitude, and its wildness. For league after league, a plain as level as a lake was spread beneath us; here and there the Platte, divided into a dozen thread-like sluices, was traversing it, and an occasional clump of wood, rising in the midst like a shadowy island, relieved the monotony of the waste. No living thing was moving throughout the vast landscape, except the lizards that darted over the sand and through the rank grass and prickly pears at our feet.

We had passed the more tedious part of our journey; but four hundred miles still intervened between us and Fort

Laramie; and to reach that point cost us the travel of three more weeks. During the whole of this time we were passing up the middle of a long, narrow, sandy plain, reaching like an outstretched belt nearly to the Rocky Mountains. Two lines of sand-hills, broken often into the wildest and most fantastic forms, flanked the valley at the distance of a mile or two on the right and left; while beyond them lay a barren, trackless waste, extending for hundreds of miles to the Arkansas on the one side, and the Missouri on the other. Before and behind us, the level monotony of the plain was unbroken as far as the eye could reach. Sometimes it glared in the sun, an expanse of hot, bare sand; sometimes it was veiled by long coarse grass. Skulls and whitening bones of buffalo were scattered everywhere; the ground was tracked by myriads of them, and often covered with the circular indentations where the bulls had wallowed in the hot weather. From every gorge and ravine, opening from the hills, descended deep, well-worn paths, where the buffalo issue twice a day in regular procession to drink in the Platte. The river itself runs through the midst, a thin sheet of rapid, turbid water, half a mile wide, and scarcely two feet deep. Its low banks, for the most part without a bush or a tree, are of loose sand, with which the stream is so charged that it grates on the teeth in drinking. The naked landscape is, of itself, dreary and monotonous; and yet the wild beasts and wild men that frequent the valley of the Platte make it a scene of interest and excitement to the traveller. Of those who have journeyed there, scarcely one, perhaps, fails to look back with fond regret to his horse and his rifle.

THE SUNFLOWER TRAIL

WILLA CATHER · 1918

All the years that have passed have not dimmed my memory of that first glorious autumn. The new country lay open before me: there were no fences in those days, and I could choose my own way over the grass uplands, trusting the pony to get me home again. Sometimes I followed the sunflower-bordered roads. Fuchs told me that the sunflowers were introduced into that country by the Mormons; that at the time of the persecution, when they left Missouri and struck out into the wilderness to find a place where they could worship God in their own way, the members of the first exploring party, crossing the plains to Utah, scattered sunflower seed as they went. The next summer, when the long trains of wagons came through with all the women and children, they had the sunflower trail to follow. I believe that botanists do not confirm Fuchs's story, but insist that the sunflower was native to those plains. Nevertheless, that legend has stuck in my mind, and sunflower-bordered roads always seem to me the roads to freedom.

I took a long walk north of the town, out into the pastures where the land was so rough that it had never been ploughed up, and the long red grass of early times still grew shaggy over the draws and hillocks. Out there I felt at home again. Overhead the sky was that indescribable blue of autumn; bright and shadowless, hard as enamel. To the south I could see the dun-shaded river bluffs that used to look so big to me, and all about stretched drying cornfields, of the pale-gold colour I remembered so well. Russian thistles were blowing across the uplands and piling against the wire fences like barricades.

From *My Antonia*, by Willa Cather. Reprinted by permission of and arrangement with Houghton Mifflin Company, the authorized publishers.

Along the cattle-paths the plumes of goldenrod were already fading into sun-warmed velvet, grey with gold threads in it. I had escaped from the curious depression that hangs over little towns, and my mind was full of pleasant things; trips I meant to take with the Cuzak boys, in the Bad Lands and up on the Stinking Water.

As I wandered over those rough pastures, I had the good luck to stumble upon a bit of the first road that went from Black Hawk out to the north country; to my grandfather's farm, then on to the Shimerdas' and to the Norwegian settlement. Everywhere else it had been ploughed under when the highways were surveyed; this half-mile or so within the pasture fence was all that was left of that old road which used to run like a wild thing across the open prairie, clinging to the high places and circling and doubling like a rabbit before the hounds.

On the level land the tracks had almost disappeared—were mere shadings in the grass, and a stranger would not have noticed them. But wherever the road had crossed a draw, it was easy to find. The rains had made channels of the wheel-ruts and washed them so deeply that the sod had never healed over them. They looked like gashes torn by a grizzly's claws, on the slopes where the farm-wagons used to lurch up out of the hollows with a pull that brought curling muscles on the smooth hips of the horses. I sat down and watched the hay-stacks turn rosy in the slanting sunlight.

This was the road over which Ántonia and I came on that night when we got off the train at Black Hawk and were bedded down in the straw, wondering children, being taken we knew not whither. I had only to close my eyes to hear the rumbling of the wagons in the dark, and to be again overcome by that obliterating strangeness. The feelings of that night were so near that I could reach out and touch them with my hand. I had the sense of coming home to myself, and of having found out what a little circle man's experience is. For Ántonia and for me, this had been the road of Destiny; had taken us to those early accidents of fortune which predetermined for us all that we can ever be. Now I understood that the same road was to bring us together again. Whatever we had missed, we possessed together the precious, the incommunicable past.

GRASS

PAUL B. SEARS · 1935

Man, if there were no grasses, would be just one of the animals. No plants but the grasses can endure the continued nibbling of grazing beasts; to a degree they actually thrive on it. Without roving herds of quadrupeds, primitive man would have had no means of livelihood excepting those afforded by the fish and game of the forest, and the fruits and roots which grow there. By domestication, the grazing animals enabled him to move forward into a pastoral existence. Moreover, in the domestication of certain highly favorable grasses, men found bread, repose from unceasing movement, and ultimately civilization.

No one would deny to the grasses the credit they deserve for their role in elevating mankind from the beasts, although we have seen how dismal is the treatment accorded our grazing lands and the soil upon which our bread must grow. Yet there is another reason why the grasses deserve well of man. The great grasslands, apart from the abundant wealth they yield, are the strategic buffer between civilization and the desert. While there are notable exceptions, the great centers of population are in regions whose climate would, if given a chance, produce forest. From there humanity shades out to virtual invisibility in the desert. We may pass from Massachusetts, with over five hundred people to a square mile, west to Oklahoma, with thirty-four, on through Arizona, with about three, into Nevada, which has less than one. If numbers mean anything, they tell a story here. It is not good to have the deserts grow in size. And against that growth our best defense is the tight-knit turf of the grasslands.

When a tree is cut it leaves "a hole in the sky." When forests are destroyed every one is aware of that fact. Even when the forest deteriorates one does not need to be a trained forester to sense what is taking place. Grass, on the other hand, is to most people simply a green carpet. The kinds of plants, their abundance, and their vitality are matters which escape the casual. So long as all is green, all is well. To the untrained traveler the great grasslands are a matter of indifference or even an unutterable bore as he moves through them, in automobile or train. The term "Great American Desert" was not coined for the desert at all, but for that land which was, to the writer of *My Ántonia*, alive and glowing with beauty.

The plants of the virgin sod are mostly perennials—coming up year after year from the same underground system. Once established, they depend much less upon seeds than upon new buds for their spread. This in fact is one of the most important features of that marvelous flexibility of the grasslands which we have mentioned. Each individual clump is prepared to put forth few or many new shoots each year, as conditions happen to permit, or even to suspend operations for a time and live upon its underground store. Under too frequent attacks from fire or hungry teeth the clumps of grass cannot hold their own. Shrinking in size, they leave space for brash, short-lived annual weeds of little food value. These may be in turn followed by more persistent and even more useless perennial weeds, such as the poisonous or thorny types mentioned above. All too often, if the abuse is continued, nothing can come into the tortuous spaces between the clumps in time to prevent the elements from scouring them into winding channels. It is not uncommon to find a once beautiful and uniform sod which has been reduced to isolated tufts or bunches each standing several inches above the eroded bare surfaces that separate them. There is a kind of grass which finally comes into these naked spaces after the topsoil is gone and erosion has done its worst, which the natives call "poverty grass." Its dirty pale gray will show in patches across the landscape for miles, a warning to any intelligent investor except those hardy souls who deal in royalties for wealth far below the soil.

Weeds resemble those people who thrive best under difficulties and adversity. Prosperity and peace ruin them. They cannot retain their power under a calm and stable regime. Weeds, like red-eyed anarchists, are the symptoms, not the real cause, of a disturbed order. When the Russian thistle swept down across the western ranges, the general opinion was that it was a devouring plague, crowding in and consuming the native plants. It was no such thing. The native vegetation had already been destroyed by the plow and thronging herds—the ground was vacated and the thistles took it over. It is the same with the American prickly pear, which is regarded as an unmitigated pest in Algeria and Australia. Again, the Mormons were accused of sowing sunflower seeds along their route as they crossed the continent. The truth is the sunflowers have always been there, but the hoofs and tires of the Mormon trains broke through the turf, destroying it and giving the sunflowers their chance—a temporary one at best. No one ever saw a field, protected against fire, plow, and livestock, support a permanent population of thistles, sunflowers, or any other kind of weed. Just as surely as the weeds replaced the native plants with misuse, the reverse will happen under protected conditions.

Under favorable conditions it has been found that the planting of such a thing as wheat-grass, and its subsequent careful protection will bring about a return of satisfactory pasture. Or, if ample fields of buffalo grass are near at hand, narrow strips may be cut from them, separated into small blocks, and these transplanted at intervals onto the bare and abandoned space. With reasonable rainfall the native grass will establish itself and creep out to cover the clear intervals between the blocks. Both methods involve expense, waiting, and the hazard that drought may prevent success.

But there is a great deal of loose, sandy land, once good pasture, which has blown and drifted until it has become a temporary desert. It is vital that some cover, no matter what, be developed here without delay. Nature has furnished a hint. Throughout this region after the drought was well begun the despised Russian thistle did so well that it was often the only plant available for stock-feed. Instead of seeding the area with costly grass-seed, whose success is a gamble, it might be sensible to mix in a good proportion of weed seeds. If the land is abandoned weeds will be the first cover anyhow, and as we have seen, they are a transient affair at most, preparing the way for better kinds of plants. Actually the method is not new. There is a brilliant example of its use on the bare clay slopes of the huge Ohio Conservancy dams north of Dayton, which today are held in perfect condition by a dense, well-developed sod. The success of this plant cover was insured from the start by the deliberate use of the cheapest, weediest mixtures of grass and clover seed that could be obtained. The weeds took hold at once, but their more genteel companions are now in full possession, just as the coon-skin cap and leather jacket have been replaced by the fedora and business suit in the one-time wilderness beyond the Alleghenies.

DUST

JOHN STEINBECK · 1939

To the red country and part of the gray country of Oklahoma, the last rains came gently, and they did not cut the scarred earth. The plows crossed and recrossed the rivulet marks. The last rains lifted the corn quickly and scattered weed colonies and grass along the sides of the roads so that the gray country and the dark red country began to disappear under a green cover. In the last part of May the sky grew pale and the clouds that had hung in high puffs for so long in the spring were dissipated. The sun flared down on the growing corn day after day until a line of brown spread along the edge of each green bayonet. The clouds appeared, and went away, and in a while they did not try any more. The weeds grew darker green to protect themselves, and they did not spread any more. The surface of the earth crusted, a thin hard crust, and as the sky became pale, so the earth became pale, pink in the red country and white in the gray country.

In the water-cut gullies the earth dusted down in dry little streams. Gophers and ant lions started small avalanches. And as the sharp sun struck day after day, the leaves of the young corn became less stiff and erect; they bent in a curve at first, and then, as the central ribs of strength grew weak, each leaf tilted downward. Then it was June, and the sun shone more fiercely. The brown lines on the corn leaves widened and moved in on the central ribs. The weeds frayed and edged back toward their roots. The air was thin and the sky more pale; and every day the earth paled.

In the roads where the teams moved, where the wheels milled the ground and the hooves of the horses beat the ground, the dirt crust broke and the dust formed. Every moving thing lifted the dust into the air: a walking man lifted a thin layer as high as his waist, and a wagon lifted the dust as high as the fence tops, and an automobile boiled a cloud behind it. The dust was long in settling back again.

When June was half gone, the big clouds moved up out of Texas and the Gulf, high heavy clouds, rain-heads. The men in the fields looked up at the clouds and sniffed at them and held wet fingers up to sense the wind. And the horses were nervous while the clouds were up. The rain-heads dropped a little spattering and hurried on to some other country. Behind them the sky was pale again and the sun flared. In the dust there were drop craters where the rain had fallen, and there were clean splashes on the corn, and that was all.

A gentle wind followed the rain clouds, driving them on northward, a wind that softly clashed the drying corn. A day went by and the wind increased, steady, unbroken by gusts. The dust from the roads fluffed up and spread out and fell on the weeds beside the fields, and fell into the fields a little way. Now the wind grew strong and hard and it worked at the rain crust in the corn field. Little by little the sky was darkened by the mixing dust, and the wind felt over the earth, loosened the dust, and carried it away. The wind grew stronger. The rain crust broke and the dust lifted up out of the fields and drove gray plumes into the air like sluggish smoke. The corn threshed the wind and made a dry, rushing sound. The finest dust did not settle back to earth now, but disappeared into the darkening sky.

The wind grew stronger, whisked under stones, carried up straws and old leaves, and even little clods, marking its course as it sailed across the fields. The air and the sky darkened and through them the sun shone redly, and there was a raw sting in the air. During a night the wind raced faster over the land, dug cunningly among the rootlets of the corn, and the corn fought the wind with its weakened leaves until the roots were freed by the prying wind and then each stalk settled wearily sideways toward the earth and pointed the direction of the wind.

The dawn came, but no day. In the gray sky a red sun appeared, a dim red circle that gave a little light, like dusk; and as that day advanced, the dusk slipped back toward darkness, and the wind cried and whimpered over the fallen corn.

Men and women huddled in their houses, and they tied handkerchiefs over their noses when they went out, and wore goggles to protect their eyes.

When the night came again it was black night, for the stars could not pierce the dust to get down, and the window lights could not even spread beyond their own yards. Now the dust was evenly mixed with the air, an emulsion of dust and air. Houses were shut tight, and cloth wedged around doors and windows, but the dust came in so thinly that it could not be seen in the air, and it settled like pollen on the chairs and tables, on the dishes. The people brushed it from their shoulders. Little lines of dust lay at the door sills.

In the middle of that night the wind passed on and left the land quiet. The dust-filled air muffled sound more completely than fog does. The people, lying in their beds, heard the wind stop. They awakened when the rushing wind was gone. They lay quietly and listened deep into the stillness. Then the roosters crowed, and their voices were muffled, and the people stirred restlessly in their beds and wanted the morning. They knew it would take a long time for the dust to settle out of the air. In the morning the dust hung like fog, and the sun was as red as ripe new blood. All day the dust sifted down from the sky, and the next day it sifted down. An even blanket covered the earth. It settled on the corn, piled up on the tops of the fence posts, piled up on the wires; it settled on roofs, blanketed the weeds and trees.

XV

The American

❊ ❊ ❊ ❊ ❊ ❊ ❊ ❊ ❊ ❊ ❊ ❊ ❊ ❊ ❊ ❊ ❊

CURIOSITY about the American was strong in nineteenth-century Europe, and the subject attracted a double audience, for Americans were equally curious about what Europe would say of them. The same accusations and generalizations recur in these descriptions of the abstraction who is supposed to be the composite or typical citizen of the United States. Interest lies, therefore, in the presentation of the subject. Matthews, the American, is frankly patriotic. Dickens's vigorous denunciation is a sharp contrast to Buchan's politely penetrating assessment. Dylan Thomas is wickedly clever, but disarmingly impartial; the sins of the poet and of his audience are equally venial.

In each of these appraisals the devices of qualification and persuasion are skillfully enlisted to make the "truth" acceptable. Matthews establishes a balance between positive and negative assertions. Dickens, tactfully distinguishing the individual American from the national character, sweetens his gall with introductory paragraphs of personal affection for Americans, but this is only the introduction which confirms the justice of his attack. Buchan uses the same technique in reverse. Opening with a catalogue of "the weak and ugly things in America," which establishes the penetration of his view, he then develops the numbered virtues of the American people as a whole. Dylan Thomas reproduces in his hail of phrases the lecturer "confused by shameless profusion," but from the

277

rhetorical *tour de force* emerges the ridiculous figure of the "fat poet with the slim volume"—himself.

❀   ❀   ❀   ❀   ❀   ❀   ❀   ❀   ❀   ❀   ❀   ❀   ❀   ❀   ❀   ❀   ❀

AMERICANISM

BRANDER MATTHEWS · 1901

There are many words in circulation among us which we understand fairly well, which we use ourselves, and which we should, however, find it difficult to define. I think that *Americanism* is one of these words; and I think also it is well for us to inquire into the exact meaning of this word, which is often most carelessly employed. More than once of late we have heard a public man praised for his "aggressive Americanism," and occasionally we have seen a man of letters denounced for his "lack of Americanism." Now what does the word really mean when it is thus used?

It means, first of all, a love for this country of ours, an appreciation of the institutions of this nation, a pride in the history of this people to which we belong. And to this extent *Americanism* is simply another word for *patriotism*. But it means, also, I think, more than this: it means a frank acceptance of the principles which underlie our government here in the United States. It means, therefore, a faith in our fellow-man, a belief in liberty and in equality. It implies, further, so it seems to me, a confidence in the future of this country, a confidence in its destiny, a buoyant hopefulness that the right will surely prevail.

It calls not only for love of our common country, but

From *Parts of Speech*, by Brander Matthews. Charles Scribner's Sons, publishers.

also for respect for our fellow-man. It implies an actual acceptance of equality as a fact. It means a willingness always to act on the theory, not that "I'm as good as the other man," but that "the other man is as good as I am." It means leveling up rather than leveling down. It means a regard for law, and a desire to gain our wishes and to advance our ideas always decently and in order, and with deference to the wishes and ideas of others. It leads a man always to acknowledge the good faith of those with whom he is contending, whether the contest is one of sport or of politics. It prevents a man from declaring, or even from thinking, that all the right is on his side, and that all the honest people in the country are necessarily of his opinion.

True Americanism is sturdy but modest. It is as far removed from "Jingoism" in times of trouble as it is from "Spread-Eagleism" in times of peace. It is neither vainglorious nor boastful. It knows that the world was not created in 1492, and that July 4, 1776, is not the most important date in the whole history of mankind. It does not overestimate the contribution which America has made to the rest of the world, nor does it underestimate this contribution. True Americanism, as I have said, has a pride in the past of this great country of ours, and a faith in the future; but none the less it is not so foolish as to think that all is perfection on this side of the Atlantic, and that all is imperfection on the other side.

It knows that some things are better here than anywhere else in the world, that some things are no better, and that some things are not so good in America as they are in Europe. For example, probably the institutions of the nation fit the needs of the population with less friction here in the United States than in any other country in the world. But probably, also, there is no other one of the great nations of the world in which the government of the large cities is so wasteful and so negligent.

True Americanism recognizes the fact that America is the heir of the ages, and that it is for us to profit as best we can by the experience of Europe, not copying servilely what has been successful in the old world, but modifying what we borrow in accord with our own needs and our own conditions. It knows, and it has no hestitation in declaring, that we must always be the judges ourselves as to whether or not we shall follow the example of Europe. Many times we have refused to walk in the path of European precedent, preferring very properly to blaze out a track for ourselves. More often than not this independence was wise, but now and again it was unwise.

Finally, one more quality of true Americanism must be pointed out. It is not sectional It does not dislike an idea, a man, or a political party because that idea, that man, or that party comes from a certain part of the country. It permits a man to have a healthy pride in being a son of Virginia, a citizen of New York, a native of Massachusetts, but only on condition that he has a pride still stronger that he is an American, a citizen of the United States. True Americanism is never sectional. It knows no North and no South, no East and no West. And as it has no sectional likes and dislikes, so it has no international likes and dislikes. It never puts itself in the attitude of the Englishman who said, "I've no prejudices, thank Heaven, but I do hate a Frenchman!" It frowns upon all appeals to the former allegiance of naturalized citizens of this country; and it thinks that it ought to be enough for any man to be an American without the aid of the hyphen which makes him a British-American, an Irish-American, or a German-American.

True Americanism, to conclude, feels that a land which bred Washington and Franklin in the last century, and Emerson and Lincoln in this century, and which opens its schools wide to give every boy the chance to model himself on these great men, is a land deserving of Lowell's praise as "a good country to live in, a good country to live for, and a good country to die for."

A NOTE ON AMERICAN CHARACTER

CHARLES DICKENS · 1843

On the general character of the American people, and the general character of their social system, as presented to a stranger's eyes, I desire to express my own opinions in a few words, before I bring these volumes to a close.

They are, by nature, frank, brave, cordial, hospitable, and affectionate. Cultivation and refinement seem but to enhance their warmth of heart and ardent enthusiasm; and it is the possession of these latter qualities in a most remarkable degree, which renders an educated American one of the most endearing and most generous of friends. I never was so won upon, as by this class; never yielded up my full confidence and esteem so readily and pleasurably, as to them; never can make again, in half-a-year, so many friends for whom I seem to entertain the regard of half a life.

These qualities are natural, I implicitly believe, to the whole people. That they are, however, sadly sapped and blighted in their growth among the mass; and that there are influences at work which endanger them still more, and give but little present promise of their healthy restoration; is a truth that ought to be told.

It is an essential part of every national character to pique itself mightily upon its faults, and to deduce tokens of its virtue or its wisdom from their very exaggeration. One great

From *American Notes*, 1843.

blemish in the popular mind of America, and the prolific parent of an innumerable brood of evils, is Universal Distrust. Yet the American citizen plumes himself upon this spirit, even when he is sufficiently dispassionate to perceive the ruin it works; and will often adduce it, in spite of his own reason, as an instance of the great sagacity and acuteness of the people, and their superior shrewdness and independence.

"You carry," says the stranger, "this jealousy and distrust into every transaction of public life. By repelling worthy men from your legislative assemblies, it has bred up a class of candidates for the suffrage, who, in their every act, disgrace your Institutions and your people's choice. It has rendered you so fickle, and so given to change, that your inconstancy has passed into a proverb; for you no sooner set up an idol firmly, than you are sure to pull it down and dash it into fragments: and this, because directly you reward a benefactor, or a public servant, you distrust him, merely because he *is* rewarded; and immediately apply yourselves to find out, either that you have been too bountiful in your acknowledgments, or he remiss in his deserts. Any man who attains a high place among you, from the President downwards, may date his downfall from that moment; for any printed lie that any notorious villain pens, although it militate directly against the character and conduct of a life, appeals at once to your distrust, and is believed. You will strain at a gnat in the way of trustfulness and confidence, however fairly won and well deserved; but you will swallow a whole caravan of camels, if they be laden with unworthy doubts and mean suspicions. Is this well, think you, or likely to elevate the character of the governors or the governed, among you?"

The answer is invariably the same: "There's freedom of opinion here, you know. Every man thinks for himself, and we are not to be easily overreached. That's how our people come to be suspicious."

Another prominent feature is the love of "smart" dealing: which gilds over many a swindle and gross breach of trust; many a defalcation, public and private; and enables many a knave to hold his head up with the best, who well deserves a halter: though it has not been without its retributive operation, for this smartness has done more in a few years to impair the public credit, and to cripple the public resources, than dull honesty, however rash, could have effected in a century. The merits of a broken speculation, or a bankruptcy, or of a successful scoundrel, are not gauged by its or his observance of the golden rule, "Do as you would be done by," but are considered with reference to their smartness.

It would be well, there can be no doubt, for the American people as a whole, if they loved the Real less, and the Ideal somewhat more. It would be well, if there were greater encouragement to lightness of heart and gaiety, and a wider cultivation of what is beautiful, without being eminently and directly useful. But here, I think the general remonstrance, "we are a new country," which is so often advanced as an excuse for defects which are quite unjustifiable, as being of right only the slow growth of an old one, may be very reasonably urged: and I yet hope to hear of there being some other national amusement in the United States, besides newspaper politics.

They certainly are not a humorous people, and their temperament always impressed me as being of a dull and gloomy character. In shrewdness of remark, and a certain cast-iron quaintness, the Yankees, or people of New England, unquestionably take the lead; as they do in most other evidences of intelligence. But in travelling about, out of the large cities— as I have remarked in former parts of these volumes—I was quite oppressed by the prevailing seriousness and melancholy air of business: which was so general and unvarying, that at every new town I came to I seemed to meet the very same people whom I had left behind me, at the last. Such defects as are perceptible in the national manners, seem, to me, to be referable, in a great degree, to this cause: which has generated a dull, sullen persistence in coarse usages, and rejected the graces of life as undeserving of attention. There is no doubt that Washington, who was always most scrupulous and exact on points of ceremony, perceived the tendency towards this mistake, even in his time, and did his utmost to correct it.

THE AMERICAN PEOPLE

JOHN BUCHAN · 1940

No country can show such a wide range of type and character, and I am so constituted that in nearly all I find something to interest and attract me. This is more than a temperamental bias, for I am very ready to give reasons for my liking. I am as much alive as anyone to the weak and ugly things in American life: areas, both urban and rural, where the human economy has gone rotten; the melting-pot which does not always melt; the eternal colored problem; a constitutional machine which I cannot think adequately represents the efficient good sense of the American people; a brand of journalism which fatigues with its ruthless snappiness and uses a speech so disintegrated that it is incapable of expressing any serious thought or emotion; the imbecile patter of high-pressure salesmanship; an academic jargon, used chiefly by psychologists and sociologists, which is hideous and almost meaningless. Honest Americans do not deny these blemishes; indeed they are apt to exaggerate them, for they are by far the sternest critics of their own country. For myself, I would make a double

From *Pilgrim's Way* (*Memory Hold the Door*) by John Buchan. Reprinted by permission of Hodder & Stoughton, publishers.

plea in extenuation. These are defects from which today no nation is exempt, for they are the fruits of a mechanical civilization, which perhaps are more patent in America, since everything there is on a large scale. Again, you can set an achievement very much the same in kind against nearly every failure. If her historic apparatus of government is cranky, she is capable of meeting the "instant need of things" with brilliant improvisations. Against economic plague-spots she can set great experiments in charity; against journalistic baby-talk a standard of popular writing in her best papers which is a model of idiom and perspicuity; against catch-penny trade methods many solidly founded, perfectly organized commercial enterprises; against the jargon of the half-educated professor much noble English prose in the great tradition. That is why it is so foolish to generalize about America. You no sooner construct a rule than it is shattered by the exceptions.

I am less concerned with special types than with the American people as a whole. Let me try to set down certain qualities which seem to me to flourish more lustily in the United States than elsewhere. Again, let me repeat, I speak of America only as I know it; an observer with a different experience might not agree with my conclusions.

First, I would select what, for want of a better word, I should call homeliness. It is significant that the ordinary dwelling, though it be only a shack in the woods, is called not a house, but a home. This means that the family, the ultimate social unit, is given its proper status as the foundation of society. Even among the richer classes I seem to find a certain pleasing domesticity. English people of the same rank are separated by layers of servants from the basic work of the household, and know very little about it. In America the kitchen is not too far away from the drawing-room, and it is recognized, as Heraclitus said, that the gods may dwell there. But I am thinking chiefly of the ordinary folk, especially those of narrow means. It is often said that Americans are a nomad race, and it is true that they are very ready to shift their camp; but the camp, however bare, is always a home. The cohesion of the family is close, even when its members are scattered. This is due partly to the tradition of the first settlers, a handful in an unknown land; partly to the history of the frontier, where the hearthfire burnt brighter when all around was cold and darkness. The later immigrants from Europe, feeling at last secure, were able for the first time to establish a family base, and they cherished it zealously. This ardent domesticity has had its bad effects on American literature, inducing a sentimentality which makes a too crude frontal attack on the emotions, and which has produced as a reaction a not less sentimental "toughness." But as a social cement it is beyond price. There have been many to laugh at the dullness and pettiness of the "small town." From what I know of small-town life elsewhere, I suspect obtuseness in the satirists.

Second, I would choose the sincere and widespread friendliness of the people. Americans are interested in the human race, and in each other. Deriving doubtless from the old frontier days, there is a general helpfulness which I have not found in the same degree elsewhere. A homesteader in Dakota will accompany a traveler for miles to set him on the right road. The neighbors will rally round one of their number in distress with the loyalty of a Highland clan. This friendliness is not a self-conscious duty so much as an instinct. A squatter in a cabin will share his scanty provender and never dream that he is doing anything unusual.

American hospitality, long as I have enjoyed it, still leaves me breathless. The lavishness with which a busy man will give up precious time to entertain a stranger to whom he is in no way bound remains for me one of the wonders of the world. No doubt this friendliness, since it is an established custom, has its fake side. The endless brotherhoods and sodalities into which people brigade themselves encourage a geniality which is more a mannerism than an index of character, a tiresome, noisy, back-slapping heartiness. But that is the exception, not the rule. Americans like company, but though they are gregarious they do not lose themselves in the crowd. Waves of mass emotion may sweep the country, but they are transient things and do not submerge for long the stubborn rock of individualism. That is to say, people can be led, but they will not be driven. Their love of human companionship is based not on self-distrust, but on a genuine liking for their kind. With them the sense of a common humanity is a warm and constant instinct and not a doctrine of the schools or a slogan of the hustings.

Lastly—and this may seem a paradox—I maintain that they are fundamentally modest. Their interest in others is a proof of it; the Aristotelian Magnificent Man was interested in nobody but himself. As a nation they are said to be sensitive to criticism; that surely is modesty, for the truly arrogant care nothing for the opinion of other people. Above all, they can laugh at themselves, which is not possible for the immodest. They are their own shrewdest and most ribald critics. It is charged against them that they are inclined to boast unduly about those achievements and about the greatness of their country, but a smug glorying in them is found only in the American of the caricaturist. They rejoice in showing their marvels to a visitor with the gusto of children exhibiting their toys to a stranger, an innocent desire, without any unfriendly gloating, to make others partakers in their satisfaction. If now and then they are guilty of bombast, it is surely a venial fault. The excited American talks of his land very much, I suspect, as the Elizabethans in their cups talked of England. The foreigner who strayed into the Mermaid Tavern must often have listened to heroics which upset his temper.

A VISIT TO AMERICA

DYLAN THOMAS · 1953

Across the United States of America, from New York to California and back, glazed, again, for many months of the year, there streams and sings for its heady supper a dazed and prejudiced procession of European lecturers, scholars, sociologists, economists, writers, authorities on this and that and even, in theory, on the United States of America . . .

At first, confused and shocked by shameless profusion and almost shamed by generosity, unaccustomed to such importance as they are assumed, by their hosts, to possess, and up against the barrier of a common language, they write in their notebooks like demons, generalizing away, on character and culture and the American political scene. But, towards the middle of their middle-aged whisk through middle-western clubs and universities, the fury of the writing flags . . . And in their diaries, more and more do such entries appear as, 'No way of escape!' or 'Buffalo!' or 'I am beaten,' until at last they cannot write a word. And, twittering all over, old before their time, with eyes like rissoles in the sand, they are helped up the gangway of the home-bound liner by kind bosom friends (of all kinds and bosoms) who boister them on the back, pick them up again, thrust bottles, sonnets, cigars, addresses, into their pockets, have a farewell party in their cabin, pick them up again, and, snickering and yelping, are gone: to wait at the dockside for another boat from Europe and another batch of fresh, green lecturers.

There they go, every spring, from New York to Los Angeles: exhibitionists, polemicists, histrionic publicists, theological rhetoricians, historical hoddy-doddies, balletomanes, ulterior

decorators, windbags and bigwigs and humbugs, men in love
with stamps, men in love with steaks, men after millionaires'
widows, men with elephantiasis of the reputation (huge trunks
and teeny minds), authorities on gas, bishops, best-sellers,
editors looking for writers, writers looking for publishers,
publishers looking for dollars, existentialists, serious physicists
with nuclear missions, men from the BBC who speak as though
they had the Elgin marbles in their mouths, pot-boiling philosophers, professional Irishmen (very lepri-corny), and, I am
afraid, fat poets with slim volumes . . .

See the garrulous others, also, gabbing and garlanded from
one nest of culture-vultures to another: people selling the
English way of life and condemning the American way as
they swig and guzzle through it; people resurrecting the
theories of surrealism for the benefit of remote parochial
female audiences who did not know it was dead, not having
ever known it had been alive; people talking about Etruscan
pots and pans to a bunch of dead pans and wealthy pots in
Boston. And there, too, in the sticky thick of lecturers moving
across the continent black with clubs, go the foreign poets,
catarrhal troubadours, lyrical one-night-standers, dollar-mad
nightingales, remittance-bards from at home, myself among
them booming with the worst.

Did we pass one another, en route, all unknowing, I wonder; one of us spry-eyed, with clean, white lectures and a
soul he could call his own, going buoyantly west to his re-
munerative doom in the great state university factories; another returning dog-eared as his clutch of poems and his
carefully typed impromptu asides? I ache for us both. There
one goes, unsullied as yet, in his Pullman pride, toying—oh,
boy!—with a blunderbuss bourbon, being smoked by a large
cigar, riding out to the wide open spaces of the faces of his
waiting audience . . .

He is vigorously welcomed at the station by an earnest,

crew-cut platoon of giant collegiates, all chasing the butterfly culture with net, notebook, poison-bottle, pin and label, each with at least thirty-six terribly white teeth, and nursed away, as heavily gently as though he were an imbecile rich aunt with a short prospect of life, into a motorcar in which, for a mere fifty miles or so travelled at poet-breaking speed, he assures them of the correctness of their assumption that he is half-witted by stammering inconsequential answers in an over-British accent to their genial questions. He is then taken to a small party of only a few hundred people all of whom hold the belief that what a visiting lecturer needs before he trips on to the platform is just enough martinis so that he can trip off the platform as well. And clutching his explosive glass, he is soon contemptuously dismissing, in a flush of ignorance and fluency, the poetry of those androgynous literary ladies with three names who produce a kind of verbal ectoplasm to order as a waiter dishes up spaghetti—only to find that the fiercest of these, a wealthy huntress of small, seedy lions (such as himself), who stalks the middle-western bush with ears and rifle cocked, is his hostess for the evening.

Late at night, in his room, he fills a page of his journal with a confused, but scathing, account of his first engagement, summarises American advanced education in a paragraph that will be meaningless tomorrow, and falls to sleep where he is immediately, chased through long dark thickets by a Mrs. Mabel Frankincense Mehaffey, with a tray of martinis and lyrics.

And there goes the other happy poet bedraggledly back to New York which struck him all of a sheepish never-sleeping heap at first but which seems to him now, after the ulcerous rigors of a lecturer's spring, a haven cozy as toast, cool as an icebox, and safe as skyscrapers.

XVI

The Gentleman

❀ ❀ ❀ ❀ ❀ ❀ ❀ ❀ ❀ ❀ ❀ ❀ ❀ ❀ ❀ ❀ ❀

THE CHARACTER of the gentleman is a persistent ideal, and one which commands attention today; yet the subject belongs to times more formal than ours, to the decorum of the eighteenth century or to the refinement of the Victorian Era. All these essays, whenever they were written, follow a nineteenth-century pattern of thought, development, and style. They are among the most conventional essays in this volume; therefore, they most nearly approach the traditional idea of a model essay.

Like the section on the American, this on the Gentleman is included for the study of definition and of the exposition of an abstract idea. All the devices of limitation and development —definition by description, by example, by anecdote, by figure of speech—are illustrated in one or another of the passages. The four examples were chosen to provide four common patterns of essay organization. Newman depends simply upon a series of descriptive statements based first upon human relationships and then upon ethical and religious ones. Grattan employs contrast and comparison between English and American concepts, adding local color and conviction and human interest by the quotation of news reports. Crothers uses the familiar chronological or historical pattern. Mrs. Gerould, having surveyed the methods of the others, bases her case upon a series of examples of famous men.

Definitions are not static. Through the centuries the concept behind the word "gentleman" has constantly changed. The new meanings testify to the shifting values which man has put upon birth, money, haberdashery, leisure, learning, integrity, generosity, and human understanding.

❀ ❀ ❀ ❀ ❀ ❀ ❀ ❀ ❀ ❀ ❀ ❀ ❀ ❀ ❀ ❀ ❀ ❀

DEFINITION OF A GENTLEMAN

JOHN HENRY NEWMAN · 1852

It is almost a definition of a gentleman to say he is one who never inflicts pain. This description is both refined and, as far as it goes, accurate. He is mainly occupied in merely removing the obstacles which hinder the free and unembarrassed action of those about him; and he concurs with their movements rather than takes the initiative himself. His benefits may be considered as parallel to what are called comforts or conveniences in arrangements of a personal nature: like an easy chair or a good fire, which do their part in dispelling cold and fatigue, though nature provides both means of rest and animal heat without them. The true gentleman in like manner carefully avoids whatever may cause a jar or a jolt in the minds of those with whom he is cast: all clashing of opinion, or collision of feeling, all restraint, or suspicion, or gloom, or resentment; his great concern being to make everyone at his ease and at home. He has his eyes on all his company; he is tender towards the bashful, gentle towards the distant, and merciful towards the absurd; he can recollect to whom he is speaking; he guards against unseasonable allusions or topics which may irritate; he is seldom prominent in conversation, and never wearisome. He makes light of favors while he does

From *The Idea of a University*, 1852.

them, and seems to be receiving when he is conferring. He never speaks of himself except when compelled, never defends himself by a mere retort; he has no ears for slander or gossip, is scrupulous in imputing motives to those who interfere with him, and interprets every thing for the best. He is never mean or little in his disputes, never takes unfair advantage, never mistakes personalities or sharp sayings for arguments, or insinuates evil which he dare not say out. From a long-sighted prudence, he observes the maxim of the ancient sage, that we should ever conduct ourselves towards our enemy as if he were one day to be our friend. He has too much good sense to be affronted at insults, he is too well employed to remember injuries, and too indolent to bear malice. He is patient, forbearing, and resigned, on philosophical principles; he submits to pain because it is inevitable, to bereavement because it is irreparable, and to death because it is his destiny. If he engages in controversy of any kind, his disciplined intellect preserves him from the blundering discourtesy of better, perhaps, but less educated minds; who, like blunt weapons, tear and hack instead of cutting clean, who mistake the point in argument, waste their strength on trifles, misconceive their adversary, and leave the question more involved than they find it. He may be right or wrong in his opinion, but he is too clear-headed to be unjust; he is as simple as he is forcible, and as brief as he is decisive. Nowhere shall we find greater candor, consideration, indulgence: he throws himself into the minds of his opponents, he accounts for their mistakes. He knows the weakness of human reason as well as its strength, its province, and its limits. If he be an unbeliever, he will be too profound and large-minded to ridicule religion or to act against it; he is too wise to be a dogmatist or fanatic in his infidelity. He respects piety and devotion; he even supports institutions as venerable, beautiful, or useful, to which he does not assent; he honors the ministers of religion, and it contents him to decline its mysteries without assailing or denouncing them. He is a friend of religious toleration, and that, not only because his philosophy has taught him to look on all forms of faith with an impartial eye, but also from the gentleness and effeminacy of feeling which is the attendant on civilization.

THE GENTLEMAN IN AMERICA

THOMAS COLLEY GRATTAN · 1859

To meet anything quite coming up to English notions of a finished gentleman is scarcely to be expected. The difficulty can be proved on a perfectly (popular) heraldic principle. Everyone knows that it takes three generations to make a gentleman. And as that implies three generations of liberal education and all the appliances of gentility, ergo, it is very rare, if to be found at all among Americans; for such a thing as grandfather, father, and son in one family preserving their fortune and station is almost unheard of. The fluctuations of property are sure to reduce one generation out of three to a low level; and thus it is that we see so many persons of respectable manners just bordering on good-breeding, and so few that are thoroughly well-bred.

The subject of American gentlemen is one of so much difficulty—I might say delicacy, in as far as the feelings of many are concerned—and it rises up in so many forms that I must revert to it in a desultory way, instead of having made it a topic to be treated under one distinct head, and standing, like any abstract question, by itself.

Manners in the United States are of this nature. There is no standard for them from the want of a permanent class in

From *Civilized America*, 1859.

society to be looked up to and imitated. As the whole of its ingredients are mixed and incongruous, almost each individual follows his natural bent; and we find in the same circles most striking contrasts of style, "everyone" being, as might be said, "his own gentleman." Persons are to be found in America of really good *ton*, even according to the European estimate, but they are infrequently met with in the business or political world. You must look for them on the banks of the Hudson, the Delaware, or the Ohio, in villas with the appurtenances of refinement; in the remote valleys of New England; or on the plantations of the Southern States—and there surrounded by the repulsive associations of slavery, which neutralize the graces to whose culture they administer. All the men of that superior stamp, to mix with whom it was occasionally my good fortune, were (with rare exceptions) out of the whirl of politics, and what is called in the phraseology of the cities "high life." They do not come into contact with the pushing inelegancy of the mass from which the leading party-men and the highest functionaries, whether state or federal, are chosen. Many of the secluded gentry of whom I speak have been partly educated in Europe, or have extended their adult experience there long enough to appreciate the tastes and habits of the Old World; and they do not hesitate to choose between the obscure enjoyments of their country homes and the ambitious vulgarity of public life. It was most gratifying to join those delightful circles. But it was not in them that I was to find materials for a book on the general characteristics of civilized America. It was among the motley crowd of the millions that I had to make my way, and among whom my temporary lot was cast.

In the columns of a New York paper, I find the following obituary notice of a gentleman whom I had frequently met in that city and elsewhere, without being at all aware of his antecedents or pretensions:—

Mr. Hone has long occupied a prominent position in our social, commercial, and political circles. He was of humble origin, being the son of a baker. In early life, he entered into the mercantile profession in Maiden Lane, and afterwards engaged in the auction and commission business in Pearl Street, always standing at the head of the auctioneers. In the fashionable world Mr. Hone always held a high rank, being always considered a leader of the *ton*. Indeed, it has been said that if an order of nobility had existed in this country, Mr. Hone would have claimed the right of being numbered in their ranks. His bearing, though courteous toward his fellow-citizens, was aristocratic and self-confident; and when any of the foreign nobility visited our shores they received his hospitality, while he was personally but little known to the mechanics and other middle classes of American society.

This fluent and clever auctioneer might possibly have had the patrician contempt for the class he sprang from which is here ascribed to him; and he was perhaps a Coriolanus in pride, though not in bearing; but the thing to remark in relation to him is that he is here held up as a model aristocrat and a ready-made nobleman.

Flying to a higher altitude, that of the White House itself, and without reverting to its past distinguished occupants, the *Baltimore Sun*, of the month of August, 1858, gives the following anecdote of the present incumbent, Mr. James Buchanan.

Familiar as our people are generally with the unostentatious habits of the chief officers of our government, one cannot witness them, with the knowledge of the pomp and show of royalty to invite the contrast, without involuntarily indulging it. On Saturday last President Buchanan arrived at the Relay House, or Washington Junction, as it is more properly called, en route for Washington city. There was a rumor abroad that he was to arrive, and the visitors had consequently grouped about the house when the train came along. We soon perceived the President coming from the cars to the platform, looking heartily, but thoroughly travel-soiled, smiling and cheerful. By his side, and evidently offering with gentlemanly deference the courtesy of attention, was a rather rough-looking individual, whom we took for a conductor or brakesman. The gentleman will excuse our blundering in such a matter; but, upon inquiry, we were informed he was Sir William Gore Ouseley. On passing into the bar-room the President threw off his coat and his white neckcloth, carelessly pitching them over a chair, opened his shirt-collar, and tucked up his sleeves for a wash, conveniences for this purpose being in the apartment. At the time, however, both basins were occupied by two young men, neither of whom seemed to be aware that the President was about. He waited patiently some time when some one spoke and invited him upstairs. He declined, however, quietly remarking that he would wait for his turn. And as soon as the basins were vacated he "took his turn" in a jolly good wash in the public bar-room. This done, he seemed rather perplexed about the arrangement of his neckcloth, and seemed likely to tie his nose and mouth up in it. Somebody just then offered assistance, and the President was briefly equipped. At about this time, a person who had come into the room sang out pretty near to him, "Look here, I thought the old Pres. was to be here to-day—" The speech was cut short by a nudge, while a momentary comical expression passed across the face of that same "old Pres." A cigar was handed to him by a friend; he took a good satisfying drink of—not "old rye," which he is said to affect, when prime—but ice-water, had barely fired up his cigar, when the bell rang, and "all aboard" summoned the chief magistrate of the United States to his seat in the cars, and away they went to Washington. We took our admiration of this scene of republican simplicity quietly with us into the cars for Baltimore, and mused with some complacency over the sterling honor of being an American citizen.

I record these small matters to show that I have good reasons for saying that American ideas about gentleman-like manners and habits are different from ours. No one more despises instances of over-fastidious coxcombry. All who, like me, have seen a good deal of the rough work of life in various countries, have often been reduced to far greater straits than that which the President of the United States here voluntarily chose for himself. In his case it was a matter of taste, not necessity, and he had a perfect right to indulge it. But the striking moral of the story is contained in the concluding words of the foregoing article. Here we find the editor of an American newspaper of well-established credit, and to a certain degree (like all persons of his profession) a censor, or at least a critic of manners as well as morals, glorifying himself for "the sterling honor of being an American citizen," not from pride in the greatness of his country or the virtue of its people; not from the contemplation of any deed of heroism, piety, or benevolence, on the part of a compatriot; but simply because President Buchanan, in preference to decently performing his ablutions in a private room, chose to take "a jolly good wash" in a public bar, out of a basin recently used, and in all probability imperfectly rinsed.

THE EVOLUTION OF A GENTLEMAN

SAMUEL MC CHORD CROTHERS · 1903

It is not easy to define a gentleman, as the multitudes who have made the attempt can testify. It is one of the cases in which the dictionary does not help one. Perhaps, after all, definitions are to be looked upon as luxuries, not as necessities. When Alice told her name to Humpty Dumpty, that intolerable pedant asked,—

" 'What does it mean?'

" 'Must a name mean something?' Alice asked doubtfully.

" 'Of course it must,' Humpty Dumpty said with a short laugh. 'My name means the shape I am,—and a good handsome shape it is, too.' "

From *The Gentle Reader*, by Samuel McChord Crothers. Reprinted by kind permission of and arrangement with Houghton Mifflin Company, the authorized publishers.

I suppose that almost any man, if he were asked what a gentleman is, would answer with Humpty Dumpty, "It is the shape I am." I judge this because, though the average man would not feel insulted if you were to say, "You are no saint," it would not be safe to say, "You are no gentleman."

And yet the average man has his misgivings. For all his confident talk, he is very humble minded. The astral body of the gentleman that he is endeavoring to project at his neighbors is not sufficiently materialized for his own imperfect vision. The word "gentleman" represents an ideal. Above whatever coarseness and sordidness there may be in actual life, there rises the ideal of a finer kind of man, with gentler manners and truer speech and braver action.

In every age we shall find the true gentleman—that is, the man who represents the best ideal of his own time, and we shall find the mimicry of him the would-be gentleman who copies the form while ignorant of the substance. These two characters furnish the material, on the one hand for the romancer, and on the other for the satirist. If there had been no real gentlemen, the epics, the solemn tragedies, and the stirring tales of chivalry would have remained unwritten; and if there had been no pretended gentlemen, the humorist would have lost many a pleasure. Always the contrasted characters are on the stage together; simple dignity is followed by strutting pomposity, and after the hero the braggart swaggers and storms. So ridicule and admiration bear rule by turns.

The idea of the gentleman involves the sense of personal dignity and worth. He is not a means to an end; he is an end in itself. How early this sense arose we may not know. Professor Huxley made merry over the sentimentalists who picture the simple dignity of primitive man. He had no admiration to throw away on "the dignified and unclothed savage sitting in solitary meditation under trees." And yet I am inclined to think that the gentleman must have appeared even before the advent of tailors. The peasant who followed Wat Tyler sang,—

> "When Adam delved and Eve span
> Who was then the gentleman?"

But a writer in the age of Queen Elizabeth published a book in which he argued that Adam himself was a perfect gentleman.

We turn to the Analects of Confucius and we see the Chinese gentleman. Everything with him is exact. The disciples of Confucius are careful to tell us how he adjusted the skirts of his robe before and behind, how he insisted that his mince-meat should be cut quite small and should have exactly the right proportion of rice, and that his mat must be laid straight before he would sit on it. Such details of deportment were thought very important. But we forget the mats and the mince-meat when we read: "Three things the master had not,—he had no prejudices, he had no obstinacy, he had no egotism." And we forget the fantastic garb and the stiff Chinese genuflections, and come to the conclusion that the true gentleman is as simple-hearted amid the etiquette of the court as in the tent in the desert, when we hear the master saying: "Sincerity is the way of Heaven; the wise are the unassuming. It is said of Virtue that over her embroidered robe she puts a plain single garment."

When we wish to see a masculine virtue which has no need of an embroidered garment we go to Plutarch's portrait gallery of antique gentlemen. What a breed of men they were! There were no holiday gentlemen. With the same lofty dignity they faced life and death. How superior they were to their fortunes. No wonder that men who had learned to conquer themselves conquered the world.

The romances of the Middle Ages are variations on a single theme, the appearance of the finer type of manhood and its struggle for existence. In the palace built by the enchantment of Merlin were four zones of sculpture.

"And in the lowest beasts are slaying men,
And in the second men are slaying beasts,
And on the third are warriors, perfect men,
And on the fourth are men with growing wings."

Europe was in the second stage, when men were slaying beasts and what was most brutal in humanity. If the higher manhood was to live, it must fight, and so the gentleman appears, sword in hand. Whether we are reading of Charlemagne and his paladins, or of Siegfried, or of Arthur, the story is the same. The gentleman has appeared. He has come into a waste land,

"Thick with wet woods and many a beast therein,
And none or few to scare or chase the beast."

The ballads and romances chronicle a struggle desperate in its beginning and triumphant in its conclusion. They are in praise of force, but it is a noble force. There is something better, they say, than brute force: it is manly force. The giant is no match for the gentleman. The evolution of the gentleman has its main line of progress where there is a constant though slow advance; but, on the other hand, there are arrested developments, and quaint survivals, and abortive attempts.

In each generation there have been men of fashion who have mistaken themselves for gentlemen. They are uninteresting enough while in the flesh, but after a generation or two they become very quaint and curious, when considered as specimens. Each generation imagines that it has discovered a new variety, and invents a name for it. The dude, the swell, the dandy, the fop, the spark, the macaroni, the blade, the popinjay, the coxcomb,—these are butterflies of different summers. There is here endless variation, but no advancement. One fashion comes after another, but we cannot call it better. One would like to see representatives of the different generations together in full dress. What variety in oaths and small talk! What anachronisms in swords and canes and eye-glasses, in ruffles, in collars, in wigs! What affluence in powders and perfumes and colors! But "will they know each other there"? The real gentlemen would be sure to recognize each other. Abraham and Marcus Aurelius and Confucius would find much in common. Launcelot and Sir Philip Sidney and Chinese Gordon would need no introduction. Montaigne and Mr. Spectator and the Autocrat of the Breakfast-Table would fall into delightful chat. But would a "swell" recognize a "spark"? And might we not expect a "dude" to fall into immoderate laughter at the sight of a "popinjay"?

There was Beau Nash, for example,—a much admired person in his day, when he ruled from his throne in the pump-room in Bath. Lord Chesterfield himself had nothing in common with the absurd imitation gentlemen, and yet the gentleman whom he described and pretended to admire was altogether artificial. He was the Machiavelli of the fashionable world. He saw through it, and recognized its hollowness; but such as it was it must be accepted. The only thing was to learn how to get on in it. "In courts you may expect to meet connections without friendships, enmities without hatred, honor without virtue, appearances saved and realities sacrificed, good manners and bad morals."

It is a relief to get away from such a world, and, leaving the fine gentleman behind, to take the rumbling stagecoach to the estates of Sir Roger de Coverley. His is not the great world at all, and his interests are limited to his own parish. But it is a real world, and much better suited to a real gentleman. His fashions are not the fashions of the court, but they are the fashions that wear. Even when following the hounds Sir Roger has time for friendly greetings. "The farmers' sons thought themselves happy if they could open a gate for the good old knight, which he requited with a nod or a smile, and a kind inquiry after their fathers and uncles." But even dear old Roger de Coverley cannot rest undisturbed as an ideal gentleman. He belonged, after all, to a privileged order, and there is a force at work to destroy all social privileges. A generation of farmers' sons must arise not to be so easily satisfied with a kindly nod and smile.

What becomes of the gentleman in an age of democratic equality? Just what becomes of every ideal when the time for its fulfillment has come. It is freed from its limitations and enters into a larger life. Let us remember that the gentleman was always a lover of equality, and of the graces that can only grow in the society of equals. The gentleman of an aristocracy is at his best only when he is among his peers. There is a little circle within which there is no pushing, no assumption of superiority. Each member seeks not his own, but finds pleasure in a gracious interchange of services.

But an aristocracy leaves only a restricted sphere for such good manners. Outside the group to which he belongs the gentleman is compelled by imperious custom to play the part of a superior being. It has always been distasteful and humiliating to him. It is only an essentially vulgar nature than can really be pleased with the servility of others.

An ideal democracy is a society in which good manners are universal. There is no arrogance and no cringing, but social intercourse is based on mutual respect. This ideal democracy has not been perfected, but the type of men who are creating it has already been evolved. Among all the crude and sordid elements of modern life, we see the stirring of a new chivalry. It is based on a recognition of the worth and dignity of the common man.

BEING A GENTLEMAN

KATHERINE FULLERTON GEROULD · 1926

"Being a gentleman" ("gentlemanliness" is not quite a synonym) constitutes moral solvency: a state which makes it possible for other people to do human and social business with you. Yet, though its significance (on which depends its correct implication) is immensely important now and then, if not constantly, to all of us, it is extraordinarily difficult to define. Indeed, I do not think it is much discussed. To speak paradoxically, it is too important for discussion. There is always the danger of wounding someone else by the statement of implications that we ourselves find resident in the term.

There have been many much-quoted definitions of "gentleman"; but, so far as I know, no perfect one. Cardinal Newman, we recall, had a famous page on the subject; and Newman's tentative definition is as often quoted, surely, as any. "Hence it is," he says, "that it is almost a definition of a gentleman to say that he is one who never inflicts pain." I remember once hearing a brilliant Englishman comment on this to the effect that Newman omitted a necessary adverb: that a gentleman is one who never inflicts pain unwittingly; who is never objectionable unless he wishes to be. The proposition covers a lot of cases, but it does not cover the case of the man whose instincts are impeccable yet who may wound people through his fundamental stupidity. Newman's definition, I fancy we should all agree, is too finicking. We all know cases where a gentleman has inflicted pain, though he may have done it with distaste or regret. How, otherwise, should any of the ends of justice be served?

In considering the term, there is no point in burdening ourselves with foreign definitions. The average Englishman puts into it certain connotations that America cannot accept. It is part of our social creed, for example, that a man either is or is not a gentleman, regardless of his social inheritance. We reject it as a class-name. The people who use it as a class-name only are apt to find themselves constantly challenged. Careful individuals, indeed, are more likely to say "a man of breeding," or "a man of good family," than "a gentleman" when they are excluding all moral implications. "A man in whom gentle birth is accompanied by appropriate qualities and behavior; hence, in general, a man of chivalrous instincts and fine feelings," says the Oxford Dictionary; and elsewhere, "A man of superior position in society . . . often, one whose means enable him to live in easy circumstances without engaging in trade, a man of money and leisure." Neither definition helps American questioners much. We have no heraldry of our own to determine "gentle birth"; our heraldry is purely derivative, and if a man brought no coat-of-arms from Europe, he could find none here.

What, then, do we mean by this important, this almost sacred term? That, alas! it is difficult to say; for we mean different things, each according to his temperament and tradition. There are those who mean by it, like Oliver Wendell Holmes, "three generations of portraits in the family"; there are those who mean by it the habit of literate speech; others who mean having money in one's purse, or being able to wear evening clothes without looking like a waiter, or being sexually virtuous. The gentlemen who prefer blondes are a different category from the gentlemen who prefer grammar. In some groups it means willingness to put up a fight with your bare fists; in some it means having a pew in church. I once knew an eminent scientist who had a way of saying—not simply in the interests of humor—"a geologist, and, therefore, a gentleman." And so on, indefinitely. To find a common denominator for the myriad definitions would be well-nigh impossible.

Yet I think we can say that to every group the word "gentleman" expresses a certain ideal of masculine bearing. When it is used satirically it is only someone's else definition that is being satirized—never one's own. We can also say, I believe, that in spite of the loosening use of the word, it has never lost its importance. Usually, when a word comes to be used loosely, inexactly, it becomes discredited. "Gentleman" as a term has never lost caste. We—the great body of the people—agree less than ever on its meaning, yet we do not cease to carry it, as a kind of gauge, in our private consciousness. The same, indeed, might be said, in all reverence, of the word "God," which has never before been so variously defined, yet never more reflected upon.

It is not, for most of us, a matter of external manners alone. I can think, as can you, of men born in such purple as America affords, adequate to the whole gamut of social exigencies, concerning whom I have no information that they have ever done a questionable thing, whom, none the less, I cannot bring myself to call gentlemen. I have known, though more rarely, men born with no social advantages and possessed of no innate social gift to whom I should find myself readily applying the term. Nor is it a matter of external morals, though both manners and morals somehow count. Shelley was a gentleman and Swinburne was a gentleman, both much more certainly than Wordsworth or Keats; yet the balance of morals, as they are popularly appraised, is heavier on the side of the two latter. Some of the best work in the political and social world has been done by men who were not, very certainly, gentlemen; some of the greatest harm has been done by those who indubitably were. Look at Cromwell and Charles I. It was the gentleman who made the thug necessary. Lancelot's honor rooted in dishonor stood, and faith unfaithful kept him falsely true, yet is there anyone to maintain that Lancelot was less of a gentleman than King Arthur?

No: you cannot define it. Yet each of us "feels" it, as some individuals "feel" the north. A certain inflexibility is always implied, something in a man that is not to be swayed by tempest or melted by fire; a certain selfishness, also, an orientation of the spirit away from his own mere advantage. A gentleman will never let you down. Yet, bearing in mind those who have, in their time, been let down by men indubitably gentlemen, I would add that the gentleman has to make his own estimate of any situation, and that we may, deceived by our own egotism, be making invalid claims upon him. It is not our summing up of the evidence, but his, that must control his gestures. Who is to say, except the man himself, where his greatest loyalty lies? And what is the use of confessing that you cannot make an omelette without breaking eggs if you are going to cry out, as soon as they are broken, that it is no omelette? Calling a man a gentleman is an expression of high faith.

XVII
Tragedy

✳ ✳ ✳ ✳ ✳ ✳ ✳ ✳ ✳ ✳ ✳ ✳ ✳ ✳ ✳ ✳

THE CLASSIFICATION of tragedy is a literary preoccupation, which has often consisted in writing a play or seeing one upon the stage and then shaping a definition to "fit the crime." Aristotle, who first engaged in this exercise, based his discussion upon the works of the four great Greek dramatists. Dryden defended his own heroic tragedies by writing new definitions. Plays, however, depend for their importance upon an audience, and the definitions which grow out of the theater are evidence of public interest and popular belief. *Death of a Salesman* has stimulated a recent clamor for new criteria.

The eighteenth century, which was particularly conscientious about searching for principles, has contributed half of these excerpts. The other half consists of essays, generally more extended, by modern critics. No attempt has been made to include in this short space a complete representation of the theories of tragedy. Some of the most influential definitions are not included here except perhaps by reference or reflection. Aristotle, Milton's preface to *Samson Agonistes*, Dryden's numerous statements, Joseph Warton, Hegel, Bradley, and many other important voices are unrecorded. In the light of all the centuries of argument one can confidently say only that this is a collection of varied, often contradictory, opinions upon the connections between literature and man's condition.

✳ ✳ ✳ ✳ ✳ ✳ ✳ ✳ ✳ ✳ ✳ ✳ ✳ ✳ ✳ ✳

I

CLIFFORD LEECH · 1950

The gulf between the learned use and the popular use of the same word is nowhere better illustrated than in 'tragedy'. The term is used from day to day in referring to incidents of a distressful nature, and, in so far as it is popularly used as the name of a literary type, it is applied to any play or story with an unhappy ending. This is unfortunate, for the wide-spread vague use of the term makes it more difficult for students to clarify their ideas on the significance of *King Lear* and the *Agamemnon:* if our labels are smudged, we are forced to make a continual effort to remind ourselves of the contents of each package. Yet here we cannot blame the journalist for the blurring of the word's meaning, for the vague use of 'tragedy' goes back to medieval times. Moreover, even those who have aimed at using the word precisely have not reached agreement concerning the nature of the literary type to which the word is, by them, applied.

The most famous definition of tragedy in medieval times is given by Chaucer in the Prologue to *The Monk's Tale:*

> Tragedie is to seyn a certeyn storie,
> As olde bokes maken us memorie,
> Of him that stood in greet prosperitie
> And is y-fallen out of heigh degree
> Into miserie, and endeth wrecchedly.

He adds that tragedies are commonly written in hexameters, but that 'many oon' has been written in prose.

But whenever tragedy has come into being, its customary and right dress has been poetry. The equilibrium of Pride and

Terror is, as we have seen, an opposition of persistent forces, and consequently the tragic play is characterised by strong tension. An appearance of casualness in the play will weaken the tension, and contradict the implication of a preordained pattern of event. Moreover, in order that the spectator's mind may more fully respond to the vision of evil and of human strength in defeat, the language must be finely turned. The medium of tragedy must be poetry, or at least a kind of prose which in its formal properties is clearly distinguished from the prose of the everyday, haphazard situation—not because the beauty of the words will atone for the presentation of evil, soothing our nerves and dulling our perceptions, but because only by a co-ordination of our faculties can we reach a full realisation of any complex picture of the world.

II

DAN S. NORTON AND PETERS RUSHTON · 1941

Tragedy, which has found its fullest expression in drama, is the artistic presentation of human suffering. In spite of the fact that its subject is pain, it is regarded as the highest literary type, the one that gives the greatest aesthetic pleasure. In a tragedy we find a man in powerful conflict with other men and circumstances, and we watch him go down to defeat, almost always to death. Yet this spectacle does not depress us. On the contrary its effect has been variously described as a sense of calm, a sense of exultation, and a sense of emotional understanding.

This can be put in another way: tragedy represents the

struggle of man against evil, which he can never wholly avoid. This conflict has value because it is significant to all men, and its significance depends on accepted beliefs regarding the good and bad effects of action. If there is no such standard of judgment there can be no evaluation of the things man does. Moral standards have always been based in large part upon religious beliefs. We shall see, however, that a recognized moral standard based upon religion is not in itself a sufficient background for tragedy. We shall see also that a moralistic theory of tragedy does not produce tragic drama.

Medieval tragedy, according to Chaucer's monk, is the story of a man who reaches great happiness on earth but is hurled from it suddenly into misery. Collections were made of such tales to prove that wordly activity was vain. Man's lot on earth was trouble, and good fortune and bad had no permanent significance.

III

SAMUEL JOHNSON · 1751

As the design of tragedy is to instruct by moving the passions, it must always have a hero, a personage apparently and incontestably superior to the rest, upon whom the attention may be fixed, and the anxiety suspended.

From *The Rambler*, No. 156, Saturday, September 14, 1751.

IV

RICHARD STEELE · 1710

When unhappy catastrophes make up part of the history of princes, and persons who act in high spheres, or are represented in the moving language and well-wrought scenes of tragedians, they do not fail of striking us with terror; but then they affect us only in a transient manner, and pass through our imaginations, as incidents in which our fortunes are too humble to be concerned, or which writers form for the ostentation of their own force; or, at most, as things fit rather to exercise the powers of our minds, than to create new habits in them. Instead of such high passages, I was thinking it would be of great use (if anybody could hit it) to lay before the world such adventures as befall persons not exalted above the common level. This, methought, would better prevail upon the ordinary race of men, who are so prepossessed with outward appearances, that they mistake fortune for nature, and believe nothing can relate to them that does not happen to such as live and look like themselves.

From *The Tatler*, No. 172, May 16, 1710.

V

JOHN DENNIS · 1701

I conceive, that every Tragedy, ought to be a very Solemn Lecture, inculcating a particular Providence, and shewing it plainly protecting the Good, and chastizing the Bad, or at least the Violent; and that, if it is otherwise, it is either an

From *The Advancement and Reformation of Poetry*, 1701.

empty Amusement, or a scandalous and pernicious Libel upon the Government of the World. The killing of Julius Caesar in Shakespear, is either a Murder, or a Lawful Action; if the killing Caesar is a Lawful Action, then the killing of Brutus and Cassius is downright Murder; and the Poet has been guilty of polluting the Scene, with the Blood of the very Best and Last of the Romans. But if the killing of Caesar is Murder, and Brutus and Cassius are very justly punish'd for it, then Shakespear is, on the other Side, answerable for introducing so many Noble Romans, committing, in the Face of an Audience, a very horrible Murder, and only punishing Two of them; which Proceeding gives an Occasion to the People, to draw a dangerous Inference from it, which may be destructive to Government, and to Human Society.

VI

JEREMY COLLIER · 1697/8

The Business of Plays is to recommend Vertue, and discountenance Vice; To shew the Uncertainty of Humane Greatness, the suddain Turns of Fate, and the Unhappy Conclusions of Violence and Injustice: 'Tis to expose the Singularities of Pride and Fancy, to make Folly and Falsehood contemptible, and to bring every Thing that is Ill under Infamy, and Neglect. This Design has been odly pursued by the English Stage. Our Poets write with a different view, and are gone into another Interest. 'Tis true, were their Intentions fair, they might be Serviceable to this Purpose. They have in a great measure the Springs of Thought and Inclination in their Power. Show, Musick, Action, and Rhetorick, are moving Entertainments;

From *A Short View of the English Stage*, 1697/8.

and, rightly employ'd, would be very significant. But Force and Motion are Things indifferent, and the Use lies chiefly in the Application. These Advantages are now, in the Enemies Hand, and under a very dangerous Management. Like Cannon seized, they are pointed the wrong way; and by the Strength of the Defence the Mischief is made the greater. That this Complaint is not unreasonable, I shall endeavour to prove by shewing the Misbehaviour of the Stage, with respect to Morality, and Religion. Their Liberties in the Following Particulars are intolerable, *viz.* Their Smuttiness of Expression; Their Swearing, Prophaneness, and Lewd Application of Scripture; Their Abuse of the Clergy, Their making their top Characters Libertines, and giving them Success in their Debauchery. This Charge, with some other Irregularities, I shall make good against the Stage, and shew both the Novelty and Scandal of the Practice. And first, I shall begin with the Rankness and Indecency of their Language.

VII

JOSEPH ADDISON · 1711

The English Writers of Tragedy are possessed with a Notion, that when they represent a virtuous or innocent Person in Distress, they ought not to leave him till they have delivered him out of his Troubles, or made him triumph over his Enemies. This Error they have been led into by a ridiculous Doctrine in Modern Criticism, that they are obliged to an equal Distribution of Rewards and Punishments, and an impartial Execution of Poetical Justice. Who were the first that established this Rule I know not; but I am sure it has no Foun-

From *The Spectator,* Monday, April 16, 1711.

dation in Nature, in Reason, or in the Practice of the Ancients. We find that Good and Evil happen alike to all Men on this Side the Grave; and as the principal Design of Tragedy is to raise Commiseration and Terror in the Minds of the Audience, we shall defeat this great End, if we always make Virtue and Innocence happy and successful. Whatever Crosses and Disappointments a good Man suffers in the Body of the Tragedy, they will make but small Impression on our Minds, when we know that in the last Act he is to arrive at the End of his Wishes and Desires. When we see him engaged in the Depth of his Afflictions, we are apt to comfort our selves, because we are sure he will find his Way out of them; and that his Grief, how great soever it may be at present, will soon terminate in Gladness. For this Reason the ancient Writers of Tragedy treated Men in their Plays, as they are dealt with in the World, by making Virtue sometimes happy and sometimes miserable, as they found it in the Fable which they made choice of, or as it might affect their Audience in the most agreeable Manner. Aristotle considers the Tragedies that were written in either of these Kinds, and observes, that those which ended unhappily, had always pleased the People, and carried away the Prize in the publick Disputes of the Stage, from those that ended happily. Terror and Commiseration leave a pleasing Anguish in the Mind; and fix the Audience in such a serious Composure of Thought, as is much more lasting and delightful than any little transient Starts of Joy and Satisfaction. Accordingly we find, that more of our English Tragedies have succeeded, in which the Favourites of the Audience sink under their Calamities, than those in which they recover themselves out of them.

VIII

F. L. LUCAS · 1953

The world of everyday seems often a purposeless chaos, a mangy tiger without even the fearful symmetry of Blake's vision; but the world of tragedy we can face, for we feel a mind behind it and the symmetry is there. Tragedy, in fine, is man's answer to this universe that crushes him so pitilessly. Destiny scowls upon him: his answer is to sit down and paint her where she stands.

From *Tragedy*, by F. L. Lucas. Used by kind permission of The Hogarth Press, Ltd., and Dufour Editions, publishers in Great Britain and the United States.

IX

UNA ELLIS-FERMOR · 1946

In great tragedy there is an element common to the individual plays, though differing in form and theme, an element which marks both the treatment of the material and the nature of the resulting interpretation: it is the presence of that conflict, to which we have just referred, between two impressions made by his experience upon the poet's mind.

The part of this experience which is most clearly revealed is the intense awareness of evil and pain. But in conflict with this specific response to fact and event is another of a wholly different kind; the intuitive and often undefined apprehension of another universe implying other values. Beyond the

From *The Frontiers of Drama*, by Una Ellis-Fermor. Used by permission of Methuen & Co. Ltd., publishers.

realization of evil and pain (and the work of art will be great in proportion as this is profound), beyond the apprehension of an alien destiny that appears to shape man's action, there is the perception, at once more comprehensive and less explicit, of a possible resolution, of some reconciliation with or interpretation in terms of good. The impressions in conflict may be of various kinds; of a malevolent and a beneficent world-order; of apparent lawlessness against underlying law, a casual against a causal, a chaotic against a patterned universe. And the unresolved conflict between them will at first give rise to a sense of mystery; to the assumption that evil can never be sounded, however thoroughly it be analysed, that its causes will never fully reveal themselves, even to the most passionate questioning.

It is here that, in the finest tragic writing, there is equilibrium. The reality of evil and pain is not denied; if it were, tragedy would not speak to man's condition as it has done from the time of Aeschylus to the present day. Nevertheless, something is revealed which makes possible the transvaluation of the values upon which this rests; the works of art which we call tragedies are distinguished from others, not only by technical characteristics of subject-matter or form, but also by the balance maintained between conflicting readings of the universe and of man's condition and destiny. The supreme works in this kind reveal that balance in the highest degree, thus satisfying most nearly man's need to find his complex and contradictory experience transmuted into the enduring form of art. Certain tragedies, it is true, fail to maintain complete balance, some lessening their hold on the imagination by presenting irremediable evil and a satanic universe, and some, with similar consequences, indicating remedies so immediate or so easily defined that men's judgement and innate sanity mistrust them. Both kinds may nevertheless remain within the category of tragedy, provided they do not destroy either of the elements in whose conflict the average man recognizes an essential part of his own dual experience.

The characteristic balance thus obtained results, as we have said, in a play of a certain quality. In content and in thought tragedy is, like all great art, an interpretation of some part of the universe of man's experience, but inasmuch as it is dramatic it is primarily an interpretation by implication, by the emphasis it lays on certain parts of that experience, the significance with which it invests them, rather than by explicit or direct commentary. The part of this experience which it selects involves suffering and some kind of catastrophe, and these significant of something more than the bare facts actually present. Balance is thus maintained in all great tragedy; suffering and catastrophe upon the one hand and upon the other a relation (often unspecified and undefined) with some fundamental or universal law whose operation justifies or compensates them. From this arises the conflict of impressions; evident evil against partially hidden yet immanent and overruling good. Thus far all tragedy is akin.

X

JOHN SMART · 1922

The most powerful influence in modern discussions of Tragedy has been that of Hegel, either directly, or indirectly through his disciples. It seems no longer permissible to allow that Tragedy is in its very nature mysterious. As far as may be, mystery is to be eliminated: all things are to be understood, explained, and justified. There must, therefore, be a *reason*

From "Tragedy," by John Smart, *Essays and Studies*, viii, 1922. Used by kind permission of the English Association.

for Tragedy itself. It is not the result of blind forces: there is no such thing as mere fatality: everything that happens can be vindicated as what was right and inevitable. It must be so; it would be wrong if it were otherwise. Hegel's object is, therefore, to justify Tragedy; and he finds the explanation in the character of the tragic hero himself. He is responsible for his own fate. By some guilty act, some fault of judgement, or some defect in his nature, he sets in motion the events which prove at last to be the cause of his own undoing. He cannot blame fate; he cannot blame anything but himself. In his final fall the principle of justice is vindicated. By putting the Individual in the wrong, we put the Universe in the right.

Although Hegel's theory proceeds from a philosophic basis, yet, when it is applied to certain tales or dramas, it ends by being little more than the old doctrine of poetical justice expressed in a new way. Indeed, it almost begins to resemble the familiar morality of the Sunday School: be good and you will be happy; be wicked and you will be punished. By this process of interpretation Tragedy is not so much explained as explained away. Every one can consider the significance which he attaches to the word *Tragedy*, and what process of feeling and reflection passes through his mind when reading or witnessing a tragic work. The reader is invited to make such a process of introspection, and to decide for himself whether an element of *mystery* is not inseparable from Tragedy in his conception of it, and whether he does not associate the idea of Tragedy with that of something *wrong* in the world, an inexplicable failure in the general justice of things; whether, in short, a tragedy in which everything can be explained and justified is actually a tragedy at all.

THE TRAGIC FALLACY

JOSEPH WOOD KRUTCH · 1929

Though we still apply, sometimes, the adjective "tragic" to
one or another of those modern works of literature which
describe human misery and which end more sadly even than
they begin, the term is a misnomer since it is obvious that the
works in question have nothing in common with the classical
examples of the genre and produce in the reader a sense of
depression which is the exact opposite of that elation generated
when the spirit of a Shakespeare rises joyously superior to the
outward calamities which he recounts and celebrates the
greatness of the human spirit whose travail he describes. Tragedies, in that only sense of the word which has any distinctive
meaning, are no longer written in either the dramatic or any
other form and the fact is not to be accounted for in any
merely literary terms. It is not the result of any fashion in
literature or of any deliberation to write about human nature
or character under different aspects, any more than it is of
either any greater sensitiveness of feeling which would make
us shrink from the contemplation of the suffering of Medea
or Othello or of any greater optimism which would make
us more likely to see life in more cheerful terms. It is, on the
contrary, the result of one of those enfeeblements of the human spirit, an illustration of that gradual weakening of man's
confidence in his ability to impose upon the phenomenon of
life an interpretation acceptable to his desires.

Milton set out, he said, to justify the ways of God to man,
and his phrase, if it be interpreted broadly enough, may be
taken as describing the function of all art, which must, in

some way or other, make the life which it seems to represent
satisfactory to those who see its reflection in the magic mirror,
and it must gratify or at least reconcile the desires of the be-
holder, not necessarily, as the naiver exponents of Freudian
psychology maintain, by gratifying individual and often ec-
centric wishes, but at least by satisfying the universally human
desire to find in the world some justice, some meaning, or, at
the very least, some recognizable order. Hence it is that every
real tragedy, however tremendous it may be, is an affirmation
of faith in life, a declaration that even if God is not in his
Heaven, then at least Man is in his world.

Thus for the great ages tragedy is not an expression of
despair but the means by which they saved themselves from
it. It is a profession of faith, and a sort of religion; a way of
looking at life by virtue of which it is robbed of its pain. The
sturdy soul of the tragic author seizes upon suffering and
uses it only as a means by which joy may be wrung out of
existence, but it is not to be forgotten that he is enabled to
do so only because of his belief in the greatness of human
nature and because, though he has lost the child's faith in
life, he has not lost his far more important faith in human
nature. A tragic writer does not have to believe in God, but
he must believe in man.

And if, then, the Tragic Spirit is in reality the product of
a religious faith in which, sometimes at least, faith in the
greatness of God is replaced by faith in the greatness of man,
it serves, of course, to perform the function of religion, to
make life tolerable for those who participate in its beneficent
illusion. It purges the souls of those who might otherwise
despair and it makes endurable the realization that the events
of the outward world do not correspond with the desires of
the heart, and thus, in its own particular way, it does what all
religions do, for it gives a rationality, a meaning, and a justification to the universe. But if it has the strength it has also the

weakness of all faiths, since it may—nay, it must—be ultimately lost as reality, encroaching further and further into the realm of imagination, leaves less and less room in which that imagination can build its refuge.

Like the belief in love and like most of the other mighty illusions by means of which human life has been given a value, the Tragic Fallacy depends ultimately upon the assumption which man so readily makes that something outside his own being, some "spirit not himself"—be it God, Nature, or that still vaguer thing called a Moral Order—joins him in the emphasis which he places upon this or that and confirms him in his feeling that his passions and his opinions are important. When his instinctive faith in that correspondence between the outer and the inner world fades, his grasp upon the faith that sustained him fades also, and Love or Tragedy or what not ceases to be the reality which it was because he is never strong enough in his own insignificant self to stand alone in a universe which snubs him with its indifference.

Poetry, said Santayana in his famous phrase, is "religion which is no longer believed," but it depends, nevertheless, upon its power to revive in us a sort of temporary or provisional credence and the nearer it can come to producing an illusion of belief the greater is its power as poetry. Once the Tragic Spirit was a living faith and out of it tragedies were written. Today these great expressions of a great faith have declined, not merely into poetry, but into a kind of poetry whose premises are so far from any we can really accept that we can only partially and dimly grasp its meaning.

We read but we do not write tragedies. The tragic solution of the problem of existence, the reconciliation to life by means of the tragic spirit is, that is to say, now only a fiction surviving in art. When that art itself has become, as it probably will, completely meaningless, when we have ceased not only to write but to *read* tragic works, then it will be lost and in all real senses forgotten, since the devolution from Religion to Art to Document will be complete.

THE TRAGIC THEATRE

WILLIAM BUTLER YEATS · 1912

One dogma of the printed criticism is that if a play does not contain definite character, its constitution is not strong enough for the stage, and that the dramatic moment is always the contest of character with character. In poetical drama there is, it is held, an antithesis between character and lyric poetry, for lyric poetry—however much it move you when read out of a book—can, as these critics think, but encumber the action. Yet when we go back a few centuries and enter the great periods of drama, character grows less and sometimes disappears, and there is much lyric feeling, and at times a lyric measure will be wrought into the dialogue, a flowing measure that had well-be-fitted music, or that more lumbering one of the sonnet. Suddenly it strikes us that character is continuously present in comedy alone, and that there is much tragedy, that of Corneille, that of Racine, that of Greece and Rome, where its place is taken by passions and motives, one person being jealous, another full of love or remorse or pride or anger.

Tragedy must always be a drowning and breaking of the dykes that separate man from man, and it is upon these dykes comedy keeps house. There is an art of the flood, the art of Titian when his "Ariosto," and his Bacchus and Ariadne, gives new images to the dreams of youth, and of Shakespeare

From *The Cutting of an Agate*, by William Butler Yeats. Used by permission of The Macmillan Company.

when he shows us Hamlet broken away from life by the passionate hesitations of his reverie. And we call this art poetical, because we must bring more to it than our daily mood if we would take our pleasure; and because it takes delight in the moment of exaltation, or excitement, of dreaming (or in the capacity for it, as in that still face of "Ariosto's" that is like some vessel soon to be full of wine). And there is an art that we call real, because character can only express itself perfectly in a real world, being that world's creature, and because we understand it best through a delicate discrimination of the senses which is but entire wakefulness, the daily mood grown cold and crystalline.

We may not find either mood in its purity, but in mainly tragic art one distinguishes devices to exclude or lessen character, to diminish the power of that daily mood, to cheat or blind its too clear perception. If the real world is not altogether rejected, it is but touched here and there, and into the places we have left empty we summon rhythm, balance, pattern, images that remind us of vast passions, the vagueness of past times, all the chimeras that haunt the edge of trance; and if we are painters, we shall express personal emotion through ideal form, a symbolism handled by the generations, a mask from whose eyes the disembodied looks, a style that remembers many masters that it may escape contemporary suggestion; or we shall leave out some element of reality as in Byzantine painting, where there is no mass, nothing in relief; and so it is that in the supreme moment of tragic art there comes upon one that strange sensation as though the hair of one's head stood up. And when we love, if it be in the excitement of youth, do we not also, that the flood may find no stone to convulse, no wall to narrow it, exclude character or the signs of it by choosing that beauty which seems unearthly because the individual woman is lost amid the labyrinth of its lines as though life were trembling into stillness and silence, or at last folding itself away? Some little irrelevance of line, some promise of character to come, may indeed put us at our ease, "give more interest" as the humour of the old man with the basket does to Cleopatra's dying; but should it come as we had dreamed in love's frenzy to our dying for that woman's sake, we would find that the discord had its value from the tune. Nor have we chosen illusion in choosing the outward sign of that moral genius that lives among the subtlety of the passions, and can for her moment make her of the one mind with great artists and poets. In the studio we may indeed say to one another "character is the only beauty," but when we choose a wife, as when we go to the gymnasium to be shaped for woman's eyes, we remember academic form, even though we enlarge a little the point of interest and chose "a painter's beauty," finding it the more easy to believe in the fire because it has made ashes.

When we look at the faces of the old tragic paintings, whether it is in Titian or in some painter of mediaeval China, we find there sadness and gravity, a certain emptiness even, as of a mind that waited the supreme crisis (and indeed it seems at times as if the graphic art, unlike poetry which sings the crisis itself, were the celebration of waiting). Whereas in modern art, whether in Japan or Europe, "vitality" (is not that the great word of the studios?), the energy, that is to say, which is under the command of our common moments, sings, laughs, chatters or looks its busy thoughts.

Certainly we have here the Tree of Life and that of The Knowledge of Good and Evil which is rooted in our interests, and if we have forgotten their differing virtues it is surely because we have taken delight in a confusion of crossing branches. Tragic art, passionate art, the drowner of dykes, the confounder of understanding, moves us by setting us to reverie, by alluring us almost to the intensity of trance. The persons upon the stage, let us say, greaten till they are humanity itself. We feel our minds expand convulsively or spread out slowly like some moon-brightened image-crowded sea. That which is before our eyes perpetually vanishes and returns again in the midst of the excitement it creates, and the more enthralling it is, the more do we forget it.

XVIII

The Idea of Comedy

❋ ❋ ❋ ❋ ❋ ❋ ❋ ❋ ❋ ❋ ❋ ❋ ❋ ❋ ❋ ❋ ❋ ❋ ❋

EVERY MAN firmly believes that, whatever faults or virtues he may possess, he unquestionably has a sense of humor. He may think that he holds this faculty in high regard because it proves him to be an amusing companion or because it is a guarantee that he is never left out when the laugh goes around. Actually the reasons are far more fundamental. A sense of humor is basically a sense of proportion, a perception of relationships and of values which is the beginning of wisdom.

These essays on comedy are devoted to definition as were those on tragedy, but the scope is larger. Definition, in the sense of establishing boundaries, becomes in this case a census of the various provinces of the comic. These areas are vast and many-sided. Tragedy can come to a man in solitude; the simplest pun demands an audience. Comedy is central to the complex of human relationships. It is as large as living and can hardly be separated from either frivolity or high seriousness.

Charged with the capture of a spirit so pervasive and yet so elusive, critics employ various stratagems. Some of them approach comedy cautiously, calling it many names by which they hope to come closer to its true character: wit, humor, fun, laughter, mirth, jest, drollery, quip. Others pursue the opposite of comedy, talking about tragedy and tears. Sometimes they proceed indirectly, using figures of speech and symbols: Addison's allegory and Bergson's echo, Morris's use of light, Meredith's comic spirit. Often they do not try to capture comedy itself but to grasp its characteristics or causes or effects: Eastman's four laws, Morris's seven, Bergson's dancers, Kronenberger's literary examples.

Reading in this group of essays becomes, then, an exercise in discrimination and understanding and a study in method. Addison presents the different elements in comedy by means of an ingenious figure. Morris tries by a series of antitheses to discriminate between two of its components, wit and humor. Bergson, Hazlitt, and Kronenberger turn every facet of the idea to reveal its complexity and to discourage easy generalization. Truly understood, says Meredith, the comic offers material for endless meditation.

✳ ✳ ✳ ✳ ✳ ✳ ✳ ✳ ✳ ✳ ✳ ✳ ✳ ✳ ✳ ✳ ✳ ✳

THE GENEALOGY OF HUMOUR

JOSEPH ADDISON · 1711

It is indeed much easier to describe what is not Humour, than what is; and very difficult to define it otherwise than as Cowley has done Wit, by Negatives. Were I to give my own Notions of it, I would deliver them after *Plato's* manner, in a kind of Allegory, and by supposing Humour to be a Person, deduce to him all his Qualifications, according to the following Genealogy, TRUTH was the Founder of the Family, and the Father of GOOD SENSE. GOOD SENSE was the Father of Wit, who married a Lady of a Collateral Line called MIRTH, by whom he had issue HUMOUR. HUMOUR therefore being the youngest of this Illustrious Family, and descended from Parents of such different Dispositions, is very various and unequal in his Temper; sometimes you see him putting on grave Looks and

From *The Spectator*, No. 35, April 10, 1711.

a solemn Habit, sometimes airy in his Behaviour and fantastick in his Dress: Insomuch that at different times he appears as serious as a Judge, and as jocular as a *Merry-Andrew*. But as he has a great deal of the Mother in his Constitution, whatever Mood he is in, he never fails to make his Company laugh.

FUN AND FUNNY

MAX EASTMAN · 1936

The first law of humor is that things can be funny only when we are in fun. There may be a serious thought or motive lurking underneath our humor. We may be only "half in fun" and still funny. But when we are not in fun at all, when we are "in dead earnest," humor is the thing that is dead.

The second law is that when we are in fun, a peculiar shift of values takes place. Pleasant things are still pleasant, but disagreeable things, so long as they are not disagreeable enough to "spoil the fun," tend to acquire a pleasant emotional flavor and provoke a laugh.

The third law is that "being in fun" is a condition most natural to childhood, and that children at play reveal the humorous laugh in its simplest and most omnivorous form. To them every untoward, unprepared for, unmanageable, inauspicious, ugly, disgusting, puzzling, startling, deceiving, shaking, blinding, jolting, deafening, banging, bumping, or otherwise shocking and disturbing thing, unless it be calamitous enough to force them out of the mood of play, is enjoyable as funny.

The fourth law is that grown-up people retain in varying

From *The Enjoyment of Laughter*, by Max Eastman. New York: Simon and Schuster, 1936. Used by kind permission of the publishers.

degrees this aptitude for being in fun, and thus enjoying unpleasant things as funny. But those not richly endowed with humor manage to feel a very comic feeling only when within, or behind, or beyond, or suggested by, the playfully unpleasant thing, there is a pleasant one. Only then do they laugh uproariously like playing children. And they call this complicated thing or combination of things at which they laugh, a joke.

LAUGHTER

HENRI BERGSON · 1900
Translated by Cloudesley Brereton and Fred Rothwell

The first point to which attention should be called is that the comic does not exist outside the pale of what is strictly *human*. A landscape may be beautiful, charming and sublime, or insignificant and ugly; it will never be laughable. You may laugh at an animal, but only because you have detected in it some human attitude or expression. You may laugh at a hat, but what you are making fun of, in this case, is not the piece of felt or straw, but the shape that men have given it,—the human caprice whose mould it has assumed. It is strange that so important a fact, and such a simple one too, has not attracted to a greater degree the attention of philosophers. Several have defined man as "an animal which laughs." They might equally well have defined him as an animal which is laughed at; for if any other animal, or some lifeless object, produces the same effect, it is always because of some resemblance to man, of the stamp he gives it or the use he puts it to.

From *Laughter, An Essay on the Meaning of the Comic,* by Henri Bergson. Used by kind permission of the Estate of Fred Rothwell.

Now step aside, look upon life as a disinterested spectator: many a drama will turn into a comedy. It is enough for us to stop our ears to the sound of music, in a room where dancing is going on, for the dancers at once to appear ridiculous. How many human actions would stand a similar test? Should we not see many of them suddenly pass from grave to gay, on isolating them from the accompanying music of sentiment? To produce the whole of its effect, then, the comic demands something like a momentary anesthesia of the heart. Its appeal is to intelligence, pure and simple.

This intelligence, however, must always remain in touch with other intelligences. And here is the third fact to which attention should be drawn. You would hardly appreciate the comic if you felt yourself isolated from others. Laughter appears to stand in need of an echo.

Let us clearly mark the point towards which our three preliminary observations are converging. The comic will come into being, it appears, whenever a group of men concentrate their attention on one of their number, imposing silence on their emotions and calling into play nothing but their intelligence.

WIT AND HUMOUR

CORBYN MORRIS · 1744

Wit is the Lustre resulting from the quick Elucidation of one Subject by a just and unexpected Arrangement of it with another Subject. This Definition of WIT will more clearly appear by a short Explanation. It is the Province of WIT to

From *An Essay towards Fixing the True Standards of Wit, Humour, Raillery, Satire, and Ridicule,* 1744.

elucidate, or enlighten a Subject, not by reasoning upon that Subject, but by a just and unexpected Introduction of another similar, or opposite Subject; whereby, upon their Arrangement together, the original Subject may be set off, and more clearly enlighten'd, by their obvious Comparison. It may be proper, for the sake of Distinction, to call the Subject, which is the Basis and Ground-work, the original Subject; and that which is introduced, in order to elucidate it, the auxiliary Subject. That there be always an apparent Chain or Connexion, or else an obvious Agreement or Contrast, between the two Subjects, is absolutely requir'd, in order that the Auxiliary one may be justly introduced; otherwise, instead of WIT, there will only appear a rambling Vivacity, in wild, unprovoked Sallies. And yet every just or natural Introduction of an auxiliary Subject will not produce WIT, unless a new Lustre is reflected from thence upon the original Subject.

It is further to be observed, that the Introduction of the auxiliary Subject ought not only to be just, but also unexpected, which are entirely consistent together; For as every Subject bears various Relations and Oppositions to other Subjects, it is evident that each of these Relations and Oppositions upon being exhibited, will be unexpected to the Persons, who did not perceive them before; and yet they are just by Supposition. It is upon such unexpected Introductions of auxiliary Subjects, that we are struck with a Surprize; from whence the high Brilliancy, and Sparkling of WIT, result.

It is easy to be perceived, that HUMOUR, and WIT are extremely different. HUMOUR appears only in the Foibles and whimsical Conduct of Persons in real Life; WIT appears in Comparisons, either between Persons in real Life, or between other Subjects. HUMOUR is the whimsical Oddity, or Foible, which fairly appears in its Subject, of itself; whereas WIT, is the Lustre which is thrown upon one Subject, by the sudden

Introduction of another Subject. To constitute HUMOUR, there need be no more than one Object concern'd, and this must be always some Person in real Life;—whereas to produce WIT, there must be always two Objects arranged together, and either or both of these may be inanimate. However, though HUMOUR and WIT are thus absolutely different in themselves, yet we frequently see them blended together. Thus if any Foible of a Character in real Life is directly attacked, by pointing out the unexpected and ridiculous Affinity it bears to some inanimate Circumstances, this Foible is then ridiculed with WIT, from the Comparison which is made.— At the same time, as the whimsical Oddity of a Character in real Life is the Ground of the whole, there is also Humour contain'd in the Attack.

HUMOUR and WIT, as they may thus both be united in the same Subject, may also separately appear without the least Mixture together. Thus, if in order to expose the Foible of a Character, a real Person is introduc'd, abounding in this Foible, gravely persisting in it, and valuing himself upon the Merit of it, with great Self-sufficiency, and Disdain of others; this Foible is then solely ridiculed with HUMOUR.

Again, if a gay unexpected Allusion is made from one inanimate Object to another, or from one Person in real Life to another, without any Reference to their whimsical Oddities or Foibles; there WIT only appears.—

That HUMOUR gives more Delight, and leaves a more pleasurable Impression behind it, than WIT, is universally felt and established; Though the Reasons for this have not yet been assign'd.—I shall therefore beg Leave to submit the following.

1. HUMOUR is more interesting than WIT in general, as the Oddities and Foibles of Persons in real Life are more apt to affect our Passions, than any Oppositions or Relations between inanimate Objects.

2. HUMOUR is Nature, or what really appears in the Subject,

without any Embellishments; WIT only a Stroke of Art, where the original Subject, being insufficient of itself, is garnished and deck'd with auxiliary Objects.

3. HUMOUR, or the Foible of a Character in real Life, is usually insisted upon for some Length of Time. From whence, and from the common Knowledge of the Character, it is universally felt and understood.—Whereas the Strokes of WIT are like sudden Flashes, vanishing in an Instant, and usually flying too fast to be sufficiently marked and pursued by the Audience.

4. HUMOUR, if the Representation of it be just, is compleat and perfect in its Kind, and entirely fair and unstrain'd.— Whereas in the Allusions of WIT, the Affinity is generally imperfect and defective in one Part or other; and even in those Points where the Affinity may be allow'd to subsist, some Nicety and Strain is usually requir'd to make it appear.

5. HUMOUR generally appears in such Foibles, as each of the Company thinks himself superior to.—Whereas WIT shews the Quickness and Abilities of the Person who discovers it, and places him superior to the rest of the Company.

6. HUMOUR, in the Representation of the Foibles of Persons in real Life, frequently exhibits very generous benevolent Sentiments of Heart; And these, tho' exerted in a particular odd Manner, justly command our Fondness and Love.— Whereas in the Allusions of WIT, Severity, Bitterness, and Satire, are frequently exhibited.—And where these are avoided, not worthy amiable Sentiments of the Heart, but quick unexpected Efforts of the Fancy, are presented.

7. The odd Adventures, and Embarrassments, which Persons in real Life are drawn into by their Foibles, are fit Subjects of Mirth.—Whereas in pure WIT, the Allusions are rather surprizing, than mirthful; and the Agreements or Contrasts which are started between Objects, without any relation to the Foibles of Persons in real Life, are more fit to be admired

for their Happiness and Propriety, than to excite our Laughter. —Besides, WIT, in the frequent Repetition of it, tires the Imagination with its precipitate Sallies and Flights; and teizes the Judgment.—Whereas HUMOUR, in the Representation of it, puts no Fatigue upon the Imagination, and gives exquisite Pleasure to the Judgment.

These seem to me to be the different Powers and Effects of HUMOUR and WIT. However, the most agreeable Representations or Compositions of all others, appear not where they separately exist, but where they are united together in the same Fabric; where HUMOUR is the Ground-work and chief Substance, and WIT happily spread, quickens the whole with Embellishments.

A LECTURE ON THE COMIC

WILLIAM HAZLITT · 1819

Man is the only animal that laughs and weeps; for he is the only animal that is struck with the difference between what things are, and what they ought to be. We weep at what thwarts or exceeds our desires in serious matters: we laugh at what only disappoints our expectations in trifles. We shed tears from sympathy with real and necessary distress; as we burst into laughter from want of sympathy with that which is unreasonable and unnecessary, the absurdity of which provokes our spleen or mirth, rather than any serious reflections on it.

To explain the nature of laughter and tears, is to account for the condition of human life; for it is in a manner compounded of these two! It is a tragedy or a comedy—sad or merry, as

From *Lectures on the Comic Writers of Great Britain*, 1819.

it happens. The crimes and misfortunes that are inseparable from it, shock and wound the mind when they once seize upon it, and when the pressure can no longer be borne, seek relief in tears: the follies and absurdities that men commit, or the odd accidents that befall them, afford us amusement from the very rejection of these false claims upon our sympathy, and end in laughter. If every thing that went wrong, if every vanity or weakness in another gave us a sensible pang, it would be hard indeed: but as long as the disagreeableness of the consequences of a sudden disaster is kept out of sight by the immediate oddity of the circumstances, and the absurdity or unaccountableness of a foolish action is the most striking thing in it, the ludicrous prevails over the pathetic, and we receive pleasure instead of pain from the farce of life which is played before us, and which discomposes our gravity as often as it fails to move our anger or our pity!

To understand or define the ludicrous, we must first know what the serious is. Now the serious is the habitual stress which the mind lays upon the expectation of a given order of events, following on another with a certain regularity and weight of interest attached to them. When this stress is increased beyond its usual pitch of intensity, so as to overstrain the feelings by the violent opposition of good to bad, or of objects to our desires, it becomes the pathetic or tragical. The ludicrous, or comic, is the unexpected loosening or relaxing this stress below its usual pitch of intensity, by such an abrupt transposition of the order of our ideas, as taking the mind unawares, throws it off its guard, startles it into a lively sense of pleasure, and leaves no time nor inclination for painful reflections.

The essence of the laughable then is the incongruous, the disconnecting one idea from another, or the jostling of one feeling against another. The first and most obvious cause of laughter is to be found in the simple succession of events, as in the sudden shifting of a disguise, or some unlooked-for accident, without any absurdity of character or situation. The accidental contradiction between our expectations and the event can hardly be said, however, to amount to the ludicrous: it is merely laughable. The ludicrous is where there is the same contradiction between the object and our expectations, heightened by some deformity or inconvenience, that is, by its being contrary to what is customary or desirable; as the ridiculous, which is the highest degree of the laughable, is that which is contrary not only to custom but to sense and reason, or is a voluntary departure from what we have a right to expect from those who are conscious of absurdity and propriety in words, looks, and actions.

COMEDY

LOUIS KRONENBERGER · 1952

Comedy is not just a happy as opposed to an unhappy ending, but a way of surveying life so that happy endings must prevail. But it is not to be confused, on that account, with optimism, any more than a happy ending is to be confused with happiness. Comedy is much more reasonably associated with pessimism—with at any rate a belief in the smallness that survives as against the greatness that is scarred or destroyed. In mortal affairs it is tragedy, like forgiveness, that seems divine; and comedy, like error, that is human.

One might perhaps begin by talking about comedy in its philosophic sense, as an attitude toward life, rather than as a mere technical aspect of the theater. One might begin, in

From *The Thread of Laughter*, by Louis Kronenberger. New York: Alfred A. Knopf, Inc., 1952. Used with the kind permission of the publisher.

other words, by speaking of the comedy that unites such writers and writings as Lucian and Aristophanes, the *Decameron* and *Candide,* Congreve and Peacock and Sterne, *Pride and Prejudice* and *Le Bourgeois Gentilhomme.* Coarse as Aristophanes can be and genteel as Jane Austen, broadly as Aristophanes can clown and exquisitely as Jane Austen can annihilate, the two have much the same vision of life, much the same eye for its absurdities. They have in full measure the comic point of view, as other writers have the tragic point of view.

Comedy, in brief, is criticism. If through laughing at others we purge ourselves of certain spiteful and ungenerous instincts —as through tragedy we achieve a higher and more publicized catharsis—that is not quite the whole of it. Comedy need not be hostile to idealism; it need only show how far human beings fall short of the ideal. The higher comedy mounts, the airier and more brilliant its forms, the more are we aware of man's capacity for being foolish or self-deluded or complacent; in the very highest comedy, such as the finale of Mozart's *Marriage of Figaro,* we are in a very paradise of self-deceptions and misunderstandings and cross-purposes. At the heart of high comedy there is always a strain of melancholy, as round the edges there is all gaiety and ebullience and glitter; and Schiller was perhaps right in regarding high comedy as the greatest of all literary forms.

THE COMIC SPIRIT

GEORGE MEREDITH · 1877

One excellent test of the civilization of a country, as I have said, I take to be the flourishing of the Comic idea and Comedy;

From *The Idea of Comedy,* 1877.

and the test of true Comedy is that it shall awaken thoughtful laughter.

If you believe that our civilization is founded in common-sense (and it is the first condition of sanity to believe it), you will, when contemplating men, discern a Spirit overhead; not more heavenly than the light flashed upward from glassy surfaces, but luminous and watchful; never shooting beyond them, nor lagging in the rear; so closely attached to them that it may be taken for a slavish reflex, until its features are studied. It has the sage's brows, and the sunny malice of a faun lurks at the corners of the half-closed lips drawn in an idle wariness of half tension. That slim feasting smile, shaped like the long-bow, was once a big round satyr's laugh, that flung up the brows like a fortress lifted by gunpowder. The laugh will come again, but it will be of the order of the smile, finely tempered, showing sunlight of the mind, mental rich-ness rather than noisy enormity. Its common aspect is one of unsolicitous observation, as if surveying a full field and having leisure to dart on its chosen morsels, without any fluttering eagerness. Men's future upon earth does not attract it; their honesty and shapeliness in the present does; and whenever they wax out of proportion, overblown, affected, pretentious, bombastical, hypocritical, pedantic, fantastically delicate; whenever it sees them self-deceived or hoodwinked, given to run riot in idolatries, drifting into vanities, congre-gating in absurdities, planning short-sightedly, plotting dement-edly; whenever they are at variance with their professions, and violate the unwritten but perceptible laws binding them in consideration one to another; whenever they offend sound reason, fair justice; are false in humility or mined with con-ceit, individually, or in the bulk—the Spirit overhead will look humanely malign and cast an oblique light on them, followed by volleys of silvery laughter. That is the Comic Spirit.

XIX

The Mona Lisa of Leonardo da Vinci

❋ ❋ ❋ ❋ ❋ ❋ ❋ ❋ ❋ ❋ ❋ ❋ ❋ ❋ ❋ ❋ ❋

LEONARDO'S PORTRAIT, which was an attractive subject of controversy in the nineteenth century, has become almost unacceptable in modern discussion. Bernard Berenson speaks for the rebellious "captive admirers" of the picture in an analysis of his own disaffection (*Study and Criticism*) wherein he calls the Mona Lisa "an incubus." One may wonder whether time has not, after all, in spite of Pater's confidence, turned a cold eye upon the portrait, whether it is merely excessive enthusiasm and endless controversy or something more fundamental to tides in taste which has chilled our admiration.

This is the most complex of the comparative readings, since it involves not only the techniques of exposition and expression, but the basic question: what is art? It also, of course, involves the criteria of art criticism. The five passages represent five completely different approaches to the painting. Vasari admires the physical realism of the portrait. Pater, on the contrary, is captured by the mystery and the magic he finds in it. George Moore clearly demands that a picture be evocative. Kenyon Cox studies the modeling; Barnes, the color and light. The standards for judging a work of art are basically different in each of these critiques. Considered in the light of the dates of publication, they represent several steps in the history of criticism. Studied from the point of view of the author's intention, they are a striking commentary upon selection of detail and emphasis.

❋ ❋ ❋ ❋ ❋ ❋ ❋ ❋ ❋ ❋ ❋ ❋ ❋ ❋ ❋ ❋ ❋ ❋

THE PORTRAIT OF THE MONA LISA

GEORGIO VASARI · 1550

Whoever shall desire to see how far art can imitate nature may do so to perfection in this head, wherein every peculiarity that could be depicted by the utmost subtlety of the pencil has been faithfully reproduced. The eyes have the lustrous brightness and moisture which is seen in life, and around them are those pale, red, and slightly livid circles, also proper to nature. The nose, with its beautiful and delicately roseate nostrils, might be easily believed to be alive; the mouth, admirable in its outline, has the lips uniting the rose-tints of their colour with those of the face, in the utmost perfection, and the carnation of the cheeks does not appear to be painted, but truly flesh and blood. He who looks earnestly at the pit of the throat cannot but believe that he sees the beating of the pulses. Mona Lisa was exceedingly beautiful, and while Leonardo was painting her portrait, he took the precaution of keeping some one constantly near her to sing or play on instruments, or to jest and otherwise amuse her.

From *Lives of the Most Eminent Painters, Sculptors and Architects*, first published in 1550.

LA GIOCONDA

WALTER PATER · 1873

La Gioconda is, in the truest sense, Leonardo's masterpiece, the revealing instance of his mode of thought and work. In suggestiveness, only the *Melancholia* of Dürer is comparable to it; and no crude symbolism disturbs the effect of its subdued and graceful mystery. We all know the face and hands of the figure, set in its marble chair, in that circle of fantastic rocks, as in some faint light under sea. Perhaps of all ancient pictures time has chilled it least.

What was the relationship of a living Florentine to this creature of his thought? By what strange affinities had the dream and the person grown up thus apart, and yet so closely together? Present from the first incorporeally in Leonardo's brain, dimly traced in the designs of Verrocchio, she is found present at last in *Il Giocondo's* house. That there is much of mere portraiture in the picture is attested by the legend that by artificial means, the presence of mimes and flute-players, that subtle expression was protracted on the face. Again, was it in four years and by renewed labour never really completed, or in four months and as by stroke of magic, that the image was projected?

The presence that rose thus so strangely beside the waters, is expressive of what in the ways of a thousand years men had come to desire. Hers is the head upon which all "the ends of the world are come," and the eyelids are a little weary. It is a beauty wrought out from within upon the flesh, the deposit, little cell by cell, of strange thoughts and fantastic reveries and exquisite passions. Set it for a moment beside one of those white Greek goddesses or beautiful women of antiquity, and how would they be troubled by this beauty, into

From *The Renaissance*, 1873.

which the soul with all its maladies has passed! All the thoughts
and experience of the world have etched and moulded there,
in that which they have of power to refine and make expressive the outward form, the animalism of Greece, the lust of
Rome, the mysticism of the middle age with its spiritual ambition and imaginative loves, the return of the Pagan world,
the sins of the Borgias. She is older than the rocks among
which she sits; like the vampire, she has been dead many times,
and learned the secrets of the grave; and has been a diver in
deep seas, and keeps their fallen day about her; and trafficked
for strange webs with Eastern merchants, and, as Leda, was
the mother of Helen of Troy, and, as Saint Anne, the mother
of Mary; and all this has been to her but as the sound of
lyres and flutes, and lives only in the delicacy with which
it has moulded the changing lineaments, and tinged the eyelids and the hands. The fancy of a perpetual life, sweeping together ten thousand experiences, is an old one; and modern
philosophy has conceived the idea of humanity as wrought
upon by, and summing up in itself, all modes of thought and
life. Certainly Lady Lisa might stand as the embodiment of
the old fancy, the symbol of the modern idea.

MONA LISA AND REMBRANDT'S WIFE

GEORGE MOORE · 1911

Long ago the *Mona Lisa* was my adventure, but this year
Rembrandt's portrait of his wife held me at gaze. It did not
delight me as Manet delights; the emotion was deeper, vaguer

From *Hail and Farewell*, by George Moore. Copyright, 1911, D. Appleton
and Company. Reprinted by kind permission of the publishers Appleton-
Century-Crofts, Inc.

and more intense, and I seemed to myself like a magnetic patient in the coil of some powerful enchantment. The emotion that this picture awakens is almost physical. It gets at you like music, like a sudden breath of perfume. When one approaches, the eyes fade into brown shadow, and when one withdraws, they begin to tell their story, and the story they tell is of a woman's soul. She seems conscious of her weakness, of her sex, and the burden of her own special lot—she is Rembrandt's wife, a servant, a satellite, a watcher. The mouth is no more than a little shadow, but what wistful tenderness there is in it! and the colour of the face is white, faintly tinted with bitumen, and in the cheeks some rose madder transpires through the yellow. She wears a fur jacket, but the fur was no trouble to Rembrandt; he did not strive for realism. It is fur, that is sufficient. Grey pearls hang in her ears; there is a brooch upon her breast, and a hand at the bottom of the picture passing out of the frame, and that hand reminds one as the chin does, of the old story that God took a little clay and made man out of it. That chin and that hand and arm are moulded without display of knowledge as Nature moulds. The picture seems as if it had been breathed upon the canvas. Did not a great poet once say that God breathed into Adam? The other pictures seem dry and insignificant, the *Mona Lisa*, celebrated in literature, hanging a few feet away, seems factitious when compared with this portrait; that smile, so often described as mysterious, that hesitating smile which held my youth in a little tether has come to seem to me but a grimace, and the pale mountains no more mysterious than a globe or map seems at a distance.

THE MONA LISA

KENYON COX · 1917

Much rhapsodical nonsense has been written about the "Mona Lisa" and her enigmatic smile, and there have been endless speculations as to her character and the meaning of her expression. It is all beside the mark. The truth is that the "Mona Lisa" is a study of modelling, little more. Leonardo had discovered that the expression of smiling is much more a matter of the modelling of the cheek and of the forms below the eye than of the change in the line of the lips. It interested him, with his new power of modelling, to produce a smile wholly by these delicate changes of surface; hence, the mysterious expression. Poets may find "La Gioconda" a vampire or what not —to artists with a sense of form her portrait will always be a masterpiece because it is one of the subtlest and most exquisite pieces of modelling in existence. It is perfect as the surface of a Greek marble is perfect, beautiful with the beauty of a lily-petal, and is well worth the years of study and of labor that it is said to have cost.

ANALYSIS OF THE MONA LISA

ALBERT C. BARNES · 1937

Leonardo's primary interest was in science; his deficient interest in the qualities which lend themselves to a rendering in pictorial terms is reflected in his very unequal command of plastic resources, by his bad color, overemphasis on light, and dependence upon effects adventitious to painting, even semi-literary effects, such as the smile in "Mona Lisa."

In "Mona Lisa," Leonardo really makes color function successfully, a rare achievement with him. The deep, rich brownish reds in the sleeve of the figure, duplicated in the neighboring background, are an organic part of the form, and not only contribute to tying it up and making it real, but form a definite color-design. This is unusual for Leonardo, for even in his most successful picture, "Bacchus," the color adds but little to the design. Indeed, one of the chief reasons for denying to Leonardo a place among the greatest artists is his inability to merge light with color, as they are merged whenever either appears at its best.

The figure is realized in fine three-dimensional quality, in relation to a background with perspective convincing not over-accentuated, therefore harmonizing well with the figure. One feels less the tendency of Leonardo to overlighting, probably because of the pattern formed by the lighting of the hands, which is not overdone, the upper part of the chest, and the face, against a sky with less light than the face and chest. Shadows not muddy as often in Leonardo. The landscape just back of the figure and up to the water-line is formed of a rich color, deep and charged with a brownish-red, which determines its general color-value. This color is duplicated in the sleeves, and the folds and curves of the sleeves form a harmonious design with the curves in the background just noted. Yet throughout there is a preoccupation with light which detracts from the value, and the same is true of the sentimental expression of the face.

XX

The Portraits

❋ ❋ ❋ ❋ ❋ ❋ ❋ ❋ ❋ ❋ ❋ ❋ ❋ ❋ ❋ ❋

THE BOOK REVIEWER and the critic frequently live in the same person, and their obligation to interpret and to assess the value of a literary work appears at first glance to be the same. Yet, for reasons which are revealed in this series of contemporary reviews and considered critiques, their tasks present almost diametrically different occupational hazards and produce strikingly different results. Fortunately for the reviewer his pronouncements are in most cases buried in the bound volumes of old periodicals, where time's revenges are well concealed. After a decade or more he may even be given a second chance, when the paper-bound reprint is published, to write what is truly a re-view.

The collection of these criticisms of two books which have commanded continuing attention and growing understanding is not intended to discredit the contemporary review, but rather to demonstrate the variety of approaches to a book and to illustrate the ripening perception of its significance which distinguishes the important novel. The contemporary distractions which greet the appearance of a work of art are here represented by the prejudices, anti-British and sectarian, in early reviews of the Portraits. The angry rejection of Joyce's experiments with frank statement appears naïve in the perspective of thirty years. Mr. Matthiessen and Mr. Kenner, addressing themselves with confidence to a substantial group of mature readers, can, however, penetrate to the heart of the novel. It is important to note that the book reviewers write for an audience quite different from that addressed by the critic. It is, however, equally important and very reassuring to remember that not a few members of these audiences are the same, albeit separated from their former selves by time and experience.

❀ ❀ ❀ ❀ ❀ ❀ ❀ ❀ ❀ ❀ ❀ ❀ ❀ ❀ ❀ ❀ ❀ ❀

HENRY JAMES, *The Portrait of a Lady*

FOUR CONTEMPORARY REVIEWS

1 · 1883

Mr. James, in his latest completed work—'The Portrait of a Lady'—carries out unflinchingly the theories of his school. There is no story. The book is one of the longest of recent times—767 closely-printed pages; and there is not a single interesting incident in it from beginning to end. No one can possibly care, for a single moment, what becomes of any of the characters. If an earthquake swallowed them all up in the middle of the second volume, the reader would only be tempted to thank the fates for a good deliverance. Three volumes of 'analysis' in small type is somewhat trying, even to the most sternly cultivated aestheticism. The characters are described at enormous length by Mr. James; then they describe themselves; then they are described by the other characters. Between them all, it would be strange if their 'points' were not sufficiently brought out. But nothing can relieve their inborn tediousness. Mr. James's descriptive writing is not remarkable for either grace or power, and his conversations are not brilliant. True Mr. Howells assures us that Mr. James's

From *The Quarterly Review*, clv, 1883.

style 'is, upon the whole, *better than that of any other novelist;'*
but some of us may perhaps hope for pardon if we prefer Scott,
Thackeray, or George Eliot. It is evident that the Transat-
lantic aesthetic reformers will not run the risk of placing too
low an estimate upon the services which they are rendering
to literature. And then the theory is laid down, that the silly
old custom of finishing a novel should be discarded. There is
to be no beginning, no middle, and no end. It is like a lucky-
bag at a bazaar—you thrust your hand in anywhere and take
out anything you can find. As Mr. Howells says, the reader
must be left 'arbiter of the destiny of the author's creations.'
The novelist provides the characters, and everybody is left
free to dispose of them according to his own taste. Thus, in
'The Portrait of a Lady,' the fate of all the personages in
the book is left unsettled. We are shown at the close a
glimpse of the lady and her lover—one of her lovers. 'He
glared at her a moment through the dusk, and the next instant
she felt his arms about her, and his lips on her own lips. His
kiss was like a flash of lightning.' That is about all, but let no
one do Mr. James the injustice to suppose that his scenes are all
so warm as this. The flashes of lightning are few and far apart.
As Professor Nichols observes, 'his morality [is] always reliable.' And no doubt it is worth something to be sure, when
we take up a novel, that we shall have good 'reliable' morality
in every page. That merit is possessed in an equal degree by
Mr. Howells and Mr. James. So much it is due to them to
acknowledge. Dull unspeakably dull, they may be; but they
are never improper.

II · 1882

With the introduction, a few years ago, of the "Ulster" overcoat, oddly enough came in a flood of English ideas and ab-

From *The Catholic World*, xxxiv, 1882.

surd affectations of English manners. In the same way as, when the old republican simplicity of Rome was swamped by the wealth which conquest had brought, the Roman exquisites aped the small arts and the vices of the Greeks. Our Little Britons of the press studiously boycott whatever is distinctively American, so that if one desires to get at the real sentiment of the great body of the American people he must as a rule turn elsewhere than to what is styled in the English fashion the "metropolitan" journals. Of course this is merely a momentary craze, but in the meantime, like everything else that is insincere, it is doing harm to the moral sense of the people influenced by it. A mild sort of cynicism is one of its perceptible effects.

This cynicism is apparent in all of Mr. James' writings, and shows itself especially in his studied belittling of whatever was formerly supposed to be the particular pride of Americans. Yet, after all, Mr. James is perhaps not so unjust as he is unmerciful. He aims at a minute picturing of manners rather than of character. His lotus-eating Americans abroad, with their small talk, their selfishness, their entire want of moral purpose, are perhaps not so much caricatures as some critics would have us believe. They are, in fact, the types of a generation that has practically thrown off Protestantism, and remaining without any but the very vaguest notions of religion, is guided by its natural instincts only, instead of by an educated conscience. In this volume of Mr. James', for instance, except two or three Catholic nuns and a young girl brought up by them—and who all, by the way, are given a very stupid look—not one of the personages seems to have any belief in God or any idea whatever of duty. Even their ambitions, when they have any, are petty and unsteady. Apparently they are only saved from becoming real criminals by the lack of courage and of opportunity. Mr. James himself, it is likely, has no ambition to be rated as a satirist, yet all the same he is a satirist, and a tolerably effective one.

III · 1882

The one thing which the book is not, is what it calls itself.
There are several portraits of subordinate ladies—of Mrs.
Touchett and Miss Stackpole, for example, both of which
are admirable pictures; but of the heroine, upon whom the
greatest pains have been expended, and to whom endless
space is afforded for the setting forth of her characteristics, we
have no portrait, nor, even with the enormous amount of
material supplied by Mr. James, do we find it easy to put
together anything which will serve to supply the defect. We
doubt much whether, in all the historical records that exist,
we have as much material for the construction, let us say, of
a recognisable portrait of Queen Elizabeth—no insignificant
figure—as we have for that of Isabel Archer. "Her head was
erect, her eye brilliant, her flexible figure turned itself lightly
this way and that, in sympathy with the alertness with which
she evidently caught impressions. Her impressions were numerous, and they were all reflected in a clear, still smile," is Mr.
James's description of his heroine; and it is about the clearest
view we get of the young lady. For once in a way he is outside of her: but as he goes on he gets more and more within
the circle of this irresistible young woman's personality; and
we have to receive both herself and her immediate surround-
ings, not so much as they actually are, but as they are seen
through her eyes. This is always confusing; for self-knowledge
at its closest has many limitations, and the most impartial student of his own mind will probably get more light upon it by
overhearing one sharp characterisation from outside than by
weeks of self-examination. Isabel's aspect from outside is conveyed to us only in the raptures of her adorers; for all the men
she encounters fall in love with her.

It was inevitable that such a heroine should end unhappily

From *Blackwood's Edinburgh Magazine*, cxxxi, 1882.

—even if it were not inevitable that all Mr. James's books should break off with a sharp cut of arbitrary conclusion, leaving all the questions they so skilfully raise unsolved. Isabel, through the means of a wonderful woman whom she meets in her aunt's house, and who is a sort of symbol of unusual experience, as the younger woman is of the craving for it, falls under the fascinations of a certain aesthetic and beauty-loving American, Gilbert Osmond. We confess to being quite unable to understand how it is that Isabel falls into Osmond's toils, unless it is because so elaborate and self-conscious a personality recoils instinctively, even though full of an abstract admiration for truth, from the downright and veracious, and finds in the complications of an elaborately conventional mind something that has the air of being larger and richer than the true. The reader is never for a moment taken in by the superiority of this most carefully dressed and posed figure, whose being altogether is mysterious, and of whom, notwithstanding the author's elaborate descriptions, we never penetrate the *fin mot*.

IV · 1882

The analysis of character and motive, which fills so large a part in Mr. James's writings, is here conducted with all the accuracy and completeness of a mathematical demonstration. The reader is not confronted at once with the intricacies of the problem or fatigued by its length: he is led by logical process from one point to another, his interest being riveted all through by the detail. Each conclusion is clearly marked, all possible aids are given to the memory, and when at last the demonstrator breaks off in the abrupt way which has startled all his readers, it is with the air of saying, "I have furnished all the points and shown you how to proceed. Find the answer for yourselves."

From *Lippincott's Magazine*, xxix, 1882.

Mr. James's reluctance, or rather his positive refusal, to complete a book in the ordinary sense of the word is a curious trait, and one which piques study. In the matter of detail his books are finished to the last degree, but he cannot bring himself to the vulgarity of a regular *dénouement*, and he lacks the poetic force to substitute for it a suggestive or picturesque climax. Everything in one of Mr. James's books seems to be leading to a simple and satisfactory end, but coming near the goal he sees a crowd there and turns aside in disgust. There is no time to change his destination, but he will not go out at the common turnstile, happen what may.

The process is certainly seen at its best in the portrait of Miss Archer, which in all other respects than that of reality is a brilliant success. It is original, consistent in every particular, full of distinction, and painted with wonderful delicacy and precision. Mr. James has drawn from an actual though rare type of American girlhood. He has taken it at its highest development and selected all its finer qualities. He has studied every little nerve and fibre, all the intuitions and reasonings which belong to it: as an exercise in mental anatomy the delineation is perfect. The warmth of intellectual interest, the absence of any religious motive, combined with the clearest moral sense, make Isabel a character belonging to the time perhaps rather than the country, but one which is found here at an earlier age than elsewhere. To make Isabel become Caspar Goodwood's mistress at the end would be to destroy the entire texture of her character, and we cannot believe that Mr. James intended to point to that as the solution. A sweeter nature than hers might be one more susceptible of corruption. Isabel was aloof from it rather than above it, and if moral support failed her she was certain to be saved by that other instinct with which the author has endowed her, —the dread of vulgarity.

Of the other characters, who are all intimately associated with Isabel's destiny, Goodwood is too much in the nature of a geometrical line to require any detailed analysis, but every one else is more or less complex, and there are many delicate shades in their delineation. Such is the resemblance between Madame Merle and Pansy, which is touched upon in a number of little ways and suggests their relationship to each other long before circumstances give any hint of it. Pansy is an unfledged Madame Merle, the same nature more carefully trained, as contented and as complete in her innocence as her mother is at home in intrigue. Madame Merle herself is tolerably vague. She is an ever-present idea, rather than a person. Miss Stackpole, on the other hand, is bright and vivid; and Ralph Touchett is the warmest and truest figure in Mr. James's gallery of portraits, not excepting the more elaborate and finished one of the Lady herself.

THE CODE OF LADYHOOD

EDWARD SACKVILLE WEST · 1943

The code of ladyhood received its first attacks (from within) just before the last war. After the war it was generally buffeted, both from within and from without; now there are few representatives of the species still extant, and they are mostly old, living apart and—as a standard—generally unregarded. Where a lady is detected, her vulnerability is contemptuously exploited. Virtue may be its own reward, but the adage comes ill from those who flout it. What is—what was—that virtue? To be a lady meant to possess a high degree of social responsibility and a sensitiveness to *taste* in behaviour. It was prima-

From *The New Statesman and Nation*, xxv, April 17, 1943: "Books in General," by Edward Sackville West. Used by kind permission of the publishers.

rily an aesthetic, only secondarily a moral, position: the lady did certain good things because to do them was implied by her condition, and she avoided certain others because they were (to her) obviously ugly. If she was kind it was because she was, in the nature of her case, disinterested. She was not expected to be an angel, but was continuously required to be something of an artist.

In 1881 ladies were the rule, and in drawing the portrait of one the middle-aged, cosmopolitan man of letters that was Henry James set himself to make explicit what novelists like Disraeli and Meredith took for granted, and to isolate and set in relief the specific qualities of the situation. The result is by the highest standard a most beautiful and distinguished piece of work. If, as a novel, it is not quite in the first class, the reason lies, not in any failure to realise the chief end, but rather in the relative weakness of two of the other characters. Nevertheless the standard of conduct represented by Isabel Archer will not soon be matched by any code of social behaviour we are likely to see emerge from the opening era. Indeed, to read *The Portrait of a Lady* to-day is to take the measure of the relational poverty to which modern men and women have condemned themselves.

The story is unfolded with Victorian leisureliness but with a serpentine guile in the "placing" of events and the juxtaposition of characters. As far as the creation of living character goes, James's later elaboration of method never enabled him to do better than here. As the years went on he took mother-of-pearl opera-glasses to look at things he could already see quite clearly. The result was a fascinatingly absolute completeness of detail and a soft yet bright light beautifully diffused over the whole canvas—but at the cost of lively impact and of clear-cut dialogue. It is possible that at least once (in *The Wings of the Dove*) James treated a situation with wider and deeper implications and an even greater intrinsic pathos;

he never told a more poignant story with more perception and directness.

The poignancy lies in the sweetness of Isabel's character and the brutal disillusionment to which her Bovarysme exposes it. She may have "enjoyed puzzling a lord," but she declined to marry even the nicest of them. To have chosen so much— so very much—worse would seem to argue a failure of intelligence. But this is exactly the crux of James's vision of Isabel's character, for we are told quite early in the book that her view of life reposed on a considerable self-esteem. Now innocence such as hers is made doubly vulnerable by this quality, which creates a vicious time-lag after innocence has been destroyed.

Yet these sacrifices have concomitant satisfactions, and Isabel rightly felt herself to be "in a better position for appreciating people than they are for appreciating you." And even in the ultimate abyss of disillusion, during her last meeting with the woman who had grossly betrayed her friendship, she enjoyed the luxury of silence, where mere words would have spelt a vulgar revenge. Such private subtleties are the reward of a Cornelian conception of duty being to embrace danger and unhappiness in the aesthetic fulfilment of personality.

"*L'esthétique est une justice supérieure,*" said Flaubert. Superior or not, Henry James is a novelist who never flinches from judging his characters.

THE END OF THE *PORTRAIT*

F. O. MATTHIESSEN · 1944

The end of Isabel's career is not yet in sight. That fact raises a critical issue about James' way of rounding off his narratives.

From *Henry James: The Major Phase*, by F. O. Matthiessen. Copyright, 1944, by Oxford University Press, Inc.

He was keenly aware of what his method involved. As he wrote in his notebook, upon concluding his detailed project: 'With strong handling it seems to me that it may all be very true, very powerful, very touching. The obvious criticism of course will be that it is not finished—that it has not seen the heroine to the end of her situation—that I have left her *en l'air*. This is both true and false. The *whole* of anything is never told; you can only take what groups together. What I have done has that unity—it groups together. It is complete in itself—and the rest may be taken up or not, later.'

This throws a great deal of light—perhaps more than any single passage of his published work—on how James conceived of structure. He recounted in the preface to the *Portrait* how Turgenieff had encouraged him in his belief that the important thing to start with was not an air-tight plot, but rather a character or group of characters who are so living that the main question becomes to 'invent and select' the complications that such characters 'would be most likely to produce and to feel.'

He had been particularly concerned in the *Portrait* with launching Isabel Archer into action, with presenting her so vividly that his narrative would compose itself around the primary question, 'Well, what will she do?' It has recently been assumed that James believed entirely in the rightness of his heroine's conduct, and that since our age no longer feels as he—and she—did about the strictness of the marriage vow, we can no longer respond to the book except as to a period piece. But that is to misread not merely the ending, but all of James' own 'characteristic characterization' of Isabel. He could hardly have made a more lucid summary of the weaknesses that she exposed to Europe: 'her meagre knowledge, her inflated ideals, her confidence at once innocent and dogmatic, her temper at once exacting and indulgent'—that whole passage of analysis on the evening after her arrival at

Gardencourt, a passage untouched in the revision, is meant to have our closest scrutiny.

As Isabel embarks on her 'free exploration' of life, Henrietta is outspoken in declaring that she is drifting rather to 'some great mistake,' that she is not enough 'in contact with reality,' with the 'toiling, striving' world. Ralph tells her that she has 'too much conscience'—a peculiarly American complication in the romantic temperament. Although all her diverse friends are united in their disapproval of Osmond, she proceeds to do the wrong thing for the right reasons.

In both the original and the revision Isabel lays the most scrupulous emphasis upon the sacredness of a promise. Despite all her eagerness for culture, hers is no speculative spirit. Osmond comes to despise her for having 'the moral horizon' of a Unitarian minister—'poor Isabel, who had never been able to understand Unitarianism!' But whether she understands it or not, she is a firm granddaughter of the Puritans, not in her thought but in her moral integrity. In portraying her character and her fate, James was also writing an essay on the interplay of free will and determinism. Isabel's own view is that she was 'perfectly free,' that she married Osmond of her most deliberate choice, and that, however miserable one may be, one must accept the consequences of one's acts. James knew how little she was free, other than to follow to an impulsive extreme everything she had been made by her environment and background.

Thus he leaves her to confront her future, and is satisfied if he has endowed his characters with so much 'felt life' that the reader must weigh for himself what is likely to lie ahead in her relation with Osmond. He had about Isabel a tragic sense, but he did not write a tragedy, as he was to do in *The Wings of the Dove*, since this earlier drama was lacking in the finality of purgation and judgment. But his view of his material was not at all ambiguous. He knew how romantic Isabel was, how little experienced she was in mature social behavior. He had shown that she was completely mistaken in believing that 'the world lay before her—she could do whatever she chose.' But James also knew the meaning and the value of renunciation. The American life of his day, in its reckless plunge to outer expansiveness and inner defeat, had taught him that as his leading spiritual theme. Through Isabel Archer he gave one of his fullest and freshest expressions of inner reliance in the face of adversity. It is no wonder that, after enumerating her weaknesses, he had concluded: 'she would be an easy victim of scientific criticism if she were not intended to awaken on the reader's part an impulse more tender . . .'

THE TREE OF KNOWLEDGE

F. W. DUPEE · 1951

Marriage as a reality figures more conspicuously in the *Portrait* than in any novel of James's so far. Much as the European scene colors and qualifies Isabel's adventures, they are strictly concerned with her finding a husband and then trying to live with him. If she is a kind of Elizabeth Bennet, she is one who operates on a world scale.

Marriage is the axis on which the *Portrait* turns. Everyone in it is involved in some significant union or exhibits some meaningful attitude towards the institution, whether it is the confirmed bachelor Ralph Touchett or the seemingly confirmed feminist Henrietta Stackpole, Isabel's American friend. Marriage, however, figures in the *Portrait* not as a specific social institution—as it does in, say, *A Doll's House*—but as a condition of existence—of Isabel's existence in particular.

In her energy and meaning, it must be admitted, Isabel is far from easy to reconstruct. One thing is certain: a kind of felicity attaches to her whatever she does. This James feels strongly and he makes us feel it. It consists partly in her delicate conviction of selfhood, a conviction which stops just short of self-importance. It is hers to begin with, but it matures considerably as she goes on. Indeed like the other Americans in the *Portrait* she is a *self*-seeker (Osmond and Mme. Merle are that in the usual sense as well); and it is what distinguishes the Americans, even the Europeanized Americans, from such a European *pur sang* as Warburton, whose identity is so largely defined by his inherited functions as head of the family, landlord, and member of the House of Lords. Warburton is enveloped by the serene charm of a man whose individual responsibility is necessarily qualified by his place in an established social order; he is congenitally unable to break into the American circle although he tries first with Isabel and later on with Pansy. Osmond and Mme. Merle are individuals become egoists, the corruption of the best; but they are real to Isabel as Warburton never is. And as Isabel is a true individual, so her friend Henrietta Stackpole is an individualist. The comic—and at last somewhat tiresomely comic—Henrietta is a journalist; in her view the free woman advertises her status by having a career. Nothing of the sort occurs to Isabel, fond as she is of improving herself through travel and reading. In fact she is enough of an individual to give expression to all the impulses in herself which are at odds with the theoretical New Woman. In her juvenile daydreams she had imagined herself, sometimes as the heroine in a rebel cause, more often as a martyred loyalist; and, as she playfully confesses to Ralph Touchett shortly after her arrival in England, she longs to behold the ghost which she feels certain must haunt even so pleasant a country seat as theirs. Despite her inexperience at this stage, amid all her expansive motions as a free American, she has, in other words, a premonition of the fact of evil and suffering, of the quantity of defeat that is involved in any success, of the necessary limitations of life. With all this Isabel is not unwilling to become more familiar, for she acknowledges it to be the substance of experience. Her career in Europe is thus a long process of escape from the native innocence, the innocence of imagining that you can do what you like, the innocence of inexperience.

If it is pursued honestly such a career threatens to end in a kind of tragedy, and Isabel's career does end in a kind of tragedy. She has saved Pansy from one unhappy union, but she has by no means assured the girl's marriage to the man she likes; and Osmond, thwarted and exposed, is now more Isabel's enemy than ever. She has further defied him by going to England to tend Ralph in his last illness; and there Goodwood appears and urges her to leave Osmond for him. "We can do absolutely as we please," he says in his liberal American way; "the world's all before us—and the world's very big." And seizing Isabel he forces a kiss on her—the only kiss in the novel. She feels the force of his passion: it occurs to her that she has never been loved before; yet she rejects his love as she does his argument. She is not Daisy Miller; and it is no longer her idea of life to do absolutely as she pleases. "The world's very small," she replies, and returns to Osmond. It is an austere decision but inescapable in the light of her character and quest. Not only is she still in a position to help Pansy, but the very suffering involved in her marriage has given it a kind of sanctity. It has been the means by which she has seen the ghost.

JAMES JOYCE, *A Portrait of the Artist as a Young Man*

PSEUDO-REALISM

UNSIGNED · 1917

The brilliant and nasty variety of pseudo-realism is excellently exemplified in "A Portrait of the Artist as a Young Man." Very plainly the author has set out with the intention of putting another nail in the coffin of convention—which to his mind is much the same thing as decency. What is reticence but hypocrisy? How are we to be honest with each other if we do not use the words that are written upon the fair lexicon of blank wall and private place? How are we to see life whole if we hesitate to chronicle the thoughts and experiences which those words connote for fumbling youth? This young Irish writer is determined to have it out. . . . His conscious determination is the usual sign of limit and defect. It is so hard to keep one's balance. In the act of squaring off to hit insincerity in the eye, somehow writers of talent are always forgetting what writers of supreme genius never have to remember —that one does not interpret truth by swatting at any half-truth—or by magnifying any fact. Mr. James Joyce is by no means a trifler, but it would be the best thing in the world for him if he could forget that he is a rebel. There is, in truth, an old and sound idea at the bottom of this story: it is the chronicle of youth setting out to discover the truth about life, and to interpret it. Stephen Dedalus, up to our last glimpse of him, is not a prodigy of achievement, but merely a young man destined to be an artist, an interpreter, when he shall have filled himself with living.

From *The Nation*, May 17, 1917; unsigned book review. Quoted by kind permission of the publishers.

THE NATURAL IN OUR ART

JOHN MACY · 1917

In the preface of "Pendennis" Thackeray says: "Since the author of 'Tom Jones' was buried, no writer of fiction among us has been permitted to depict to his utmost power a Man. We must drape him and give him a certain conventional simper. Society will not tolerate the Natural in our Art." If Thackeray felt that, why did he not take his reputation and his fortune in his hands and, defying the social restrictions which he deplored, paint us a true portrait of a young gentleman of his time? He might have done much for English art and English honesty. As it was, he did as much as any writer of his generation to fasten on English fiction the fetters of an inartistic reticence. It was only in the last generation that English and Irish novelists, under the influence of French literature, freed themselves from the cowardice of Victorian fiction and assumed that anything human under the sun is proper subject-matter for art. If they have not produced masterpieces (and I do not admit that they have not), they have made a brave beginning. Such a book as "A Portrait of the Artist as a Young Man" would have been impossible forty years ago. Far from looking back with regret at the good old novelists of the nineteenth century (whom, besides, we need never lose), I believe that our fiction is immensely freer and richer than the fiction of our immediate forefathers.

Joyce's work is outspoken, vigorous, original, beautiful. Whether it faithfully reflects Irish politics and the emotional conflicts of the Catholic religion one who is neither Irish nor Catholic cannot judge with certainty. It seems, however, that the noisy controversies over Parnell and the priests in which

From *The Dial*, June 14, 1917. Copyright. Used with the permission of The Dial Press.

the boy's elders indulge have the sound of living Irish voices; and the distracted boy's wrestlings with his sins and his faith are so movingly human that they hold the sympathy even of one who is indifferent to the religious arguments. I am afraid that the religious questions and the political questions are too roughly handled to please the incurably devout and patriotic. If they ever put up a statue of Joyce in Dublin, it will not be during his life time. For he is no respecter of anything except art and human nature and language.

There are some who, to turn his own imaginative phrase, will fret in the shadow of his language. He makes boys talk as boys do, as they did in your school and mine, except that we lacked the Irish imagery and whimsicality. If the young hero is abnormal and precocious, that is because he is not an ordinary boy but an artist, gifted with thoughts and phrases above our common abilities. This is a portrait of an artist by an artist, a literary artist of the finest quality.

THE SELF-IMAGE

REBECCA WEST · 1928

Seduced by his use of a heterodox technique into believing himself to be a wholly emancipated writer, James Joyce is not at all ahead of his times in his enslavement to the sentimental. That is manifest in isolated incidents. But, more important still, his sentimentality deforms the conception of one of the two protagonists, and that the one which should have been presented with the most careful sincerity and grace: the young Stephen Dedalus, whose quarrel with the gross-

From *The Strange Necessity*, by Rebecca West. London, Jonathan Cape, 1928. Used by permission of A. D. Peters, agent for the author.

ness of man's theory of living (as symbolized by the Roman Catholic Church) and the grossness of man's living (as symbolized by Leopold Bloom) is meaningless unless they are destroying in him a sincere and graceful spirit. But the young man is transparently a hero. His creator has given him eyelashes an inch long. And how he comports himself! He rolls his eyes, he wobbles on his base with suffering, like a Guido Reni. This is partly, of course, a consequence of Mr. Joyce's habit of using his writing as a means of gratifying certain compulsions under which he labours without making the first effort towards lifting them over the threshold that divides life from art. An obvious example of this is his use of obscene words. This might be a perfectly justifiable artistic device. I would hesitate to say that some artist may not at some time find it necessary to use these Anglo-Saxon monosyllables which are in a sense so little used and in a sense so much, for the completion of some artistic pattern. But that Mr. Joyce is not this artist, that his use of obscene words is altogether outside the aesthetic process is proved by that spurt of satisfaction, more actual but also more feeble than authentic artistic emotion which marks the pages whenever he uses them. Simply he is gratifying in his maturity the desire to protest against the adult order of things by the closest possible verbal substitutes for the practical actions, originating in the zone against which adults seemed to have such a repressive prejudice, by which he could register such feelings in his infancy.

It would be odd if an infantile trait should exist in such pungency alone; and, of course, it does not. There is working here a narcissism, a compulsion to make a self-image and to make it with an eye to the approval of others, which turns Stephen Dedalus into a figure oddly familiar for the protagonist of a book supposed to be revolutionary and unique.

There is a sense of portentousness in his dislike of his environment, as if the author should turn his head to his audience and say in an awe-stricken whisper, as of a curate noting that the Bishop is not pleased, "He does not like it"; there is a sense of separation from the mob in all his desirable qualities, of monopoly, of total lack of response from all others. These too are familiar, and as features in fiction of a not at all revolutionary sort. They are, in fact, the constant ingredients in almost every novel in which an Oxford or Cambridge graduate looks back on the Oxford or Cambridge undergraduate that he was five minutes previously and reverently commemorates the chrysalis. Such novels are written by talent or less, and *Ulysses* is written by genius, but there is in both the same narcissistic inspiration, which inevitably deforms all its products with sentimentality, since the self-image which it is the aim of narcissism to create is made not out of material that has been imaginatively experienced but out of material that has been selected as likely to please others.

DAEDALUS

W. Y. TINDALL · 1950

If, as some critics have claimed, there is also the enjoyment of self-pity behind this portrait and that of Stephen, then Joyce is sentimental. Rebecca West, who makes this charge in *Strange Necessity*, finds Joyce competent enough when he is writing about Mrs. Bloom, but narcissistic when writing about himself. Stephen seems to her an infantile dream of wish-fulfillment. That Joyce named his hero not only after Daedalus (surely a sign of pride) but after St. Stephen, the first martyr, seems to imply a compact of self-pity with self-love. Even

From *James Joyce,* by W. Y. Tindall. Charles Scribner's Sons, publishers.

the form taken by *A Portrait of the Artist,* that of the novel of adolescence, adds weight to this grievous charge.

Writers in this form invite the dangers of sentimentality. Few in our time have altogether escaped them. The defect of *The Way of All Flesh,* for example, is Samuel Butler's loving union with himself. Separated from an alien world, subject became one with object, and that distance which is necessary for art is nowhere to be found. A more recent example of the same defect, although somewhat redeemed by exuberance and apparent genius, is Thomas Wolfe's *Look Homeward, Angel.* These love affairs, which call for Rebecca West's rebuke, failed to get it.

In Joyce's autobiographical work the relation of subject to object or of the author to himself is different. Rebecca West's error is a confusion of Joyce with Stephen. As almost everybody knows, Joyce once said that the important words of his title are *as a Young Man.* From this remark and from a careful reading of the book it becomes evident that Joyce differs from Butler and Wolfe in having an artist's detachment from what he is using. Stephen is not Joyce but Joyce's past. Stephen is sentimental; Joyce is not. In *A Portrait of the Artist as a Young Man,* the mature man looks back at his adolescent self, not to praise it, but to give it shape as an artist must. Stephen is Joyce's material. Like any artist Joyce was fascinated with his material, but as he wrote, he formalized and "distanced" it. By this process, which is that of all art, he composed the personal and gave it that symbolic form which, freed from the emotive and the personal, permits insight into reality.

Those who find a sentimental attachment in *A Portrait of the Artist* have failed to notice the tone. To his friend Frank Budgen, Joyce once said: " 'I haven't let this young man off very lightly, have I?' " A careful reading makes it apparent that Joyce is aloof and generally ironic in his treatment of Stephen. But Joyce's attitude is never explicit. Stephen is allowed to expose himself. Joyce limits his assistance to arranging contrasts and juxtapositions and to using a style which, following the contours of the hero's passion, becomes that passion while parodying it.

THE *PORTRAIT* IN PERSPECTIVE

HUGH KENNER · 1948

It is high time, in short, to point out once and for all that Stephen's flight into adolescent "freedom" is not meant to be the "message" of the book. The Stephen of the first chapter of *Ulysses*, who "walks wearily," constantly "leans" on everything in sight, invariably sits down before he has gone three paces, speaks "gloomily," "quietly," "with bitterness," and "coldly," and "suffers" his handkerchief to be pulled from his pocket by the exuberant Mulligan, is precisely the priggish, humorless Stephen of the last chapter of the *Portrait* who cannot remember what day of the week it is (p. 206), sentimentalizes like Charles Lamb over the "human pages" of a second-hand Latin book (p. 209), conducts the inhumanly pedantic dialogue with Cranly on mother-love (pp. 281–292), writes Frenchified verses in bed in an erotic swoon, and is epiphanized at full length, like Shem beneath the bedclothes, shrinking from the "common noises" of daylight (p. 260).

The fit reader will be able to see that Stephen's introspective visions are constantly judged, and ironically, by the terms in which they are raised, and that the vision of the final pages, in fact, the total vision of the book, is murderously lambasted in *Ulysses*. The relation between Stephen and his sanctified namesake, who was stoned by the Jews after reporting a vision (Acts VII: 56), extends to parody as well as parallel.

The dashing of youthful hopes is constantly hovering, like an ironic disembodied grin, over their genesis. Stephen's repentance after the retreat, for example, is phrased throughout according to standards by which it will later be judged. The good life conceived in terms of white pudding and sausages needs no external satirist. Only an incurable tendency to identify himself, like a soap-opera fan, with the ups and downs of the hero could blind the reader to the mockery behind these passages. Joyce as an artist rather than a propagandist offers emotions for contemplation rather than participation. It is true that he scarcely expected to be understood in an age of soap-opera, but the difficulty of understanding his art is always a moral difficulty imposed by an immoral civilization; it has nothing to do, as the present instance shows, with deciphering the text.